ORGANIZATIONAL *MIS*BEHAVIOUR

Stephen Ackroyd and Paul Thompson

SAGE Publications
London · Thousand Oaks · New Delhi

SAGE Publications Ltd
6 Bonhill Street
London EC2A 4PU

SAGE Publications Inc
2455 Teller Road
Thousand Oaks, California 91320

SAGE Publications India Pvt Ltd
32, M-Block Market
Greater Kailash - I
New Delhi 110 048

British Library Cataloguing in Publication data

A catalogue record for this book is
available from the British Library

ISBN 0 8039 8735 8
ISBN 0 8039 8736 6 (pbk)

Library of Congress catalog record available

Typeset by Type Study, Scarborough, North Yorkshire
Printed and bound in Great Britain by Athenaeum Press,
Gateshead

Contents

Acknowledgements   vii

Introduction   1

1   Why Organizational *Mis*behaviour?   8

2   The Recalcritrant Worker   31

3   Irresponsible Autonomy – Self-organization as the
      Infrastructure of Misbehaviour   53

4   Management and Misbehaviour   74

5   Only Joking? From Subculture to Counter-culture in
      Organizational Relations   99

6   Ruling Passions: Sexual Misconduct at Work   121

7   The End of Organizational Misbehaviour?   144

References   166

Name Index   179

Subject Index   183

Acknowledgements

Stephen Ackroyd would like to thank the many students who have shared his enthusiasm for this subject over the years. Several former students have been disposed to take their interest in the matters discussed here further, and some of them have contributed to this field in their own right. Here the names of Farhad Analoui, Philip Crowdy, Mark Stevens and Frank Worthington deserve special mention. Numerous managers have also contributed to the understanding of misbehaviour that has now emerged, not least by allowing the organizations for which they have been responsible to be studied, and by discussing the behaviour that research uncovered. Above all in this category there is Maurice Phelps, who, many years ago now, gave me my first opportunity to research the informal organization of misbehaviour at close quarters.

Colleagues at Lancaster have not always shared a high degree of intellectual interest in misbehaviour, though they have remained supportive in other ways. The names of Keith Soothill, Frank Blackler, Mike Reed and Colin Brown must be mentioned. There are exceptions to every rule of course, and Gibson Burrell and John Hughes (both well equipped by temperament to be empathetic observers of misbehaviour) could be relied on to provide a sympathetic audience for ideas and findings in the early years. At different times, Karen Legge and Barbara Townley were also willing to listen to discussions of this material; even though neither was fundamentally sympathetic to the overall explanatory scheme. Interestingly, also, both of these friends were not above taking a disciplinary attitude to what they considered my own tendencies to misbehave. Such episodes serve as a demonstration, if any is needed, that academic work is not exempt from the political processes through which self-organization is developed. However, it would be unfortunate indeed if readers were to get the impression that conflict was pervasive. Karen Legge, in particular, not only has read and commented on sections of this manuscript, much to their benefit, but is owed a huge debt for many other practical and intellectual contributions.

Paul Thompson adds that after a lifetime's experience of observing his own and others' workplace misbehaviour, there are too many people and places to mention by name. But he would like to thank Heidi Gottfried, Julia O'Connell-Davidson and Fiona Wilson for help with Chapter 6. MBA students at Edinburgh have been a stimulating audience for these ideas, and have provided valuable means of road testing the ideas in many of these chapters. They have also contributed many examples and illustrations of misbehaviour, some of which have found their way into these pages. Colleagues at Edinburgh, particularly Tricia Findlay and Jim Hine, have given valued support during the long gestation period of this book. Like anyone who knows me, they will no doubt be glad never again to hear any reference to 'The book on organizational misbehaviour I'm working on with Steve Ackroyd'. They can now read the book for themselves.

There are some people to whom both authors feel indebted. The work of David Collinson and that of Paul Edwards has been imporant to us, as anyone will see who reads the book. Paul Stewart and Miguel Martinez-Lucio have also been consistent sources of (more pointed) stimulation and for us both their ideas are matters of lively interest. Pam Ackroyd read the manuscript through on several occasions, and helped us to avoid a number of errors. She also prepared the bibliography. Special thanks are due to Sue Jones of Sage Publications who originally commissioned the book and was consistently in our corner. More recently Sue's task was taken over by Rosemary Nixon, who is also to be thanked for her consistent support and encouragement.

Stephen Ackroyd and Paul Thompson,
Universities of Lancaster and Edinburgh

Introduction

The project of writing this book began with a simple concern that the account of organizational behaviour expressed or implied in academic work often did not give an accurate picture of what it is like. Initially, we thought of our task as writing an alternative organizational behaviour book, one which redressed the inaccurate account of organizational behaviour contained in many texts in our field. Standard textbooks in this area actually say surprisingly little about the character of the phenomenon with which they are centrally concerned – the behaviour routinely exhibited by people in organizations. What they do say suggests, as much by implication as direct assertion, that behaviour in organizations is, almost exclusively, conforming and dutiful.

And yet this assumption simply did not square with what we know of organizational behaviour as researchers, what we know of it as academics with a knowledge of the relevant research literature, and, not least, what we know of it as organizational members ourselves. Thus, we thought it would be a good idea to correct this imbalance, and to draw a richer picture of behaviour in organizations. This would not be simply a matter of giving more serious attention to such things as absenteeism, pilferage, soldiering, sabotage and vandalism, which have been studied at length by scholars from time to time (see, especially, Chapter 2 of this volume); but, since such things are recurrent features of organizations, to connect them with the orientations of employees towards their work. In this way we thought we could consider more realistically the problems of misbehaviour as they are known to managers and employees. To give an account of behaviour 'warts and all', would be to rebut an obvious and ultimately unhelpful normative bias in the study of organizational behaviour.

Such an account of organizational behaviour would have the substantial merit of being interesting for readers, and likely to incline them to read what we have to say. The novelty of our book would be that it offers a view of behaviour that rings true, and which would account for the experience of organizations as it is known to people who work in them. We remain hopeful that a good many readers will find their way into the narrative we have written by enjoying the jokes and examples of behaviour arrayed in what follows, especially as they appear in the boxes sprinkled through the text. At the very least this is a useful antidote to the sanitized accounts of behaviour that appear in many books on organizational behaviour. Thus we emphasize the working definition of misbehaviour with which we began, which includes the widest range of behaviour – from failure to work very hard or conscientiously, through not working at all, deliberate output restriction, practical joking, pilferage, sabotage and sexual misconduct. We define misbehaviour in a similar way to the definition of sabotage advanced by Sprouse (1992). As with Sprouse, our interest extended to 'anything you do at work you are not supposed to do' (1992, 3).

Our concern is, however, mainly, with what ordinary employees do at work. As a result of a definite decision rather than oversight, there are some things excluded from this book, which readers might expect to find discussed. There is some consideration of managerial misbehaviour in what follows, but we do not consider the types of managerial misbehaviour that hit the headlines, such as major fraud, cheating and chicanery (Franklin, 1990). Nor do we look at the grey fringes of business – where it connects with organized crime and the black and grey economies. We have also excluded from consideration the topic of whistle-blowing, which is one of the ways in which managerial misbehaviour may be curbed when it sharply offends public morality (Adams, 1984). These topics are large, and have rightly become a focus of serious debate in recent years (Punch, 1996; Hobbs, 1995). We have judged them to be beyond the scope of this book.

Yet, in some respects, the behaviour of managers is much the same as that of the ordinary employees with which we are principally concerned. Managers are also capable of recognizing that there is not a precise correspondence between their own interests and those of their employing company, and acting accordingly. As shareholders and others have become aware from time to time, the interests of managers are not necessarily the same as those of their companies. The salaries and other rewards of managers are not, in fact, usually justified in terms of precise calculations of the benefits accruing to companies as a result of their activities. So far as senior managers are concerned, indeed, there are many, many cases of the opposite, where the emoluments of senior personnel continue to go up whilst the fortunes of the companies they manage go down (Crystal, 1991). More generally, it is difficult for people – not least ordinary company employees – to accept that any manager (no matter how gifted, prescient or hard-working) is really worth an annual salary of £2 million per year, share options and benefits amounting to a further £4 million not to mention the various perks that go along with such a position, as in one example recently reported in the press. But the point to note is that what managers do defines what behaviour should be, so that it is difficult to envisage what they do (including what they choose to pay themselves) as involving malfeasance.

Such considerations underline the basic point that what groups get as remuneration and conditions of work reflects their powers to command resources. That the modest proposals of the Greenbury and Cadbury Committees (Charkham, 1994) for checking senior managerial conduct have nonetheless met rejection – a combination of outright denial and refusal to consider reform – serves to underline the point. It is consistent and unremarkable that ordinary employees also are likely to exercise what modest powers they have in ways that they think fit, and to continue to define their interest and identity as being, in some ways, distinct from those of their employing company. Like managers, ordinary employees also do not assume that their interests are precisely the same as their company's, or that they should reveal their actual sentiments too candidly or display their dissenting behaviour too openly. Because of this, misbehaviour is endemic in contemporary organizations, though, of course, it may not be seen for what it is.

The key difference between managers and other employees has been revealed in the above comparison. This is that employees are likely to have the results of their deviations from expected standards of conduct noticed and defined as misbehaviour. It should be clear from the outset that the identification of misbehaviour is a matter of imposed definition – something decided by the group which has the power to define the way behaviour will be regarded, and to sanction deviations from expectations. Revealing the extent of misbehaviour is an exercise in detection, identification, and of making particular definitions of what the behaviour is, apply. Although organizational misbehaviour has existed for as long as there have been modern institutions and their associated control systems (Mars, 1982b; Ditton, 1977a) showing that misbehaviour exists is, very often, not easy. Ordinary employees are sophisticated in their recognition of the realities of power. Nonetheless it is important to recognize the extent of misbehaviour in organizations, if we want to come to a realistic appreciation of the way organizations actually work.

From an early point, then, we became interested in our subject matter for additional reasons. We soon moved on from simply wishing to redress an obvious imbalance in the way organizational behaviour is thought about, to considering the extent to which it has been ignored and disregarded by behavioural experts and the reasons for this. The extent, persistence and variety of the organizational misbehaviour that we began to identify was such that it became an obvious question to consider why this behaviour is so seldom acknowledged. As our research into organizational misbehaviour, and into the existing writing about the subject continued, as our appreciation of the material discussed in our book became deeper, this second order of question became much more important. Working out not only the full extent of the misbehaviour (and the full extent of its omission from standard writing in the organizational field) but also the reasons for this, added layers of complexity to our task.

It is our conviction that both managers and organization behaviour specialists alike not only underestimate the extent of organizational misbehaviour but that they also exaggerate the extent to which organizational behaviour can be changed by them. They confuse the capacity to induce some marginal changes in behaviour (let us call this tractability) with its permanent 'correction' (let us call this corrigibility). Workplace behaviour is often tractable – in that it can be marginally and temporarily changed by managerial action. On the other hand, behaviour is seldom corrigible in the sense that behaviour thenceforth generally conforms with management expectations. The reality of managerial control is that it is one of the forces that moves behaviour about – from one form to another, from one manifestation to another – but there is little reason to think that it will eliminate misbehaviour, because it does not act on the tendency to misbehave itself. For example, the introduction of new rules of acceptable conduct with regard to attendance, the careful keeping of records concerning the breaking of these rules and the application of penalties for those who break them, will probably cut back absenteeism in its existing forms. Clearly however, this impact on behaviour is not to be confused with a reduction in the tendency to take time off, or, more generally, to get back advantages perceived to be lost.

Quite commonly, attempts to limit customary misbehaviour seem to have little effect. When managerial persistence appears to produce some conformity, close inspection often shows that what has happened is that behaviour has simply taken new (and perhaps less tractable) forms. To continue with the example of absence, the removal of customary licence not to attend work – by the imposition of controls designed to curb casual non-attendance – is likely to contribute to the innovation of other kinds of failure to conform to time discipline, such as increased absence excused as sickness, which is less within control than customary absenteeism. Alternatively it may induce more or less obvious and tractable innovations in misbehaviour, such as irresponsibility or, even, destructiveness. The basic point to note is that the processes which are formative of organizational behaviour are, to a considerable extent, outside the control of managers. This means that behaviour can be affected only to a certain extent. It may be to some extent tractable but only degrees of conformity with managerial expectation can be produced. A good part of our consideration of misbehaviour in this book shows how incorrigible *and* innovative organizational behaviour actually is.

Our analysis serves to reinforce the conclusion that the tendency to misbehave, or, to consider the matter from the point of view of the employee, to behave in ways that seem appropriate to their situation as they perceive it, is the normal case. But this directly contradicts the assumptions embedded in orthodox studies of organizational behaviour, which take for granted a close correspondence between expected and actual behaviour. In fact, there are few differences between organizational behaviour writers and managers on this central issue: the point of studying behaviour for both groups is to contribute to its control. Many organizational behaviour specialists believe, very much as managers do, that organizational behaviour should be, for ethical as well as practical reasons, corrected (Giacalone and Greenberg, 1997). The difference between these writers and managers is, in this respect, merely a matter of degree. The former believe that the latter do not have a sufficiently sophisticated level of understanding of the phenomenon with which they are dealing; but there is no basic difference of general approach. The same argument that can be levelled against managers is also applicable to specialists in organizational behaviour. It may be possible to achieve limited compliance in a campaign to cut back misbehaviour but it is much less clear that, by doing so, general compliance with expectations will be secured, no matter how sophisticated the policy adopted.

In sum the first task we set ourselves was met by setting out and establishing the range of organizational misbehaviour. But it was only by revealing the relationship of misbehaviour to the mechanisms designed to control it, the extent of the involvement of managers in the proceses of the production and perpetuation of misbehaviour, and, finally, the complicity of organizational behaviour specialists in pretending that all this is not important, that we arrived at an acceptable account of the subject.

But there was another development which also served to make our task challenging and prolonged the time taken to complete it. This time the cause was external to the project itself as we conceived of it. As our work on misbehaviour progressed, it became clear to us that we are witnessing significant change in contemporary organizations at the present time, and changes in misbehaviour, to some extent directly caused by this, were also noticed. Many fellow social scientists noticed this too. But they, almost without exception, argued that the effect of change is to enhance the effectiveness of management in inducing the compliance of employees. They sought to persuade everyone that, if organizational misbehaviour had been relatively prevalent in the past, these days the last vestiges of non-compliance were being removed. If misbehaviour existed extensively before, current change, and especially innovation by managements, is substantially eradicating it. Whereas employees used to resist managerial controls, the powers of contemporary management are being extended to such an extent that any remaining resistance is becoming completely ineffectual. To borrow a memorable phrase from the writing of one of the early proponents of this view, management had successfully negotiated the 'last frontier of control' (Ray, 1986, 287). There is now no alternative for people at work but complete behavioural compliance with managerial dictates. Such conformity might be resigned (Ogbonna and Wilkinson, 1990) or even, apparently, voluntary and uncoerced (Willmott, 1993), but writers of very different persuasions were developing similar sorts of conclusions about the increasing conformity of people in organizations.

Even though such argument are being made by – amongst others – people with good radical credentials, these readings did not square with the history of misbehaviour or quite a lot of research in contemporary organizations undertaken by ourselves and others. It is undeniable that we are in a period of significant organizational change, and that the alteration of organizational structures is also helping to reconstruct the conventional forms in which misbehaviour finds expression. In our view, however, misbehaviour has by no means gone away; still less is it being eliminated. Much of what is now being claimed about the removal of misbehaviour is tendentious or simply wrong from a factual point of view. Moreover, the theory brought to bear on the alleged facts of the removal of misbehaviour is vulnerable to reasoned criticism. For all its radical packaging, much of the new writing with which we were confronted made claims about conformity that are not substantially different from the ideas of traditional organizational behaviour (OB). To repeat: in our view, it is not accurate to envisage the end of misbehaviour.

The empirical evidence to show that old forms of misbehaviour are becoming relatively less important is not present. Neither is enough research being done which might show the way new forms of misbehaviour are being innovated. Writers are approaching their subject with the assumption that management has become – for the first time in its history – really effective in controlling behaviour. We suggest, however, that this conclusion is as much dictated by the assumption that management is effective and any resistance to it non-existent, as it is by any disciplined inspection of organizational behaviour as it exists. By contrast, we suggest that contemporary events exhibit continuities with the past, and as the substantial evidence of past research indicates, much of the old repertoire of misbehaviour is to be found in organizational settings. Much of this book is taken up with accounting for the range of misbehaviour traditionally found in organizations, and in considering its possible direction and patterns of change. This is treated at length in Chapters 3 and 4. However, we have also taken time to consider contemporary innovations and change in misbehaviour (in Chapters 5 and 6).

The result of our work is a book that falls into three parts, linked by a common point of view. The first part is mainly conceptual and comprises two chapters. The first chapter criticizes the assumptions of orthodox OB and discusses the reasons why the rich and varied phenomena of misbehaviour have been neglected. This discussion is concluded with the argument that there is a wide 'terrain' of misbehaviour, with a number of different dimensions, in which the tendency to misbehave can find scope for expression. We end this chapter by drawing a map of the potential terrain which misbehaviour can occupy. In this mapping exercise – in which we set out the dimensions of the misbehaviour – we accommodate the historically significant types of misbehaviour as well as covering the terrain in which emerging contemporary forms find greater expression. In Chapter 2 we show that, from time to time, there has been some exposure of parts of the terrain – and its associated forms of misbehaviour – in the work of a large number of researchers and writers. However, it is only when these writings are assembled in a different and distinctive way that the full extent and significance of misbehaviour in organizations can be understood.

In the next two chapters we consider organizational misbehaviour as it has expressed itself in recent history. To achieve this, we substantially recast existing accounts of misbehaviour and its properties, and we do so by drawing on examples from existing work, much of which has been published for some time. We show that all the important dimensions of misbehaviour mapped in Chapter 1 – in which the point of misbehaviour is the limitation of working effort or the reappropriation of time or product – have been revealed by many specialist writers in the past. In Chapter 3, we deepen the analysis by showing the interconnection between pursuit of self-interest and

processes of identity formation by workgroups, in the spontaneously generated informal organization found in such groups. We suggest that the
pursuit of autonomy (which is, from the managerial point of view, for the
most part irresponsible), is the basis of organizational misbehaviour.
Understood in this way, the tendency to misbehave can be recognized to be
deeply embedded. In Chapter 4 we add to this by considering the manageability of misbehaviour, and suggest that it has proved extremely difficult
for managers to control the behaviour of employees in practice. The result
of their efforts has been, we argue, the proliferation of discrete and recognizable forms of misbehaviour – 'soldiering', 'absenteeism', 'pilferage' and
so on. These forms of behaviour suggest that the best that can be achieved
by management is the containment of misbehaviour in discrete and manageable packages. By their continued existence they illustrate our point
about the incorrigibility of this behaviour. In this way, Chapter 4 completes
our discussion of traditional patterns of misbehaviour.

The two chapters which follow consider contemporary innovations in
organizational misbehaviour. In Chapters 5 and 6 our argument is that
organizations are in a period of significant change and that this is marked
by considerable innovation in the behaviour of employees as well as in
managerial actions. In our discussion we place far more emphasis on
employee innovation than on other things. This makes our approach distinctively different from that taken by other organizational analysts. In
these chapters we discuss the innovative use of humour in organizations and
the emerging politics of sexuality. Although both workplace joking and the
expression of sexuality have been part of the terrain of misbehaviour in the
past, these forms of misbehaviour are now becoming much more significant.
This emphasis on employee-initiated innovation is consistent with the line
taken in earlier chapters. We argue that behind changes of organization
being introduced, new kinds of employee behaviour and misbehaviour are
currently emerging: it is only to be expected that significant new misbehaviour in organizations is developing. Yet these are often only dimly perceived
by managers for what they are. We argue that management, by and large,
has not appropriately anticipated these innovations in behaviour. As has
been the case many times before, innovation by employees occurs in
advance of management development, and management often fails to
recognize it. When management finally perceives something, it is initially at
a loss to know what to do.

We conclude the book with Chapter 7, in which there is a careful analysis and critique of the writing which suggests the elimination of misbehaviour from contemporary organizations.

1 Why Organizational *Mis*behaviour?

This book has been written with the object of revising perceptions of the basic subject matter of the discipline variously called organizational behaviour, organization studies or organizational analysis. It is written in the conviction that organizational misbehaviour is very much more prevalent and varied in content than is normally acknowledged; certainly more than the token chapters on conflict in textbooks or specialist contributions on strikes would suggest. We offer a detailed consideration and interpretation of some of the many varieties and forms of misbehaviour that exist, drawing on the findings and insights of a wide variety of sources: specialist, journalistic and personal. The book may be read as an interesting and diverting review of the reality of organizational life, but, at the same time, there is a more serious purpose. This is to argue that much of the subject matter of organizational behaviour has been generally misunderstood and neglected. The attempt to understand and account for the extent and character of misbehaviour in organizations offers a considerable intellectual challenge to the student, to practitioners, and indeed to anyone with an interest in organizations and what happens in them.

Unfortunately there is an assumption in the discipline of organizational behaviour that employees are largely if not invariably constructive and conforming. Luthans is typical: 'Virtually all available evidence indicates that actual behaviour is orderly and purposeful, and appears to support the goals of the organization' (1972, 287). Thus 'normal' behaviour is that which is programmable, that which is compliant with managerial norms and rules. This view in a curious way resembles commonsense notions of behaviour. When someone is told 'behave yourself', it is as if behaviour is doing what we are told. This comforting, but hopelessly unrealistic, view has to be questioned and revised. Indeed, one of the reasons why teachers of OB encounter so much scepticism from practising managers and others with extensive experience of organizations, concerns their cosy assumptions about the basic disposition of employees and others. People in organizations actually get up to all sorts of tricks. To a considerable extent, the organization not only produces organizational behaviour but produces organizational misbehaviour as well. It is recurrent and is produced in the normal working of the organization. That is the reality of organizational life.

In the UK and some other European countries, organization studies is a diverse field, which has only been separated from other disciplines in the last decade or so. In this sense, its practitioners have varied greatly in the extent to which they have acknowledged the existence of organizational misbehaviour. Some of them have been oriented explicitly to the more formally organized kinds of behaviour, being concerned only to bring into focus those activities which are highly conflictual. We will return to such strands of thinking later. Traditional organization studies, embodied in mainstream and largely American OB, has, by contrast, ignored misbehaviour almost entirely; suggesting by implication that all behaviour is basically well intentioned when it is not poorly managed or led.

Paradoxical though it may seem, what organizational behaviour is like in its ordinary forms has not been subjected to considerable analysis and discussion. Though the possibility is envisaged that behaviour will, in some limited instances, fall short of managerial expectation, it is seldom acknowledged to be subversive of it. Nor is there usually any implication, direct or indirect, that management may connive in and even undertake misbehaviour.

An examination of the development of standard texts in this tradition reveals a persistent pattern of neglect and trivialization. Conflict may be largely denied through reasoning such as, 'for the most part members of a group cooperate, since this is one of the reasons they are in a group in the first place' (Von Haller, 1971, 62). This text claims that it is about 'people in organizations and how they behave', yet only seven out of 700 pages concern conflict. Others such as Leavitt (1973), Luthans (1972) and Wilson and Rosenfeld (1990) have token single chapters. Elsewhere, many indexes have nothing at all under such headings as 'conflict' or 'resistance'.

When such issues are dealt with, their location in texts tells us a lot about how they are viewed. Resistance and conflict is frequently dealt with under 'change', as a means to explain why the latter doesn't happen. Such action is seen as a defensive or irrational response – the psychology of fear rather than the sociology of opposing interests. Meanwhile change itself is assumed to be benign and change agents the purveyors of valid knowledge (Bennis, 1966).

There are also chapters or specialist texts on 'managing conflict' (e.g. Likert and Likert, 1976). Conflict itself and its causes are quickly leapt over to get to conflict resolution. Such contributions are resolutely upbeat. The message is that conflict isn't all that bad; in fact it can be positive for the organization as long as it is tame, trivial and managed appropriately. Win–win has to replace win–lose, as if managers can perform processual conjuring tricks to overcome the inequalities of the material and symbolic resources that underpin conflict. Where causes are discussed the emphasis tends to be on factors external to the organization such as tensions associated with the introduction of technology or new values and rights that lack adequate institutionalization.

Regardless of where it is located, misbehaviour is therefore largely marginalized or psychologized as a part of a bundle of abstract wants or drives. For Luthans (1972), conflict is a 'class of frustrations' that arise when goals are wrongly set. Again these need not be harmful. Kelly's (1972) advice on how to 'Make Conflict Work for You', states that there is 'an optimal level of anxiety, arousal and conflict for man to function efficiently'. Persistent troublemakers may be interpreted in terms of personal pathology. Leavitt (1973) refers to a minority of chronic anti-authoritarians, while Wilson and Rosenfeld (1990) argue that conflict resolution depends on 'the reasonable person'. However, 'all organizations are not staffed by such reasonable people' (1990, 141), and unfortunate parallels are drawn with terrorists and hijackers.

It must be admitted that there are some exceptions to the above rule. Texts or chapters dealing with organizational politics and power do have to come to terms with conflict. The emphasis here is predominantly on inter-group conflict and coalitions based on competition for scarce resources (Hickson and McCullough, 1980; Pfeffer, 1981; Lee and Lawrence, 1985). This is solid enough stuff, though focusing on the visible exercise of power rather than its structural origins. More importantly for our purposes, it is narrowly conceived, emphasizing a limited range of activities, notably those of formal sub-units such as departments; and highly specialist with little impact on conventional organizational analysis as a whole.

Occasionally you come across something that promises the real 'low down' on organizational life, such as Fournie's *Why Employees Don't Do What They're Supposed to Do and What to Do About It*. In that folksy way that managerial self-help books have, it begins 'As you know, most people at work do most of what they are supposed to do most of the time. They are co-operative, hard-working and dependable . . . . But there are those few bad performers who don't seem to do anything right' (1988, viii). The book gives 16 reasons why employees non-perform, including 'They don't know how to do it', 'obstacles beyond their control' and 'personal problems'. No sign here of any conflicting interests or oppositional norms.

Since we started writing this book OB has just begun to show some inkling that there may be a problem. The preface to a recent volume from Giacalone and Greenberg (1997, ix) rightly observes that management scholars have been content to relegate to security officials an examination of a whole range of issues that should be in the OB domain. Unfortunately their own approach treats misbehaviour as antisocial. Indeed this word appears in the title of the volume. It is difficult to imagine a term more unlikely to capture the reality of the workplace. For, as many of their chapters show, sabotage, theft and other misbehaviours are profoundly social, frequently, as the authors admit, underpinned by informal workgroup norms. What they really mean by antisocial is something which does not conform to established goals or power relations. One of the chapters defines workplace or employee deviance as 'voluntary behaviour that violates significant organizational norms and in doing so threatens the well-being of an organization, its members or both' (Robinson and Bennett, 1995, quoted in Giacalone and Greenberg, 1997, 137). The language again gives the game away. We are firmly on the terrain of 'deviancy'. With some exceptions the chapters treat their topics as if they were personal mal-functions or abnormal behaviour. Yet one of the chapters refers to research which shows that up to 80 per cent of samples of employees admitted having been engaged in some type of what they call (rather nicely) 'counterproductive behaviour', ranging from using illicit drugs at work to working in a slow or sloppy manner (Boye and Jones, 1997, 172). This example illustrates a further problem: the list of antisocial behaviours is mind-boggling – including arson, blackmail, fraud, lawsuits, lying, sabotage and whistle-blowing. Not only are some of these extremely curious even by their own definitions. Since when was whistle-blowing antisocial? A number – lying comes to mind – lack sufficient organizational specificity for study as a distinctive form of behaviour. Some scepticism arises in the mind of the reader when homicide is included in the discussion of work-place aggression. Fortunately, we are reassured that, 'Although workplaces may contain many disaffected workers, these persons do not typically resort to murder' (Neuman and Barron, 1997, 44).

We shall return to the discipline later. The real question is how and why the organization produces misbehaviour. A basic point can be made at the outset. This is, that only when there is a precise correspondence between directive and responsive aspects of organizational behaviour will there be no perceived problems concerning behaviour. When direction – what is expected of people – precisely corresponds with response – what people are willing to do – there is no perception of organizational misbehaviour. Since there is often not a precise correspondence, misbehaviour is properly regarded as endemic to organizations. Moreover, as we shall see, it is common not only for there to be toleration of forms of misbehaviour, but degrees of dependency on it.

The purpose of this chapter is to explain how and why misbehaviour is neglected and to provide a conceptual framework to understand its nature and processes. Let us begin with the former task.

Explaining the neglect of misbehaviour

There are a variety of reasons why much of what we propose to discuss here is seldom acknowledged. We need to start at a fairly basic point concerning the perception of behaviour. Despite the complexity of behaviour itself, not to mention the complexity of the processes involved in recognizing it, the perception of people behaving typically involves simplification. Physiologi-cally, perceptions are patterns of light and colour falling on the retina of the eye. The brain is receiving and processing millions of impressions per minute in the normal day. From these impressions, complex behavioural events are being actively constructed and identified by observers. Some of them are being selected, simplified and stored away for later reference, reportage and other use. In this set of processes, observations are routinely resolved into reportable events. This is to note the all-important point that all accounts of behaviour are precisely that – constructions and accounts. Hence, what is represented as organizational behaviour – as if it were simply and straightforwardly a factual matter – is really a highly packaged and organized set of observations.

Part of the process of social construction is ideological. For example, many academics and managers work with the recognizably liberal philosophy that may be formulaically expressed as follows: treat people right and they will behave right. This leads them to minimize the importance of much that they see in the way of misbehaviour in organizations. This philosophy is not so much false as irrelevant: it is more often than not impossible to operate on this sort of basis whether managers would like to do so or not.

It is also about power. The assumptions of those who direct behaviour in organizations typically define whether misbehaviour occurs or not. It is when there is a lack of correspondence between direction and responses that misbehaviour is identified, and the presumption is made that what needs to change is the response rather than the direction. However, it should not be assumed that the perceived problem of misbehaviour will be resolved by its elimination. Organizational misbehaviour is actually, in large part, a chronic feature of the exercise of direction and control. Indeed, the definition of problems of misbehaviour may be as far as attempts to exert control actually proceed. In addition, misbehaviour may be partly acknowledged in some times and places and overlooked at others.

For example, although organizational behaviour such as pilferage – as Jason Ditton (see especially 1977a) has extensively argued – is officially defined as wrong or not allowed, it is quite often positively encouraged in practice. Management cannot and does not own up to the fact that it knows pilferage goes on or that it is not particularly against the practice.

What we have here is not just the ability to change the operative criteria of good performance from time to time – to move the goalposts – but to evaluate the same behaviour in different ways. This is reflected in an extended ironic joke which is current in organizations. It runs as follows: my boss has vision whilst I lack attention to detail; my boss's disrespect for bureaucracy is my failure to follow procedure; my boss's concern for change and innovation is my lack of consistency.

The research process

Social construction is also embedded in the organization of research. Much research in organizational settings is not concerned to observe all the behaviour that might be present. This is because there is a tendency to focus only on certain categories of things – things that are deemed in principle as being relevant to the purposes of the research. So even when one is in an organization expressly in order to analyse behaviour, behaviour in general is often not being examined. What happens is that instances of behaviour are appraised through the focused perception of the research worker. Sometimes this is quite remote from any kind of direct observation of behaviour. In this, the perception of the research worker and the ordinary observer are actually little different. They both involve highly selective perceptions according to pre-selected criteria. In the case of the ordinary observer, commonsense criteria concerning what happens in workplaces are in use. In the case of the research worker, operational definitions of what needs to be observed are what matters.

To make this point more credible, let us consider an example. Absenteeism is a common form of organizational misbehaviour much studied by academics. But extended studies of absenteeism do not involve much direct observation of behaviour; absence from the workplace is, by definition, behaviour that is difficult to observe! Partly for this reason, absence studies almost never involve direct observation as a research technique. In fact the most prevalent activity in much research into absenteeism involves poring over documents – making operational decisions as to what to count as instances of absence from records and files, adding up and summarizing the numbers produced, etc. This is admittedly an extreme case, but even where researchers generate their own data, and so observe behaviour directly as a prelude to converting it into 'data', much of their work involves deciding how to classify instances of behaviour before it can be observed. When this happens the success of research can only too easily be judged in terms of the efficiency with which instances of absence (or whatever) have been accurately recorded.

There are, of course, research strategies that have as their basic justification the directness with which they observe social situations and their initial openness. We have in mind here particularly the method of participant observation in which the researcher joins an organization as an ordinary member and observes what is going on in the organization at close quarters for relatively long periods of time. While some of the richest and most provocative findings to be reported in this book have been thrown up by research involving these methods, we do not believe that such methods in themselves eliminate the basic problem of selective observation. Even when the direct observation of behaviour is being used in research, there are filtering mechanisms at work ordering perception. In sum, whatever research methods are employed, there is a good deal of what the American economist Thorstein Veblen called 'trained incapacity' to see things. In addition, what can be seen is limited by the contentious nature of some of the practices. As Analoui (1992, 3) notes of his own participant observation at a large night club, 'It would have been naive if not idiotic to approach a member of staff, just after he and two of his mates, had "neutralized" (as the saboteurs put it) a large freezer, and enquire, "Excuse me, I am conducting my Doctoral research and I wish to ask you why you and your colleagues destroyed that freezer?" '

One of the basic problems we have to contend with is related to the selective perception of different kinds of researcher. Researchers tend to be interested in different aspects of the subject. To write this account, we have collected scattered observations on behaviour and misbehaviour from many sources. But the accounts offered have been constructed within several disciplines with different assumptions and concerns. One of the ways in which the partiality of accounts of behaviour can be illustrated is in the limited coverage of phenomena by different academic disciplines. For reasons that are perhaps worthy of study in their own right, social psychologists have favoured the study of absenteeism and turnover; labour historians are interested in riot, insurrection and sabotage; whilst criminologists have been concerned about theft and, to a lesser extent, vandalism and destructiveness. Specialists in industrial relations have been concerned primarily with formally organized industrial relations, particularly in strike activity. Industrial sociologists have been a little more inclusive, but their main focus has been work limitation practices and related behaviour. Both sociologists and anthropologists have made some attempts to develop frameworks of thought to cover the whole range of misbehaviour, but even these have been partial and inadequate in other ways.

There are many forms of behaviour and misbehaviour that are not the stock in trade of any discipline and, though they might be quite common, only enter the academic literature in a partial and inadequate way. They receive scant attention from textbook writers and are not regarded as important features of organizational life. We have in mind here such things as practical joking and badinage, bullying and sexual harassment, rituals and rites of passage. No academic group has been concerned to think about the whole range of misbehaviour or the implications of this variety. Certainly no one has attempted to relate the range of misbehaviour to the emerging subjective subject of organizational behaviour. Our task of bringing together scattered accounts of misbehaviour offers a considerable intellectual challenge to the investigator. This concerns the way that the different forms of misbehaviour are connected to each other, and what is the appropriate way to think about them as a collectivity.

Both managements and social scientists studiously overlook a good deal of organizational misbehaviour. Although they know it is there, it is bracketed off as being somehow peripheral or inessential without any attempt to quantify or analyse its contribution to organizations. This perception brings home how normative the consideration of organizational behaviour actually is much of the time. There is also a certain complicity with other employees about misbehaviour in this respect. Employees do not go out of their way to exhibit behaviour that is not officially allowed. Hence there is substantial agreement that unless such behaviour interferes with the purposes of the organization as construed by its representatives, or intrudes noticeably on the interests of constituent groups within the organization, it is likely to pass unnoticed. But it should be the role of the specialist discipline of organization studies to show just how such behaviour is integral to the working of organizations.

The evolution of organizational analysis

Mainstream organization studies draw from a variety of traditions. The two most prominent historical influences – Taylorism and human relations – demonstrate an inherent incapacity to deal with misbehaviour. Taylor's legacy was his system of 'scientific management'. The whole rationale for his system derived from a form of misbehaviour that Taylor described as 'soldiering'. Essentially this consisted of deliberate restriction of output, organized by highly skilled craft workers around the turn of the century. These workers not only restricted output, they limited the amount of knowledge that managers had access to, thus constraining the capacity of capital to organize production as they saw fit. For Taylor the solution was to appropriate the knowledge and skills from the worker, gathering them together as a 'science'; or more accurately a set of managerial rules for organizing work.

This battle, so graphically described in his 1911 account of life at the Midvale Steel Works (1947), should have given Taylor profound insights into misbehaviour. In one sense it did. Soldiering was seen as a rational response by workers. But it was not so much a rational means of raising wages or maintaining job security, as a natural reaction to forms of management that were inefficient and unplanned. Once management had been made 'scientific', such misbehaviour was incomprehensible. For management was no longer the 'crack of the whip' and arbitrary authority, but relied instead on teaching best practices and 'constant and intimate cooperation' between management and employee based on an appropriate division of labour (one group thinking, the other doing) and on shared rewards from greater efficiency. Taylor, in his evidence to the American House of Representatives, therefore spoke of finding that 'almost universally', workers 'kept their word absolutely and faithfully', and that 'in the main . . . they were the most satisfied and contented set of labourers I have ever seen anywhere' (1947, 11). Unfortunately for the logic of his argument there were contradictory passages, as can be seen in the box below.

Every one of them knew that after he had received three or four yellow slips a teacher would be sent down to him from the labour office. Now, gentlemen, this teacher was no college professor. He was a teacher of shovelling; he understood the science of shovelling; he was a good shoveller himself, and he knew how to teach other men to be good shovellers . . . . The workman, instead of hating the teacher who came to him . . . looked upon him as one of the best friends he had around there. Now this teacher would find, time and time again, that the shoveller had simply forgotten how to shovel: that he had drifted back to his old wrong and inefficient ways of shovelling, which prevented him earning his 60 per cent higher wages . . . . And the teacher would stay by him two, three, four days, if necessary, until he got the man back again into the habit of shovelling right. (Taylor, 1947, 12)

The language of forgetting reveals more about the way in which Taylor's illusions about the nature of science limit his capacity to understand workplace relations than it does about the phenomenon itself. A similar lament was repeated to one of the authors by the training manager of a large Merseyside factory. In a puzzled tone he complained that workers who had been hitting managerial targets in the training school, just could not match it when back on the shop floor. Workers do not forget how to behave. Rather, soldiering is concerned with the appropriation of time and product within the effort bargain. Just in case workers carried on 'forgetting', Taylor issued a clear threat:

> just remember that on your side we want no monkey business of any kind . . . you fellows will have to do just what you are supposed to be doing; not a damn bit of soldiering on your part . . . if you start to fool this same young chap with the paper and pencil he will be onto you fifteen minutes from the time you try to fool him, and just as surely as he reports you for soldiering you will go out of this works and you will never get in again. (1947, 12)

Those who complained, for example about job losses, became 'permanent grouches'. So much for constant and intimate cooperation.

Of course, mainstream organization theory has always dismissed Taylorism as out of date and barbarous. What about the historic alternative, that of human relations? It has long been recognized that the influential writers – Mayo (1933), Roethlisberger and Dickson (1964), Whitehead (1938) – of this school proceeded on the basis of Durkheimian and Paretian theories that stressed equilibrium based on a social system of interrelated and interdependent parts (Ackroyd, 1976). Accounts of the famous Hawthorne experiments, which provided the empirical rationale for human relations, are littered with references to the inevitability or desirability of social and economic cooperation; though material progress inside and outside the factory did not guarantee collaboration.

In their experiments in the assembly test rooms and the bank wiring room, and in the extensive interviewing and counselling sessions, the Hawthorne researchers observed considerable evidence of misbehaviour. In this sense their work resembled Taylor's. He expected cooperation on the basis of science and got continued monkey business. Taylor managed to partially ignore the consequences of this for his 'theory' by claiming loss of memory. This was not the route taken by human relations researchers, though they too set aside or ignored the consequences of misbehaviour, as we shall see if we examine the most detailed account of Hawthorne (Roethlisberger and Dickson, 1964). Though the 'girls' in the early experiments enjoyed being the centre of attention and having researcher supervisors instead of real bosses, the researchers complained of 'gross insubordination' and continued work limitation. This misbehaviour is never adequately explained in terms of the pre-existing theoretical orientation. Nor was the action of excluding workers who were 'uncooperative' from the group explained in terms given any convincing rationale.

However, what we do get is a tendency to attribute such misbehaviour to psychological or biological causes. In Roethlisberger and Dickson's account of the research (1964), an astonishing amount of time is spent detailing insubordinate operators' apparent nervousness or ill-temper; their anaemic physical condition or obsessive thinking: although such workers were admitted not to be fully fledged psychoneurotics impervious to changes in the immediate work situation (1964, 314–15). But this recourse to psychologizing and pathologizing worker attitudes and action can be seen in other ways. The researchers are repeatedly dismissive of 'apprehensiveness of authority', and employees' continued fears about earnings and jobs were dismissed with comments such as: 'It is needless to say, of course, that these fears were not justified and that the girls were being "irrational" in having such anxieties' (1964, 48). It got worse in the interview stage. Grievances were the result of 'concealed, perhaps unconscious, disturbances in the employees' situation' (p. 266), to be further revealed by investigation of the inner person. Malcontents had 'morbid preoccupations' and 'psycho-neuroses', while, 'Certain complaints were no longer treated as facts in themselves, but as symptoms or indicators of personal or social situations which need to be explored' (p. 269).

But the key test as to whether the researchers could comprehend misbehaviour was the famous bank wiring room. Here, instead of finding compliant and cooperative groups, they found systematic misbehaviour taking the form of collective work norms which were imposed on all the group members – in other words, soldiering.

Though there is an unfortunate tendency to over-attribute causal influence to individuals as scapegoats or ringleaders, the reaction of the human relations tradition was different to that of Taylor. Whereas Taylor wished to attack the group head on and reconstitute employment relations on an individual basis, human relations recognizes the social and informal foundation of group behaviour, but attempts to create a framework within which

---

The supervisory control which is set up by management to regulate and govern the workers, exercises little authority except to see that they are supplied with work. It is apparent that the group is protected from without by A. He absorbs the brunt of the arguments which might upset the group's morale. The behaviour of the group itself is regulated by B. He teaches them their work and sees to it that their behaviour does not jeopardize the group security. For instance, he sees that they look busy even when they are through work, that they do not tell others that their work is easy or that they are getting through work early . . . . One day an interviewer entered a department unobserved. There was a buzz of conversation and the men seemed to be working at great speed. Suddenly there was a sharp hissing sound. The conversation died away, and there was a noticeable slowing up in the work pace. The interviewer later discovered from an acquaintance in the department that he had been mistaken for a rate setter. One of the workmen, who acted as a lookout, had stepped on a valve releasing compressed air, a prearranged signal for slowing down. (Roethlisberger and Dickson, 1964, 384–6)

it will be compliant to management goals. What the two traditions do have in common, however, is a shared incapacity to come to terms with the misbehaviour they encountered. Though the emphasis differed between the Hawthorne researchers, they frequently focused on psychological factors. This can be seen clearly in their well-known formulation of management as driven by a logic of efficiency and a workforce whose 'codes, customs and traditions of work are not the product of logic, but of deeply rooted sentiments' (Roethlisberger and Dickson, 1964, 55, 567). Examples of the latter included the 'right to work' and a 'living wage'. Resistance does take place, not as a response to exploitation and domination, but when technical and other changes are too rapid or undertaken without concern for their social implications. The subsequent lack of adjustment echoes Durkheim's concern that anomic reactions to social change disrupt social equilibrium. The previously discussed volume on 'antisocial behaviour' (Giacalone and Greenberg, 1997) provides a good example of modern writing that continues to see misbehaviour in terms of the psychology of individual deviancy.

This is one small indication of the way in which human relations continued as a strong influence in the post-war period. It has been rediscovered more recently with an emphasis on groups and the social need to belong in the Japanese management and corporate culture literatures (Peters and Waterman, 1982). We return to this territory in the final chapter. But OB developed in other directions in the intervening period, most notably with the neo-human-relations work on motivation of Maslow (1943), McGregor (1960) and Herzberg (1959), as well as the work of expectancy theorists such as Vroom (1960). The differences need not concern us here (see Rose, 1988; Thompson and McHugh, 1995). Indeed the favoured story of OB texts is one of a largely linear path in which new theories added layers of complexity to 'models of man', moving from economic, through social to employees as a collection of differing psychological needs.

But that was precisely the problem. Such perspectives did not start from the reality of observed behaviour, but from a variety of preconceived starting points – either abstract and highly generalized conceptualizations of human needs (Maslow, 1943) or ideas rooted in conceptions of biological drives originating in behaviourist notions (Skinner, 1953; Homans, 1950). But the ultimate starting point of such conceptions is irrelevant. Whatever its intellectual origins, the whole problematic of motivation built into OB assumes that a compliant and programmable worker is possible. Indeed the object of these conceptions is to develop ways of thinking about the compliant worker, and the situations in which he or she can be produced. This mirrors the interest of managerial practitioners in understanding 'motivation' in order to control performance and increase productivity.

There are of course other specialist areas in OB, but their orientation is essentially the same. The modern textbook is divided up into a number of discrete subjects – work motivation, leadership, job design, communication, decision-making and so on. Behaviour is considered, organized and

classified according to criteria that have obvious relevance to those direct-
ing organizations. The field is presented as a number of discrete but evidently manageable problems. They are manageable in the sense that they
are strictly delimited and that understanding them is relevant if one occu-
pies a given position to which knowledge of this neatly packaged kind is relevant. There is, clearly, an implicit idea in this sort of conception that
studying organizational behaviour is about achieving and enhancing managerial control. Indeed the whole point of considering organizational behaviour at all is, in this definition of the subject, only justified if one can the
better contrive to meet managerial objectives by doing so. The assumption
is that by the discreet application of behavioural science, organizational performance can be tweaked and adjusted to higher levels. Organizational
analysis improves performativity. Occasional problems of low motivation or
instances of groups defining projects for themselves in ways that are not
wholly constructive from the organizational point of view will be encountered even in the best organization; but it is in precisely such circumstances
that a knowledge of the springs of organizational behaviour can prove its
worth.

This kind of perspective can be illustrated within the work of Analoui
(1992) and Analoui and Kakabadse (1993), who have made the most systematic attempt in recent years to examine what they call 'defiance' or
'unconventional practices' from within an OB framework. They are rightly
careful to establish the normal, rational and purposeful character of such
practices as pilferage, rule-breaking and non-cooperation and reject the
common tendency towards 'stigmatising, stereotyping and ostracising the
behaviour and the actor, at the expense of exclusion of the "meaningful-
ness" of the behaviour as the actor's self-expression' (Analoui, 1992, 8).
Useful descriptive accounts are also given of misbehaviour at a large night
club they dub 'Alpha'.

But they are irresistibly drawn to the OB illusion that if something can
be understood, it is manageable. If unconventional practices can be understood as normal then they can be conventionally dealt with through effective communication, proper planning and control and the provision of
means through which employees can express their voice. Whatever slips
through this net is confinable: 'Managers in industry should provide the
foundation for the creation of the appropriate workplace culture in which
only the least disruptive and damaging forms of discontent are promoted,
rewarded and are naturally adopted as the logical response to situations of
discontent' (Analoui and Kakabadse, 1993, 58). To reach a conclusion that
both motivation and control are of equal importance in dealing with misbehaviour (Analoui, 1992, 28) is hardly breaking new ground. The weakness of the diagnosis reveals that despite their injunctions to managers, the
authors do not understand the nature of 'unconventional practices'. The
basic problem is that their understanding of rationality is too individualistic. Employees' value orientation leads them to choose a misbehaving
response which feeds a clash of interests. By changing structures and

leadership styles, managers can alter such choices, minimizing or negating discontent (Analoui and Kakabadse, 1993, 56–8). Notions of rationally opposed interests based on structural sources of unequal power and resources are written off as 'extreme'.

It is difficult to accept the idea that these approaches understand organizational behaviour adequately or can deliver effective control over misbehaviour. Nevertheless, organizational analysis has not been confined to a behavioural framework. The other major post-war direction – including the Aston Studies, neo-Weberians and contingency theories – has emphasized organizational design and structural differentiation. In his defence of mainstream organizational theory, Donaldson (1985) defines the object of analysis as the relations between structure, contingency and performance. A large body of work has been created which concerns typologies of bureaucracy; the relations between size, markets, technologies (and other variables) and organizational structure; and the fit between the social and technical dimensions of organization (for reviews see Clegg, 1975; Clegg and Dunkerley, 1980; Thompson and McHugh, 1995; Brown, 1992).

In one sense these studies could be said simply to neglect issues of conflict and misbehaviour other than relatively routine 'office politics'. But such approaches tend to make deterministic assumptions about the link between environment, structure and behaviour; with people cast as largely passive adapters. Indeed this was the basis of the successful critique made by Silverman (1970) and other action theorists. In addition there is an implicit or explicit underpinning of much of the theorizing by a functionalist, systems approach which accepts goal consensus and interdependence of the component parts of the organization. Brown notes with respect to the open, socio-technical systems research, that there is a 'failure to acknowledge the inherent conflicts of interest of employer and employee' (1992, 75). For whatever the reason, the messy reality of behaviour and misbehaviour was again absent. Even those critics who attempted to insert human action back into the picture tended to focus on the negotiation of order, albeit an order with multiple goals and fluid, informal processes (Day and Day, 1997).

The inadequacies of such approaches have led, since the late 1970s, to successive attempts to reconceptualize the study of work organizations through radical Weberian and Marxian conceptual frameworks (Salaman, 1979; Clegg and Dunkerley, 1980; Hill, 1981; Reed, 1985; Thompson, 1983; Thompson and McHugh, 1995; Morgan, 1990). A focus on the varieties of conflict and resistance in organizations has not always been a priority, partly because the central orientation has been towards reconceptualizing the subject in general, seeking to penetrate behind the surface appearance of organizations to consider their structure and the basic processes that are held to constitute organizing. Nevertheless, given that a central starting point of such analysis has been a critique of the tendency of mainstream theories to neglect control, power and conflict, these texts have been in a much better position to understand misbehaviour. The workplace is, in the words of Richard Edwards (1979), a contested terrain, primarily because employers and managers are compelled by the logic of profit maximization to seek the cheapening of the costs of production and control over the labour process. In doing so they inevitably enter into conflict with workers seeking to protect and extend their own interests in production. The idea that a pattern of control and resistance is a fundamental dynamic of organizational life is associated with labour process theory. Reed sums up the associated research programme as: 'the specific ways in which the "dialectic of control" operates within workplaces to produce changes in the patterns of conflict that emerge out of the struggle between dominant and subordinate groups, as well as the wider impact of these changing patterns of conflict on the control strategies of employers and managers' (1992, 101).

We will further examine its character and limits in the next section.[1] But whatever criticisms have been made, it remains the case that labour process and other radical analyses have generated a much more realistic picture of organizational life and its attendant conflicts of interest. Our quarrel is simply that the project does not go far enough. We wish to expand its scope and define its purpose in somewhat different ways. This can best be explained by locating the discussion inside a wider framework which examines more systematically the main ways in which analysis of the workplace classifies misbehaviour.

Understanding and classifying misbehaviour

We have been using misbehaviour, so far, largely as synonymous with other terms such as conflict or resistance. Conceptual clarity was not necessary in order to make our basic argument about the neglect and misunderstanding of a 'class' of actions. However, we also want to make a case for misbehaviour as a distinct set of practices and this section aims to develop a classification schema appropriate to this task. It will be helpful to start with existing classifications of workplace conflict. We have already seen that the dominant strands of OB carry a baggage of unitary assumptions about the harmonious workplace and, even where conflict is 'seen', it can only be conceived of as pathological, irrational, marginal or temporary. Given that this kind of approach registers an absence rather than explanation, we can shift to 'real' frameworks, using a diagram to illustrate the differences and overlaps (see Figure 1.1).

The dimension of conflict that social science has best understood has been that behaviour that can be described as organized non-compliance. There has been a systematic examination of that behaviour which is deliberately organized, often by trade unions, to assert the interests of employees and

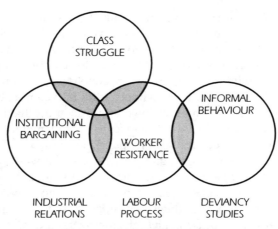

Figure 1.1 **Existing classifications of workplace conflict**

resist the encroachments of management. In terms of discipline framework, such activity has mostly gone under the heading of industrial relations (IR) and is shown as the far left circle in Figure 1.1. The object of analysis began as the IR system: a relatively formal account of the organized actors (capital, labour, state), the normative and procedural rules of the game, and the legal, political and economic conditions that make up the context for action (Dunlop, 1958; Eldridge, 1968). With this in mind the most common focus has been systems of bargaining, mechanisms to institutionalize conflict inside and outside the workplace, the range of industrial action and incidence of strikes, and the forms of trade union organization and ideology (Clegg, 1976, 1979). Such analysis is certainly necessary, but its limitations are obvious in that it tends to take a narrower institutional perspective and focuses on a specific range of actions and organizations. Even when Britain had a reputation for industrial militancy and strike-proneness in the 1960s and 1970s, the vast majority of workers never engaged in such action, or in any other formal dispute (Hyman, 1972; Crouch, 1982). Yet it would be foolish to believe that the British workplace was or indeed is a haven of harmony and cooperation. For this reason, there had long been a 'second' IR which focused more on the internal dynamics of the workplace, notably the conflicts of interest and expectation that arise in effort bargain – the gap between promise of effort and promise of reward. Such studies have also tried to elaborate 'systems' and rules governing processes such as output restriction or absenteeism, but of a largely informal and supposedly 'unorganized' kind.

A different means of escaping from the narrow limits of conventional IR is sought by social scientists whose object of analysis is capitalism as a system and class struggle as the key form of conflict (Mann, 1973; Clarke and Clements, 1977). This area of interest is depicted as the top circle in Figure 1.1. Such writers want to broaden the framework of analysis to ask under what conditions workplace conflict reflects or leads to wider struggle between capital and labour as societal, not just industrial actors. Traditionally, of course, this has largely been a debate between Marxists who see the industrial working class as the potential gravedigger of capitalism and a variety of more sceptical non-Marxists. Both sides of this debate place an impossible burden on worker resistance by judging it in terms of its capacity to transform society.

Labour process writers are influenced by Marx, but have generally abandoned any attempt to 'read off' a theory of class struggle and broader social transformation from the relations between employers and employees in the workplace. In this sense the object of analysis is particular types of capitalism and capitalist institutions and their relations, rather than capitalism as a general system. More concretely, we can say that such research is aimed at demonstrating patterns of control and resistance, and is depicted in the central circle in Figure 1.1. In this area of work Braverman (1974) focused on the characteristics of control rather than employee initiatives, while many other prominent contributors (Friedman, 1977; Edwards, 1979) attempted to establish a dialectic of managerial control and worker resistance as the central dynamic that can explain why the capitalist labour process takes on particular forms in given periods or circumstances. Alternatively they elaborated a politics of production in which workers' struggles are part of the process of producing a series of dominant factory regimes. Such frameworks are flawed by their over-ambitious attempts to create overarching models which explain the sequence or central characteristics of periods of capitalist production. A more circumspect and more sophisticated attempt to develop a full account of workplace conflict from a labour process perspective has been provided by Edwards and Scullion (1982), who look at a much wider range of conflict, utilizing seven case studies of British firms. When we talk of output restriction, sabotage or resistance it presupposes that workers have the capacity to exert some control over their working lives. That control is exerted within the space between promise of effort and promise of reward; or as it is put in labour process theory, between the purchase of labour power and its translation into profitable production. Edwards and Scullion argue that the concept of the effort bargain is insufficient because it doesn't explain the origins of the conflict in the wider workings of capitalist political economy. But though wider social influences on workplace behaviour are recognized, they distinguish their view from those who see forms of conflict such as sabotage, absenteeism and labour turnover as the direct product of class relationships. A more specific focus is developed which explains patterns of conflict in terms of the intensity and means of managerial control in each factory. For all the impressive scope and rich data, the study still tries to infer the character and direction of resistance from control alone. Nor is it accurate to define all the observed employee motives and practices by using the concept of resistance to control, or to judge its effectiveness primarily through the degree of formal, collective action achieved by workers (see Chapter 2 for a more detailed discussion).

For example, at ten o'clock on a very quiet Wednesday night, the bar staff carried out what was clearly a well-rehearsed scenario. When the majority of the customers who had been standing by the bar went on to the dance floor for a dance, one of the staff pretended to be wiping the top of the bar. The rest of the staff whilst helping her to restore some semblance of order and cleanliness, swopped around the half-consumed drinks which had been left on the bar top. When the customers returned to the bar much confusion arose. Eventually some succeeded in finding their drinks while others inadvertently took those belonging to other customers. This situation usually created many arguments. The staff, who had nothing better to do, would then place bets on which customer would become the most irate in the shortest space of time. (Analoui, 1992, 20)

Yet it is clear that there is a realm of misbehaviour beyond resistance to control. One group of writers with a perception of this is indicated by the final circle in Figure 1.1, which we have described as deviancy studies. Radical social scientists (Cohen, 1971; Ditton, 1977b, 1978; Mars, 1982b) increasingly began to challenge the idea that certain types of activity were 'abnormal'. Though the initial focus was often criminology, many of the best-known studies focused on the workplace. To create a realistic picture of the underlife of organizations the object of analysis had to be informal behaviour: 'we cannot understand how our society operates unless we consider the informal side of our social institutions' (Mars, 1982b, 7). Such studies sought to show that 'the fiddle' was a normal part of organizational life. But whereas Edwards (1986b) talks of fiddles largely in terms of the classic territory of the effort bargain and output restriction, deviancy studies are more likely to emphasize theft of goods or time, though some studies also look at issues such as sabotage (Taylor and Walton, 1971). It is the strength and weakness of the approach that it reveals 'a "subterranean" version of the conventional culture of business' (Ditton, 1977a, 173). For while it pokes into corners that normally remain in darkness, the results could be too easily marginalized as exotic or subcultural.

So, although there are insights gained from each of the disciplines and frameworks for analysis, misbehaviour does not neatly map onto them. Misbehaviour consists of non-compliant or 'counter-productive' practices that take a wider variety of forms (and have more varied motives) than can be encompassed through the available models. Formal actions can involve misbehaviour, and informal behaviour can be conforming. As an analytical category, worker resistance assumes a dialectic with managerial control that is an outcome of antagonism between capital and labour within the capitalist labour process. That is fine. But clearly, managerial control and other forms of authority exist outside of those relations, and therefore so does non-compliance with them. An example, dealt with in Chapter 6, would be sexual misbehaviour, in which employees disrupt workplace order or appropriate time in pursuit of romance or conquest. Even within

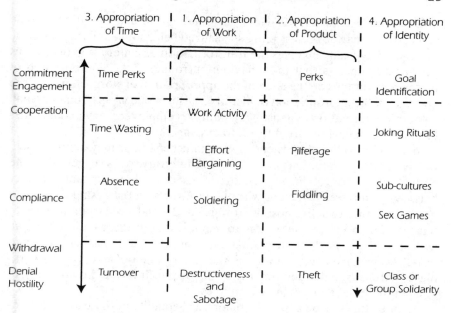

Figure 1.2   **Dimensions of misbehaviour**

the capitalist workplace, not all activities can be directly related to a pattern of control and resistance. Absenteeism is a case in point. While managerial attempts to regulate the phenomenon do shape its form and subsequent responses, it remains true that employees go absent for a variety of reasons; for example, linking the last two points together, in order to pursue an affair every Wednesday afternoon. Similarly sabotage may be part of the struggle over the frontier of control, but equally it may be employed to relieve boredom and have fun.

Our goal is not to claim misbehaviour for organizational theory or any other discipline, but rather to produce a full account of the variety of practices, an account which combines insights from traditional frameworks without being trapped within them. Again we try to map out the terrain in question, before going on to explain it further.

Broadly speaking, we contend that there are four directions that misbehaviour can take. These we suggest actually arise from four areas of contention – labelled 1 to 4 across the horizontal dimension of Figure 1.2. We envisage the possibility of: 1, disagreement over the appropriation of work; 2, over the appropriation of the materials used in work; 3, over the appropriation of the time spent on work; and 4, over the extent to which employees identify with their work activity and employers, or more simply, the appropriation of employee identity. We regard each of these as of equal significance theoretically, regardless of where they appear on the map. True, misbehaviour around the appropriation of work is fundamental in the sense that it is directly related to the material issue at the heart of the capitalist labour process. But misbehaviour surrounding the appropriation of time and material may be seen as more specialized behaviour similar to the basic form: work typically involves the transformation of materials in operations which take time, so that misbehaviour surrounding the appropriation of these are variations on the issue of the appropriation of work. However, the question of the appropriation of identity is also, in one aspect, fundamental: without the formation of a distinct identity by employees, any and all other forms of misbehaviour are difficult to envisage.

In addition to the dimensions in which misbehaviour may express itself, we also envisage variations in its degree or intensity. As is suggested by the vertical dimension of Figure 1.2, the intensity of disagreement can vary between positive engagement with the task through increasing degrees of non-compliance to active hostility towards and withdrawal from the task. In this way four areas of contention are mapped in our diagram in which the appropriation of working effort, material, time and identity are actively contested. Management and employees, the major groups of actors in the workplace, are engaged in a continual struggle to appropriate and reappropriate relevant material and symbolic resources.

Despite points made about the theoretical equality of these areas of contention, the most prevalent area in the present century, and certainly the most frequently noticed and carefully examined, has been work limitation. Certainly from Taylor's emphasis on 'soldiering' to modern research on the effort bargain, this aspect of behaviour has been recurrently analysed. In our 'map' we have represented this as misbehaviour on the terrain of work activity, whose most extreme form is sabotage.

In most work, time and materials are combined to produce products or provide services. Work limitation is in many ways an obvious recourse for people because they retain degrees of control over their activities at work, however tightly their work is specified or closely their activities regulated. Moreover, the extent and effectiveness of work limitation are seldom fully appreciated. The extent of the manipulation of the wage–work exchange is often considerable, as the work of such well-known authors such as Lupton, Cunnison, Roy, Burawoy, and so on suggests. There is almost always active manipulation of the wage–work exchange – secondary adjustments to the effort bargain – including such things as working slowly to achieve a 'loose' rate, or being booked into one job while working on another (Edwards, 1988, 190).

But such practices overlap with two other areas of activity. As we have suggested, work typically combines time and resources, and each of these can become the subject of activity aimed at reclaiming or reappropriating them separately. First, there are various attempts to appropriate time. The most obvious instance here is absence from work, but there are also the many variants of 'time-wasting', from disappearing to the toilet in the factory to going walkabout around the office, or otherwise being what Ditton (1972) has memorably called being 'absent at work'.

Second, there is the appropriation of the products of work. The most important phenomenon here is 'pilferage', but historically this has been known as anything from embezzlement to contemporary euphemisms such as 'stock shrinkage' or 'unplanned overheads'. This phenomenon has been studied by criminologists, as we shall see, and they note the connection of this kind of activity with the practice of fiddling in which money rather than goods is appropriated, and the so-called 'grey economy', in which pilfered goods become part of networks of exchange relationships outside the workplace.

It is fundamental to our account that we identify a fourth dimension – activities which feature the appropriation of identity. Not everything that happens in the workplace can be directly connected to struggles over material resources. Symbolic resources are also a terrain of informal action and misbehaviour, and the primary focus of such activity is the variety of identities carried into or developed within the workplace. Once it has been pointed out it is obvious that self-organization is necessary for all the activities we have so far discussed. Behaviour that reappropriates work, time and product depends on the self-organization of workgroups. This is particularly obvious with some kinds of activity. For example, joking rituals based on horseplay and banter are a recurrent feature of workplace life. Amongst the most prominent are initiation ceremonies, where the new worker is subject to some form of ritual test or humiliation to incorporate them into the informal organization, or 'subculture'. Many of these ceremonies have a strong connection to the affirmation of gender identities. Assertion of masculinities and femininities can take place in a variety of what we call 'sex games': informal interactions within and between men and women on the shop or office floor. However it is important not to treat such practices as highly distinctive. All misbehaviour is associated with processes of identity formation and self-organization.

This matter of identity at work is becoming more rather than less important. On the one hand, employees are becoming more aware of their capacity to sustain identity at work. At the same time, employers have interests in this area too. This is noticeable in the suggestions of management pundits and academics that the sentiments and informal social organization of employee groups should be captured and turned to the advantage of employing organizations. But these motivations are by no means the same. The view of the employer and manager – that the employee will be willing to identify with their company – is no more nor less than a startling piece of wishful thinking.

The dimensions we have considered often overlap and examples of behaviour are sometimes difficult to distinguish in these terms. Indeed, work limitation can be thought of as involving attempts to manipulate both time and product as a package. Considered in this way, active manipulation of the economic relationship between employers and employees is just a more complex form of negotiation than pilferage or time-wasting. However, we would contend that what unites these practices is not only some conceptual similarity, but that they are social practices, in a way that has often been neglected or unnoticed. Informal self-organization is a necessary accompaniment to all these activities. It is also the case that struggles over work, time and resources necessarily draw on symbolic resources, though in varying ways and degrees.

Our 'map' signals that the nature and intensity of employee practices varies with respect to each terrain. Those whose positional power or normative orientation predisposes them appropriately may have highly committed or engaged relationships to the organization characterized by a variety of 'perks'. At the opposite extreme, those who are marginal or marginalized are often characterized by withdrawal, destructive actions or oppositional value systems. A final point is that none of the actions in themselves have a fixed meaning in how they are regarded as misbehaviour or whether they are regarded as misbehaviour at all. In a flour mill worked in by one of the authors, one of the basic tasks was to take bags of flour from a pallet and throw them down a chute, where they would eventually be collected and stored for later distribution. Workers had cultivated small jagged edges at the side of the chute, so that, when they were bored, they could play solitary games of aiming the bags at the sharp edges, bursting some of them open. Though the practice was visible and had a clear, if minor, destructive intent and consequence, neither workers nor supervisors ever defined or acted upon it as if it was sabotage.

The organizational production of misbehaviour

Our purpose is not to re-examine or indeed create causal explanations for conflict and resistance in the workplace, but to produce a provisional mapping of the misbehaviour that many managers and social scientists have tended to neglect. The notion of organizational behaviour presumably designates practices that occur in organizations and not elsewhere, or differently elsewhere. People do behave differently in alternative social contexts, for example inside organizations and in their families. They see themselves and act as part of the web of relations that is the organization.

On the one hand employees have to operate inside the constraints of rules set by those who own and control resources. Behaviour in work organizations is directed and controlled in a manner not found elsewhere. People are required to do things in their work: often job specifications or descriptions make certain actions and responsibilities obligatory. Work is usually supervised, and there is a panoply of disciplinary devices, from the threat of reduction in wages to the termination of employment if workers are not sufficiently compliant. This directive aspect is most obvious for lower level participants and for certain manual kinds of work, but it is there, in some degree, for all. Even where there seem to be no specific duties attached to a job, people are constrained to accept and work within definitions of appropriate conduct.

Organizational behaviour is not however to be understood simply as the result of control and direction imposed on people in organizations. For at the same time they are adapting, interpreting and challenging those rules, in part because they are orienting their conduct to a conception of informal norms, and in part because it is a product of a relationship – albeit unequal. Organizational behaviour can therefore be thought of as a mixture of those dispositions – the directive and the responsive. These two aspects do not exactly correspond with organizational roles: employees can initiate and managers follow. Furthermore, directive and responsive aspects of organizational behaviour can only be separated analytically. In practice they are always to a large extent reciprocal, but attempts to locate clear cause and effect are usually fruitless. If any workplace is examined closely a 'dialectic of innovation' will be found that arises from the interaction between the organization as directive system and the self-organization of participants.

Though we can produce in-depth accounts of such interactions at a specific place and time, we do of course recognize the historical and social embeddedness of misbehaviour. It is shaped by social motivations in the broadest sense. People bring with them into the organization expectations about work or various gender, class and other identities which predispose them to behave or misbehave in particular ways. For example, those who sexually harass their fellow employees have been affected by a wider social construction of masculinity and femininity. But it still requires a context to create opportunities or shape the form and content of action. Similarly, effort bargain conflicts are in part a product of a broader structural antagonism between capital and labour in a specific mode of production. Such a framework establishes parameters for interests to form and action to be undertaken. But groups and individuals still have to develop strategies and tactics within specific workplaces and companies that have their own histories, cultures and resources. Our general point still stands: even though it may be innovative, misbehaviour is organizationally produced. In addition, it will be affected by the influence of traditions and past experiences, notably the ways in which organizations have attempted to shape and direct behaviour and by the sedimented experience of what it is reasonable to do at work that has been laid down over time.

With all this talk of absence and neglect, we do not want to give the impression that this is uncharted territory. Rather, it is charted with different maps. It is part of our case that social science investigations of the workplace have produced a very rich array of studies of many of the phenomena discussed in this chapter. In Chapter 2, we examine the literature produced on 'the recalcitrant worker'. Our aim is to bring it together and explore its strengths and limitations.

Note

1 Radical organization theory is increasingly influenced by those (Jermier et al., 1994) who prefer to use the work of Foucault on power and resistance, and who are heavily critical of labour process perspectives. We examine their own, in our view unsuccessful, attempts to theorize resistance in the final chapter.

2 The Recalcitrant Worker

In this chapter we consider the extent to which organizational misbehaviour is already known to social scientists. Although we argued in Chapter 1 that the terrain of misbehaviour has not been fully or adequately mapped, re-discovery of the recalcitrant worker has been one of the most persistent motifs of industrial sociology. Dictionary definitions are seldom very useful in exercises of this sort, but that given to recalcitrance is apt for our purposes: 'the refusal to submit to authority, obstinate, disobedience' (*Penguin Oxford Dictionary*). The recalcitrant worker may be engaged in absenteeism, sabotage, fiddles, or straightforward restriction of output. He or she may be characterized as deviant or rebellious. But whatever the focus or label, the important fact remains the long and largely honourable tradition in social science of seeing beneath the surface of formal organization and the apparent consent of employees in the capitalist employment relationship. Though often highly specialized or subsumed under over-ambitious attempts to construct general social theory, this tradition is a necessary antidote to the image of the willing and conforming employee too often found in management and organizational literature.

In the past, much of the emphasis has been on finding that there is a link between recalcitrance and work limitation. However, this chapter will also show that industrial sociology and related traditions have explored, often implicitly and unevenly, behaviour in which there is the appropriation of time and product and, to a lesser extent, the appropriation of identity. We have not the space to discuss all the different specialisms in social science that could be reviewed. Instead we will focus on some of the most significant attempts to describe and understand recalcitrance. These we have divided into a number of interrelated and overlapping categories of our own, rather than following any established temporal or conceptual sequence.

Soldiers of fortune

Systematic work limitation is a ubiquitous phenomenon of organized work. Historians have located a 'critical conflict for control' over the labour process in many trades as far back as the 1820s (Behagg, 1990, 5). The independent producer who pursued a belief in the right to organize work through systems of subcontract was eventually displaced by craft workers struggling to erect a series of job rules.

There were, for example, sixty-six 'Rules for Working' in the bylaws of the window-glass workers' Local Assembly 300 of the Knights of Labor. They specified that full crews had to be present 'at each pot sitting'; that skimming could be done only at the beginning of blowing and at meal time; that blowers and gatherers should not 'work faster than at the rate of nine rollers per hour'; and that the 'standard size of single strength rollers' should 'be 40 x 58 to cut 38 x 56'. No work was to be performed on Thanksgiving Day, Christmas, Decoration Day or Washington's Birthday, and no blower, gatherer or cutter could work between June 15 and September 15. In other words, during the summer months the union ruled that the fires were to be out. (Montgomery, 1980, 15)

Much work limitation is more informal, disguised and hidden. Nevertheless, the fact that it occurs is difficult to hide from sustained observation. Historically much of the work in the field of management studies, industrial sociology and the social psychology of work and occupations has been concerned with giving acceptable accounts of work limitation. The basic phenomenon has commonly been named 'soldiering', but a number of other descriptions have also been developed, among them the 'reverie' into which Mayo suggested bored operatives would lapse, and the instrumental output restriction proposed by several schools of thought in the 1950s and 1960s. In fact it is possible to argue that management theory came into being primarily in order to confront work limitation. As we have seen in Chapter 1, Taylor defined this 'enemy of efficiency' as soldiering.

Scientific management did not eliminate such practices. If anything, time study, incentive pay and dilution of skills stimulated what one union leader described as 'sabotage, syndicalism [and] passive resistance' (Montgomery, 1980, 101–2). The agency of resistance, Montgomery goes on to report, was the small informal workgroup, perhaps less explicit than before, but still a submerged, impenetrable obstacle to managerial sovereignty. He refers to a study of one group of steel workers who had not the slightest interest in the operations of the mill and who did as little as the boss would allow. Their favourite saying was 'What the hell!' Montgomery is, however, somewhat romantic in presenting such struggles for autonomy by skilled craftsmen as inherently part of a movement for workers' control (1980, 4).

A more realistic assessment, made in 1920, talked instead of a 'frontier of control' (Goodrich, 1975). Though there were indeed movements for workers' control, employee action was overwhelmingly reactive and protective. Goodrich rightly referred to restriction of output as more a method of warfare than a form of control. The popular British name for such activity was 'ca'canny', which designated a 'stay-in strike', go-slow or other type of restrictive practice; Sidney and Beatrice Webb referring to it as 'an insidious diminution of . . . energy without notice to the employer' (quoted in Brown, 1977, 8). While the army of Taylorite efficiency experts continued their low level warfare against soldiering, the focus of attention of academic social science in the workplace shifted to the human relations movement.

Again, as we saw in the previous chapter, informal, but organized work limitation was drowned in a sea of psychologizing and rendered 'irrational'. The rationality of soldiering surfaced only in the work of researchers discussed in the next section.

Rational 'man'

In the period following the Second World War, analysis of the workplace was dominated by a human relations approach in which this form of misbehaviour was interpreted as the result of group social sentiment and pressure, inadequate communication, or a disjuncture between the formal, technical and the social, informal structures of the organization. Introducing the influential study of Jaques into the problems of changing the managerial and industrial relations structures of the Glacier Metal Company, the chairman of the Tavistock Institute noted that: 'The specific study reported here shows how unconscious forces in group behaviour, and the unwitting collusion between groups for purposes of which they are only dimly aware, are important factors in the process of social adaptation' (1951, xvii).

By contrast, in this section we group together accounts of work behaviour which emphasize the rational adaptation of operatives to management. There are two important post-war strands of this work, one British (Lupton, 1963; Cunnison, 1964) and one American (Dalton, 1948; Roy, 1952, 1953, 1954), which were both strongly influenced by the outlook and methods of anthropology. Both discovered, through very close observation of particular industrial organizations, the extent of the adaptation of operatives to the methods of scientific management, and the variation that is possible in the extent and nature of this. Though the studies focused on the social factors underpinning production norms, their key finding was the economic rationality of the responses of workers to industrial regimes, and the way that practical behaviour at work aimed at adjusting wage–effort exchanges in favour of the employee. Lupton explicitly attacks human relations and the findings of the Hawthorne, bank wiring room research in particular for emphasizing that work limitation is a result of a logic of sentiment and group solidarity. In contrast he argues that the 'fiddle' worked, and was a knowledgeable and logical means to the end of regulation of the job environment (1963, 172). This even leads him to reject the term 'restriction of output' for the 'odour of disapproval' that accompanies it; he prefers to talk of 'controls over behaviour'.

These writers give a new slant to misbehaviour in that although there are a few 'fiddles' which border on dishonesty, by and large the misbehaving responses of workers are in their interests, implying that management has inadequately gauged the extent of economic rationality and the effectiveness of informal organization in supporting effective, economically rational behaviour. By being collectively in agreement about the level at which timings allow 'gravy' to be earned, a degree of control is achieved by operatives who generally respect customary output norms. The work of the American authors, in particular, identifies and describes the politics of informal relations which grows up surrounding the administration of piecework payments systems (Collins et al., 1946). Collective organization arises in response to the pursuit of economic rationality.

Although less dramatic in the way that it describes the politics of informal work relations under piecework, the research of British investigators makes similar points about the effects of and responses to scientific management regimes. The influential research report of Tom Lupton, for example, showed that the extent to which piecework payment systems produced conformity and elicited high levels of productive effort was variable, and that different combinations of circumstances, many of them not considered by management to be relevant, actually had a considerable impact. In the machine shop he studied, part of which was the unfortunately named Small Erection Section, he found a marked collectivist response, even more overtly organized than the situation investigated by Roy. Here, workers colluded in quota restriction, and effectively imposed such norms on all operatives. Some of the practices such as informal tea breaks had become customary throughout the plant. But the various forms of work limitation were openly described by workers as 'the fiddle'. More typical were standard means of influencing the effort bargain such as putting time 'in the bank' through inflated claims for work done. Every worker kept a notebook in which he or she recorded details of jobs allocated. Evidence of hostility to time study was rife. When one such engineer appears unexpectedly, he is unceremoniously greeted by an operative with the words, 'Fuck off; who invited you?' (Lupton, 1963, 149). Workers who deviated from the group's standard of 'proper behaviour' were also brought into line.

In his other case of a garment factory employing mainly female workers there were also some typical fiddles; notably the 'dead horse' practice of booking in dockets for work not yet completed, and corner cutting such as 'sweating' which produced an inferior product in less time. But by and large, piecework incentives did effectively induce greater effort and increased output. Lupton explained this variation in terms of the organization of the workforces in the two industries: workers were more individuated by the

---

Harry Birtwhistle and Lofty reported to me that they were having a great deal of difficulty in 'making out' on a new job. They had been asking Cyril to add another hour to the allowed time, but they learned that Garvey had spoiled the job and by 'tear-arsing' had shown that it was possible to make a bonus on it. On Syd's advice, Harry and Lofty told Garvey of their difficulties. It turned out that Garvey had in fact completed one of the new jobs in considerably less than their allowed time. He had not booked in any of the time to the job. He said he was quite prepared, when booking in time for the job, to make it appear as if the time was really very 'tight' so that Harry and Lofty would have good grounds for requesting an extra hour. (Lupton, 1963, 167)

organization of production and by the tradition of a volatile industry that 'taught' employees to 'look after number one'. Jobs were highly specialized and thus the development of output norms would have to cover some very different tasks. In contrast to the machine shop, the power of the union was not used as an additional leverage. If anything the reverse applied, on one occasion the union official telling 'girls' worried by time and motion that they 'mustn't stand in the way of science in industry' (1963, 44).

Lupton rejects the argument that the gender of the workforce was a significant factor. Though reference is made to the higher levels of absenteeism caused by domestic responsibilities and the preference for friendship groups because they create identification with the company, he argues that the absence of a 'will to control' arises from women adapting to the dominant customs and conventions of the industry. In her parallel study of different clothing firms, in which she accounts for some very similar findings, Sheila Cunnison (1964) places much firmer emphasis on the importance of factors external to the workplace in shaping behaviour, pointing to the intersection of domestic and work roles in the family and the community. She is aware of the limited employment prospects for women in the garment industry, and points to the fact that the insecurity of employment in this industry, seasonal and other fluctuations in the demand for product, are related to the fact that the industry is dominated by women, and it is this that has prevented organization from taking hold.

The studies discussed in this section were valuable, not merely for restoring the rationality of workplace action, but for highlighting the gap between managerial expectation of 'ideal behaviour' and the reality of misbehaviour. As the steps that workers take to assert their interests are reasonable given their position in workplace and society, 'it would seem that management would be better employed in putting its technical house in order than complaining about the restrictive practices of workers' (Lupton, 1963, 201). Such a dose of realism was welcome in theoretical and practical terms, but the analytical framework of this generation of studies remained underdeveloped. We will return to work limitation, including its relationship to gender. For now we turn to a further contribution to reclaiming the normality of misbehaviour.

Industrial deviants

In the 1970s there were a number of new attempts to think again about the nature of misbehaviour. To the realization that non-compliance was a permanent feature of work organization, was added the understanding that it was not restricted to soldiering or the sphere of the wage–effort bargain, but that there was a whole range of related practices as well. Sociological studies of deviancy in industrial settings in the late 1960s, and renewed efforts at industrial anthropology, produced studies of the underlife of institutions, and in particular the discovery of pilferage and theft.

On the fiddle

A different angle on workplace 'fiddles' was part of efforts by radical sociologists to critically interrogate received wisdom on a variety of forms of deviancy, in effect by challenging that label and restoring the meaning of such acts by showing how they were continuous with normal life (Cohen, 1971). Though the workplace was just one site for such studies, it generated important insights into the way in which a shadow economy existed in which workers appropriated invisible wages and other covert reward systems. Our understanding of misbehaviour was enhanced by the very detailed studies of particular work situations which demonstrated that theft and pilferage (the latter designating managerially acknowledged theft) was integral to the standard functioning of the firm.

Although it was easy to dismiss such studies on the grounds of untypicality, as the research increased the extent of such activity became impossible to discount. The case studies sometimes covered traditional soldiering territory. A seminal study by Ditton in a bakery, for example, suggested that the same kinds of work limitation practices as were prevalent under piecework systems were also present with day work (1977a), and that absenteeism could be connected with time-wasting (1972, 1978). Ditton's studies, notably that undertaken at the Wellbread bakery (1977a, 1978), made clear that, like output restriction, the fiddle was a particular form of making out. The skills of passing out stolen bread were identical to those required for conventional service transactions. His study suggested that the worker was active and innovative in his attempts to survive in employment, recurrently breaking rules and actively renegotiating them on a continuous basis. Individuals were aware of wrongdoing, but could justify it by reference to their own subordinate position in the workplace hierarchy and the activities of managers and customers. Indeed such rule-breaking was sustained by an oppositional subculture in which the heroic, skilful deeds of fiddling sales staff were counterposed to the haplessness of gullible customers and mendacious managers.

But the most revealing of Ditton's discoveries was that management had knowledge of, and, in some circumstances encouraged, fiddling, in this

---

In the despatch department, it was the same story. 'The wholesale boys', one said, 'are up to all their tricks'. 'They all', the others agreed, 'make a bit on the side', 'have their little perks', 'make tea money', 'take the odd loaf'. And always the meta-communicative wink: 'Y'know?', 'know what I mean?' . . . The night manager just thought of it as tolerable shrinkage: 'I mean, you've got to allow for losses, you do get a percentage of loss in every bakery . . . you get the odd loaf being taken home and not being paid for, a box of cakes goes, somebody has a nibble'. But always the insidious, 'You know [laugh] we all make a bit on the side . . . know what I mean?' No I didn't, but by God, I was going to. (Ditton 1977a, 7)

case of the customer. The 'moral career' of sales staff could only make sense in the context of the support that fiddling received from the broader context of service activities. To add to the toleration of stock shrinkage as perk and wage subsidy, salesmen were encouraged during training to over-charge customers so that the company never paid the price for staff 'coming back short' or making 'mistakes'. As Ditton observes, 'The firm will only tolerate honesty if it doesn't provide additional organization problems.' Sales staff relied on shop or individual customer ignorance of the detail of prices or orders to add to the price or the order. There were, of course, limits to managerial indulgence. When a salesman flashed a brand new Mercedes around, 'the fucking manager hit the roof, he said, "Right the hospital's coming off your route, and so's the co-op"' (sales-man quoted in Ditton, 1977a, 178). The fruits of fiddling must not become too visible.

Another writer whose work began with detailed studies of particular occupations was Gerry Mars, who studied pilferage initially in hotels and catering (1973) and subsequently in the docks (1982a). These are both trades in which casual employment and theft are widely known to be preva-lent, and, for many, his ideas initially seemed to apply only to a few cases of unusual kinds of work. Indeed these cases were only of interest because of their presumed difference from more normal work behaviour. However, as his work developed and he collected more and more examples of fiddling and theft from different kinds of workplace, he developed an argument to the effect that this kind of behaviour existed in all kinds of workplace, varying only in the typical forms and incidence (1982b). Like other studies from a more mainstream tradition of industrial sociology, the thesis was that controls of work generate characteristic forms of conformity and noncon-formity as well. Some kinds of 'cheating' and pilferage will be more preva-lent (and more obvious), but that is all.

Mars's main concern was to develop the rich description into a more generalizable set of categories that linked type of occupational crime to type of occupation. In one sense this was the deviancy equivalent of indus-trial relations, with analysis of fiddle-proneness replacing strike-proneness (1982b, 3). The differences are represented to us through the labels – hawks, donkeys, wolves and vultures. Unlike the categories used by some in the OB tradition, these are not individualistic or psychological, but rather explained by their occupational characteristics. Ditton's salesmen would be vultures as they relied on a common base of information and support to indulge their feasting activities. Wolves are more collectivist, stealing in packs according to their own rules and division of labour. Occu-pational settings, such as docks or oil rigs, which rely on considerable autonomy for work gangs are obvious examples. At the more individual-istic end, hawks are likely to be found in entrepreneurial or competitive contexts which put a premium on innovation and cutting corners. Examples are to be found among journalists, taxi drivers, waiters and fairground buskers. Meanwhile, donkeys exist in highly rule-governed and isolating circumstances such as those of supermarket cashiers and machine minders, where power is more likely to be reappropriated through absenteeism or sabotage.

While these studies could not displace soldiering from centre stage, they did show that work limitation was not the limit of workplace misbehaviour and drew attention to ways in which forms of misbehaviour involve subtle developments of informal organization to sustain them. Their limitations arose more from the fact that the main orientation was still towards explaining workplace action within the concerns of criminology – the 'shadow side of economic transactions', as Mars put it. Fiddling may have been, in Ditton's words, 'part-time' crime, but the emphasis was on 'the social processes by which a group of men could break the law and still believe themselves to be good citizens' (1977a, 11). This concern with the moral economy of deviancy was fascinating in its own right, but tended to draw attention away from workplace misbehaviour towards the broader social consequences of different forms of consciousness and action.

Breaking up is hard to do: rediscovering sabotage

In the 1970s there were a number of interesting, if ultimately unsatisfactory, attempts at a general synthetic account of workplace misbehaviour, with sabotage as the connecting key idea. On the face of it this seems strange. After all, sabotage is associated with the most extreme, destructive forms of industrial dissent.

But that is not how it has been used in a number of influential texts. Brown's *Sabotage* (1977) is primarily a fascinating account of the introduction and spread of scientific management in Britain and workers' strenuous efforts to resist it. Instead of breaking the machine, Brown borrows the idea of deliberately 'clogging' it from the revolutionary syndicalists in the early part of this century. The centrepiece of such activity is 'ca'canny', which one commentator had described as 'an insidious diminution of energy without notice to the employer' (quoted in Brown, 1977, 8). This in turn draws from the American syndicalist union the IWW (Industrial Workers of the World, or 'Wobblies'), who utilized the blunt but effective slogan 'good pay or bum work' (Kornbluh, 1968). There are spectacular examples of applications of such perspectives in Brown and elsewhere, such as the railway strikes of 1911 in France and Britain which involved altering destination labels, causing obstructions, cutting telegraph wires and attacking signal boxes. But by and large most 'striking on the job' falls squarely within the framework of restriction of output, an honourable, but hardly extraordinary strand of labour history, which can only be taken as sabotage if the definition is broadened to actions which do not respect management interests or conform precisely with management expectations.

Dubois (1977) also takes an inclusive line. For example, he treats absence from work as an authentic act of industrial sabotage, in some ways more fundamental than strike action, which depends for its effectiveness on formal organization. The point of the analysis is to identify and reappraise the importance of any and every impulse to dissent. In this kind of analysis individual actions of non-compliance are authentic expressions of basic independence from external and impersonal control. For these writers small individual acts are in their way more significant indicators of impulses to reject control than the organized actions of unions, especially those that preserve sectional interests. Aside from the already stated links to syndicalism and anarchism, such perspectives connect with the utopian socialist idea that there is a natural repugnance to all forms of external control which will express itself in spontaneous acts of rejection and violence.

As the political and ideological landscape has changed, such connections may be less prominent, but the underlying reasoning can still be found. In a lively collection of interviews and anecdotes from the US, Sprouse (1992) argues along these lines that even the trivial breaking of attendance rules or cutting corners to make work easier, and a variety of types of pilferage, all qualify as acts of sabotage.

Inclusiveness has not been the only argument used within the literature. Taylor and Walton's (1971) celebrated and much-quoted article scaled down the definition somewhat to action which is directed towards the mutilation or destruction of the work environment, including machinery and commodities. They came up with what they admit is a 'hotch-potch' of data by trawling through journals, the popular and alternative press for examples; ranging from the satisfying though probably apocryphal story of the sweet factory workers who had embedded 'fuck off' through half a mile of Blackpool rock, to the earlier New York theatre operators who backed up their campaign for wage increases by showing films upside down, mixing reels from other films and inserting alarming noises from the sound machines. The goal was again to restore a notion of meaningful behaviour and rationality to hidden and misunderstood action. The effect was both to celebrate the industrial deviant, and to suggest that industrial sabotage may be 'an important indication of underlying industrial conflict' and 'neglected grass roots action' (1971, 221–2).

A variety of types and motives are discerned, with only a minority associated with asserting control or restructuring social relationships. Nevertheless, the growth of sabotage was explicitly seen as part of the workplace revolts of the late 1960s. Watson's (1972) 'Counter-Planning on the Shop Floor' was typical in arguing that a combination of oppressive mass production and obsolescent traditional unionism led workers to seize control of various aspects of production. Sabotage went hand in hand with high absenteeism, chronic lateness, poor workmanship and wildcat strikes (Zabala, 1989, 20).

> The inspectors organized a rod-blowing contest which required the posting of lookouts at the entrances to the shop area and the making of deals with assembly, for example, to neglect the torquing of bolts on the rods for a random number of motors so that there would be loose rods. When an inspector stepped up to a motor and felt the tell-tale knock in the water-pump wheel, he would scream out to clear the shop, the men abandoning their work and running behind boxes and benches. Then he would arc himself away from the stand and ram the throttle up to first 4,000 and then 5,000 rpm. The motor would knock, clank, and finally blur to a halt with the rod blowing through the side of the oil pan and across the shop. The men would rise from their cover, exploding with cheers, and another point would be chalked up on the wall for that inspector. This particular contest went on for several weeks, resulting in more than 150 blown motors. No small amount of money was exchanged in bets over the contests. (Watson, 1972, 24, on life in a Detroit auto plant)

While such action was stimulated and sustained by new conditions, emphasis was also placed on continuity with the previous historical tradition from the Luddites through to the Wobblies. The underground magazine *INK* referred to 'a glorious echo of a proud tradition . . . . The Luddites are alive and well in the blast-furnaces of Rotherham, on the production lines at Ford and carrying on their industrial foul play much as before' (17 December 1971, 13). Organizers and their shop floor allies picked up on individual acts of sabotage such as truck drivers pulling wires, ensuring flat tyres or getting lost in traffic, but urged the collectivization of this effective tool to 'experiment in the regulation of work by the workers themselves' (Brockway, 1975, 43).

The decline of formal workplace militancy has pushed sabotage, however defined, somewhat out of the picture, but it remains an important and often ordinary feature of workplace misbehaviour (Jermier, 1988). Indeed academics continue to identify new categories of activist, such as the technicians and managers whose skills or jobs are threatened with technological obsolescence (La Nuez and Jermier, 1990), who might be described as saboteurs. No article on white collar crime is now complete without numerous examples of computer hacking, or deliberate placing of viruses in information technology (IT) systems. In fact the 'information economy' appears to be even more vulnerable to contemporary versions of 'clogging the machinery' than previous systems of production.

The problem with the main period of (re)discovery of sabotage was that it created a double burden. Sabotage was either promoted as the generic term for all workplace dissent, or pushed to the margins by 'exoticizing' or romanticizing the more extreme end of the spectrum. As Zabala's account of events at a General Motors plant makes clear, rather than being an alternative to conventional methods, sabotage is often a small-scale though collective supplement to grievance bargaining. Its success and durability depend on the informal strength of the workgroup as well as on formal union power: 'Hence the paradox: orderly and predictable collective bargaining required disorderly, unpredictable subterranean conflict to harness the creative forces at work in the labour process' (1989, 29).

But clearly the practices are multi-dimensional. Other collective actions are attempts to relieve tedium and create an alternative and more expressive symbolic order, such as Linstead's (1985) entertaining account of games played by bakery workers. These included 'target dough' in which workers hurled lumps 30 feet at a clock, and 'blackberry golf' where the aim is to drive furthest with frozen fruit and the handle of a squeegee. Finally, sometimes sabotage may be just an individual response to work pressures. It is hard not to inwardly cheer some of Sprouse's (1992) examples of employees who spiked the office fountain with bubble bath, cut the wires of a factory muzak system that was continually playing 'Tie a Yellow Ribbon' and got their friends to send in bogus customer evaluation forms; to say nothing of the Toys R Us floor manager who displayed and sold modified versions of the dolls, including Ken in a clown outfit whipping a tied-up Barbie on the balcony!

Time off for bad behaviour

Though we do not associate an identifiable school of thought with it, the misbehaviour that has been studied most frequently has been absence from work. The language is itself interesting – absenteeism implies a habitual behaviour, something akin to an addiction. Managers and many academics have often had this sort of view of absence as a corrigible tendency that is a problem in many poorly managed plants.

After 1945 interest in absence from work grew rapidly. During the period of prosperity following the war, in particular, managements generally became more interested in collecting records of all sorts and in analysing them. In Britain and the USA literally hundreds of papers, articles and instruction manuals were published on absenteeism during the post-war decades. One British book-length study published at the end of the period (Chadwick-Jones et al., 1982) lists over 100 academic papers on the subject published in the previous ten years or so. A similar book published in America at about the same time lists as many academic studies deriving primarily from work conducted in North America (Goodman et al., 1984). These books refer exclusively to academic studies of absence. There were also many more company reports and internal documents generated by managements in their own attempts to analyse and grapple with what they saw as the problem of absenteeism. This is not to mention publications by professional bodies and employers' organizations, such as the guide produced by the British Institute of Management (BIM, 1961) or that of the Confederation of British Industry (CBI, 1970).

The scale and general character of academic interest in absence in the early decades after the war is not difficult to explain. In addition to being a problem for management, which would welcome any research into the phenomenon, absence has some features which make it appealing to researchers, particularly to social psychologists who believe that absence can be measured and recorded very precisely. Absence can be thought of as time lost to employers, and can be considered as a percentage of the total time contracted in a given period. A very precise absence rate can, in fact, be calculated by looking at the time lost as a percentage of the total time scheduled to be worked. A 'lost time' rate of absence can thus be calculated for an individual or a group, and comparisons can be drawn between departments and factories. Absence may also be measured in other ways – in terms of the frequency of separate absence events, for example. Now while there are more problems of procedure for these rates, and they are less often used, absence from work can be variously measured. In addition, absence is appealing as a subject because it is usually not excused, and so can be construed as being voluntary behaviour; a factor which also increases its appeal to psychologists. Here then is an example of a precisely measurable aspect of voluntary behaviour, which many people wish to be studied. It is perhaps hardly surprising that many people took up the challenge.

However, it is surprising, given the amount of time devoted to the study of absenteeism, how few reliable results were actually produced. What were, for the researchers, obvious hypotheses about the likely pattern of absence have not been confirmed, even after exhaustive research. For example, it was a favourite idea of researchers that the more satisfied people are with the work, the lower will be their level of absenteeism. However, demonstrating this proved to be highly problematic, despite repeated examination of measures of job satisfaction and absence levels. What such studies ignore is the situated and relative nature of the satisfaction people derive from work. Really satisfying work is difficult to find for the majority of people, and this is widely understood. If this is so, of course, it is unrealistic to seek a relationship between satisfaction and attendance. People at work are often willing to say that they are satisfied with their work, but what they mean is that they are satisfied, given that one cannot expect much satisfaction. Given the general expectation of unfulfilling work and the typically low identification that people have with it, expressions of satisfaction are likely enough to be found associated with high levels of absenteeism. In these circumstances, expressed satisfaction with work is neither here nor there. Indeed, for many, opportunities for absence and other kinds of misbehaviour may themselves be a source of satisfaction (Burawoy, 1979). If this is true, we might expect expressions of work satisfaction to be positively associated with absenteeism. This is reflected in the well-known joke which is often repeated in the course of discussions of absenteeism. Foreman to returning absentee: 'Why do you only come to work four days of the week?', to which the employee replies: 'Because I can't live on the wages I would get if I only came for three!'

Willingness and desire to limit work by taking time off is fixed by a wide variety of factors, including the general level of willingness to work found in a community. Groups of employees establish a relationship with their work based on customary standards of performance, which will include particular levels of effort expenditure and customary levels of attendance. It is plausible to think that if an employer were able arbitrarily to increase the number of hours of work, this would produce an increase in the amount of absence from work, because the new work periods would take away periods of leisure. This sort of thought experiment reveals that absence is in fact an expression of the relationship between management controls and employee accommodation to them, not something intrinsic to the behaviour of workers as such.

Such a realization has been reached by some of the more insightful researchers in industrial sociology. The early work of Gi Baldamus (1957) and Hilde Behrend (1957) is particularly rich and valuable, in this respect. It was Behrend (1957) who first clearly revealed a general connection between absence and employment levels. As she shows, the relationship between absence and unemployment, as with unemployment and strikes, is inverse. The lower unemployment tends to be, the higher is absenteeism; suggesting that as unemployment rises, the fear of the sack becomes greater, inhibiting absence. Such findings suggest that the disposition to work (and to limit work) is not only an individual one, but is also regulated by social norms which reflect general economic conditions. In this approach, organizations are thought of as the conduit through which socially produced dispositions to work are channelled. Building on this insight, Baldamus (1961) developed a powerful way of analysing the employment relation and the activity of management. Management mediates general social and economic relations, and its function is to regulate or distribute working effort rather than control its general level. In his analysis, management is relatively powerless to increase the general level of commitment and effort expenditure.

In a large engineering company manufacturing vehicles, the main production line often could not start up on Mondays because there were not enough people on the line. This meant that millions of pounds of capital equipment and quite a few employees would remain idle, whilst the last score of people straggled in. A sustained management campaign against lateness and absenteeism followed. This had various effects in different parts of the plant.

It actually made absence a good deal worse on the production line. An employee setting off for work and realising he might be late, would rather not get there at all, so horrendous and public were the sanctions attracted by the last few employees to arrive. In these circumstances, it would be better to persuade oneself that the slight hangover, which was the reason for being late out of the house, was actually the first symptom of the 'flu. False sickness absence is, of course, difficult to detect, and still more difficult to sanction.

Sanctions on casual absenteeism had a variety of identifiable effects in the plant as a whole. One that was noted was the polarisation of absence periods. Both long and short periods of absence were substituted by employees in place of the customary one or two day absences, which were now attracting severe sanctions. Quite long periods of sickness absence – of up to a week or more – became more prevalent, as did very short periods off work, say for less than half a shift which could be allowed by a foreman and might not enter the official statistics of absence. One individual found that absences on Wednesday afternoons passed without notice, and took one Wednesday afternoon in three off for the following three years without detection. In some areas, the consequences of the crackdown were dire. For one highly pressurised production team of assemblers, the crackdown on absence was felt to be quite intolerable. It took away what they felt to be their only relief from the pressure. Within a week, the group was working to rule, within three a wildcat strike resulted. (Ackroyd, extracted from unpublished fieldwork reports, 1978)

Baldamus and Behrend make central to their work a particular conception of the relationship between the employer and the employee. As Behrend memorably named it, this relationship is an 'effort bargain'. Employee willingness to put forward effort they suggest is limited, and is fixed by the customary levels of working effort accepted and sanctioned. This they refer to as the social support of working effort. This analysis also suggests distinct limits to management control. While management may be able to spread out or redistribute willingness to work somewhat – by making it more even through the working day, or through the week – in general, management cannot increase the general level of working effort. Using absence statistics, Baldamus argues for the ineffectiveness of managerial controls beyond certain obvious limits. Temporary and more permanent withdrawals of labour, Baldamus suggests, are likely to result if worker perceptions of the fairness of the wage–work exchange are fundamentally transgressed.

This way of seeing the employment relationship – as an effort bargain shaped by broader social and economic forces – has been found valuable by a large number of researchers in industrial relations and industrial sociology and has been used and developed by them. (See, for example, Hyman and Brough, 1975; Jackson, 1977.) However, despite the importance of absence in the first formulations of effort bargain analysis, it was not seen as central as the approach was developed and utilized. Unfortunately this kind of analysis has not yielded a general theory of misbehaviour, despite its promise. Even the path-breaking insights into absence from work have scarcely been given much attention in the mainstream of industrial relations or industrial sociology.

Rebels without a cause

Recalcitrance can, of course, be cast in a wider frame. Some industrial sociologists have always been concerned with the boundaries between the workplace and the wider social order: radical theorists being anxious to investigate the potential for action in the former to threaten established power in the latter. Conditions for such action seemed limited for much of the post-war period. Indeed, the dominant theme of much of Western sociology had been the social, political and industrial integration of the working class. Critics, to some extent, had to turn to the past to uncover the militancy that had been 'hidden from history', whether the 1930s sit-down strikes of American workers in the 1930s (Brecher, 1978), or industrial unrest inside and outside the workshop in Britain before and after the First World War (Hinton, 1973). In both countries a continuity of aspirations for workers' control provided a bridge between past and present (Cliff, 1974; Montgomery, 1980; Milkman, 1995). Such a link implied that new conditions and conflict were arising through which workers were learning to revolt.

Apprentice revolutionaries

The early 1970s appeared to be a promising period for uncovering that radical potential. In the UK the unravelling of the post-war social settlement, and the perceived failure of the 1964–70 Labour administrations, was resulting in domestic industrial disorder, manifesting itself in events such as the Upper Clyde Shipbuilders (UCS) Work-In, a rise in unofficial strikes and visibility for shop steward organization, and the successful struggle against the 1971 Industrial Relations Act. Inspiration from foreign parts, especially Italy and France, drew attention to new types of qualitative demands and disputes focusing on control of line speed and piecework, challenges to job hierarchies and changes to the organization of production (Crouch and Pizzorno, 1978). Referring to Italy, one commentator noted, 'at the peak of cycles of dispute in 1969–70 workers in several plants organized changes in work organization on their initiative, cutting down on work rates, altering hours, re-organizing job routines and refusing various tasks' (Dubois, 1977, 12).

While Italian theorists spoke enthusiastically of a 'revolt against work' based on the rebellious 'mass worker', the British challenge from below was not as dramatic. Rather than what some saw as the rebirth of a movement for workers' control, powerful shop floor organization in a number of key industries enabled employees to push at the frontier of job controls. Just as the official order, propelled by the Donovan Report, was preparing to accept and institutionalize the shop stewards' movement, unofficial action on pay and conditions kept reasserting itself. Radical academics focused on expanding and explaining this distinction between the institutionalization of trade unionism and the incorporation of the working class (Hyman, 1975). Labour's recalcitrance and potential for radicalism was seen to be ill-served by the dominant brand of economistic, defensive and sectional trade unionism that flourished in Britain (Lane, 1974).

In the US, unencumbered by a strong, if apparently blinkered, trade union movement, direct action could be seen more optimistically: 'A new labour movement is being born in America. It is the autonomous creation of the working class. It exists more potentially than actually, but its early seeds are appearing in wildcat strikes in the trucking, air transport, and mail-communication industries' (Aronowitz and Brecher, 1975, 28). The new militancy was thus focused on insurgent groups at local level, challenging union-negotiated contracts as well as employers. In 1972 the *New York Times* (23 January) reported that at General Motors' Assembly Division, 'Both union and management were surprised at the depth of resistance ... among the workforce, and the President of the United Auto Workers' (UAW) local declared that a decision to work at their old pace to protest that change had come from the rank and file, not from the union leadership'.

When moving beyond description and discovery, the search for seeds of the revolution tended to get bogged down in interminable discussions of

actual and potential states of consciousness. If the ideal state of class identity could not be found, other terms were invented, such as factory or micro-
level trade union consciousness. The leap from the everyday practices of
what Mann called 'aggressive economism and defensive job control' to
changing world and workplace was a large one. For Mann (1973) it could
only come exceptionally in 'explosions of consciousness'. Not surprisingly,
attention tended to shift to explanations of why workers did not have the
appropriate ideology. This problematic is typified by Clarke: 'The problem
of why the quiescent labour movement has permitted a society to continue
unchanged which is based on the ongoing exploitation of workers can only
be resolved in terms of the distortion of workers' consciousness by the
power that confronts them' (1977, 15).

Fortunately, there were more concrete alternatives. The classic empirical study of this period, Beynon's *Working for Ford* (1975), is often
remembered for its relentless critique of work on the assembly line. But
its main theme is the origins and operation of the shop-steward-dominated
workplace organization. However, the two are linked: 'Trade unionism is
about work and sometimes the lads just don't want to work. All talk of
procedures and negotiations tend to break down here' (1975, 140). The
shop steward organization that articulated and organized this action was,
according to Beynon, limited to a 'sophisticated factory class consciousness'.

Elsewhere, other prominent studies found that responses were not as
rebellious as at Ford Halewood. Those of work and workers at Chemco
(Nichols and Armstrong, 1976; Nichols and Beynon, 1977) found a largely
non-militant workforce, whose most ideologically socialist employees were
foremen from 'up North'. The rest of the workforce were divided and ruled
by ideological structures inside and outside the workplace. Such studies
made strenuous efforts to chart the contours and contradictions of how
workers negotiated their way through those structures. But while workers
didn't act as fully conscious agents engaged in class struggle, the lack of a
counter-ideology did not make Chemco operatives willing workers: 'many
of the activities (and deliberate inactivities) to which workers resorted took
an individualistic and covert form – but these workers did have their ways
of "getting back" at management and of "getting by"' (Nichols and Armstrong, 1976, 211–12).

Radical theorists, therefore, tended to move along a continuum of uncovering rebellion and explaining acquiescence. Some followed the logic, as
Glaberman (1976, 26) put it, of 'living for the peak and not the valley'. More
pessimistic perspectives inevitably moved from action to ideology. The
blame for limited progress could be laid at the door of the half-hearted com-
promises of labourist reformism (Cronin, 1979, 193), or the insidious effects
of the dominant ideology. What is wrong in both cases is that workers are
treated as apprentice revolutionaries whose behaviour and attitudes are
evaluated against an a priori and unrealistic model of social agency and
change. The next range of studies was to shift that focus.

Worker resisters

The best of the above studies returned to Goodrich's 'frontier of control', locating workplace conflict in an effort bargain transformed by new forms of labour organization and utilization. They were beginning to be influenced by what became known as labour process theory (LPT), associated initially with the work of Braverman (1974). It has been noted by all and sundry that Braverman did not describe the nature or effects of worker resistance to the controls he spelt out in such detail. In practice, he carried traditional Marxist assumptions about the potential of industrial workers to become the gravediggers of capitalism (see Thompson, 1990, 114–18). What many commentators continue to ignore is that subsequent labour process theorists largely jettisoned that baggage.

On the face of it, LPT does not depart drastically from the kind of radical analysis discussed in the last section. The structured antagonism between capital and labour is situated within the search for more profitable forms of production, and this context is regarded as the engine of employee resistance. But whereas such analyses leaned towards treating workplace conflicts as rehearsal for revolution, the second wave of LPT was not prescriptive about the character or direction of worker action (Friedman, 1977; Edwards, 1979; Littler, 1982). In part this was because of the recognition of particular influences on resistance, with research focusing on the variations according to the development of management, the organization of labour and other local conditions such as product markets.

But it was also because resistance is held to have a different object – a regime of managerial controls over the labour process – which was narrower than the class relations of capitalism identified by Marxists and broader than the simple wage–effort bargain beloved of industrial sociology. Distancing LPT from both Marx and Braverman, Friedman (1977, 48) concludes that, '[Therefore] it is important to examine how the capitalist mode of production has accommodated itself to worker resistance, rather than simply how the capitalist mode of production might be overthrown through worker resistance'. Control can never be absolute and in the space provided by the indeterminacy of labour, employees will constantly find ways of evading and subverting managerial organization and direction of work. This tendency is a major source of the dynamism in the workplace.

Elaboration of this dialectic of control and resistance became a central feature of LPT. Though studies set such processes within a context of the development of capitalism and the state, the focus of analysis is struggle at the micro level. Beyond conditions of sale of labour power, detailed attention is paid to the hidden abode of production itself, with its myriad job controls, wage–effort bargains, individual and informal, as well as collective and organized. As Littler (1982, 26–7) notes, workers do not come to the factory gates as the carriers of general opposition to the system. Once such 'universal recalcitrance' is disavowed, researchers can focus on the real and specific nature of resistance and its effects, as Littler does in a series of case studies about employer and shop floor conflicts concerning the attempted spread of the Taylorite 'Bedaux system' in 1930s Britain. Any link with formal union strategies, let alone a broader class struggle, is held to be contingent on the conditions of organization, ideology and articulation of interests.

The best-known empirical illustrations of the control/resistance paradigm are provided by the work of Richard Edwards (1979) and Andrew Friedman (1977). As Edwards charts the apparent transition from simple to technical and bureaucratic control systems, he highlights the crucial role played by worker resistance. The new forms of control based around the large-scale assembly plants were in part responses to the big strikes such as those in steel in 1919–20, and the many smaller conflicts as 'workers fought with their bosses over control of the actual process of production' (1979, 119). But the new technical controls generated their own contradictions, notably the tendency to create a common and degraded status for a mass of semi-skilled workers. This displaced rather than eliminated conflict and provided a fertile ground for unionization efforts such as those of GM employees through sit-down strikes in the 1930s. As a result, 'The resistance engendered by technical control set off a new search for methods of controlling the workplace' (Edwards, 1979, 130), leading to the kinds of bureaucratic hierarchies favoured by companies such as Polaroid, IBM and Xerox.

As is well known, Friedman (1977) does not follow such a historical sequence, but does provide a detailed historical and contemporary account of the evolution of managerial strategies of direct control and responsible autonomy as they come to terms with worker organization in different labour markets. On the familiar territory of the motor industry in the Midlands, he outlines how management made a concerted effort to extend direct control in the late 1960s and 1970s through new work measurement schemes, redundancies and the ending of traditional bargaining agreements which allowed for 'mutuality' of influence in the labour process. Such actions could only be understood when set against the responsible autonomy arrangements of the previous three decades: 'During that time Coventry workers had built up strong shop-floor organizations to protect their central position. In part those organizations were based on the shop stewards. But in part the organizations were even more informal, based on the small work groups themselves' (1977, 233).

Not all labour process theorists were as optimistic about worker resistance. In his famous, though unintended, return to the same machine shop researched by Donald Roy, Burawoy (1979) shifts focus to the production of consent. Observing the familiar attempts to manipulate the effort bargain and make out against the system, Burawoy argues that participation in labour process 'games' conceals the exploitative social relations of capitalist production and redistributes conflict away from vertical management–worker relations to intra-employee lateral disputes. Flawed and partial though his argument was (see Thompson, 1989, 165–72), it testified to the growing sophistication of LPT, notably in attempts to produce a more integrated framework in which conflict and consent could be understood within the same typology, and without recourse to the 'panacea fallacy' whereby capital is seen as always moving towards 'the' solution to its labour control problems (Thompson and Bannon, 1985; Hyman, 1987).

In this framework, numerous studies have implicated many forms of misbehaviour in resistance to managerial control. However, perhaps the most comprehensive account of the resistance in the labour process perspective is that developed by Paul Edwards in two books, an empirically based study written with Scullion (1982) and a much broader theoretical and historically grounded contribution (Edwards, 1986b). The latter confirms the point already observed that labour process theory, though remaining materialist, was breaking with its narrowly Marxian origins. Though both works engage with arguments discussed earlier in the chapter about what underpins and differentiates class, factory and other forms of 'sectional' consciousness, Edwards comments that, 'Neither is workplace struggle to be equated with class struggle. Indeed a basic argument running through this study is that conflicts in work relations have no necessary connotations for wider class conflict' (1986b, 7). Like other writers he is keen to move away from a control versus resistance model to one which recognizes a variety of forms of conflict and accommodation.

But it is in the earlier set of case studies, briefly referred to in Chapter 1, that Edwards (writing with Scullion) empirically integrates a wide range of forms of misbehaviour in the effort bargain within a complex control and resistance framework. Though there is an overall attempt to understand 'the way in which activities are constituted as aspects of conflict by different forms of organization of the labour process' (1982, 277), they are much more successful than previous studies in demonstrating the complex interactions of management and labour within particular regimes of control, as

---

The peculiarities of that factory, particularly the combination of loose effort standards, a strong piecework tradition, and an established gang system led to the emergence of early leaving as a substantial problem for management . . . . during the week there was generally a mass exodus between a quarter and a half an hour before the official shift finishing time. Management attempted to control this by stationing supervisors at the main exits from each shop and in the routes to the factory gateways. The whole process often took on the air of farce, with groups of workers assembling at strategic points ready to dash past the foreman on guard if the opportunity presented itself. Foremen attempted to hold back the tide for a while, but at some point those in one shop would give way, which was the signal for workers elsewhere to leave. ('On the problem of early leaving in a large metals factory', Edwards and Scullion, 1982, 137, 149)

workplace actors seek to adapt their behaviour to new conditions and challenges. In their conclusion, Edwards and Scullion criticize previous labour process theorists for presenting resistance as a residual category where 'management acts and workers simply react' (1982, 273). Through numerous detailed examples the case studies show both how workers adapt their actions such as absence, labour turnover, the use of sanctions, and sabotage to particular modes of control over work or payment; and how management develop policies and practices on the provision of overtime or as a means of transacting with powerful shop floor controls.

However, the analysis remains flawed in two ways. The different forms of conflict are still seen essentially as responses to the exertion of managerial control. Control strategies are presented as if they alone evoke and elicit resistance, overestimating the extent to which managerial action is cohesive and effective, and underestimating the variety of influences on and types of misbehaviour (Ackroyd, 1984). In addition, Edwards and Scullion continue to evaluate employee action and organization against a scale of effectiveness, though they see the matter as more a case of apprentice collectivism rather than rehearsal for revolution. So, the extent to which labour successfully organizes itself is the key to understanding the character of organizational action. This is reflected in the categorization – implicit and non-directed versus overt and institutionalized. The differences between events such as absence or strikes is cast in terms of the degree of formal organization needed to develop them and to make them effective instruments of class action. Informal practices such as fiddling or sabotage, lacking any formal organization, are taken to be ineffective surrogates for striking and other acts which have formal organization as their basis. Edwards has returned in more recent work to the theme of varieties of conflict (Edwards et al., 1996), which we will discuss in the final chapter as part of wider consideration of theorizing the contemporary workplace.

Unwilling women

Resistance, informal and otherwise, has always been associated with 'the lads'. For example, Brown's (1977) detailed account of twentieth-century restriction of output and other disruptive tactics contains one reference to women workers, and then as 'dilutees' who undermined the power of male craft workers. As Cockburn (1983) shows in her study of printers, this is typical of the constitution of women as problem and threat, rather than active agency. One means of challenging this and related views of compliance and complicity with capital, has been to give a gender twist to the recovery of the hidden history of conflict in the workplace. For example, Milkman collects a rich set of older and contemporary accounts of women workers' involvement in strikes and unions, despite the fact that 'there is abundant evidence of women workers' ill treatment on the part of organized labour' (1995, xi). The case studies emphasize not just the conventional forms of participation, but the innovative character of action inside and outside the workplace, reflecting the different forms of solidarity and sociability arising from interaction with wider community and family networks.

The new writings reflected the concerns of a new generation of feminist industrial sociologists that appeared on the scene in the early 1980s. In Britain, the purpose of the trio of notable studies by Pollert (1981), Cavendish (1982) and Westwood (1984) was to examine the nature of female wage labour, but ethnographic methods allowed a close observation of informal practices. The very fact of neglect and marginalization of the concerns of women workers by the local and national trade union apparatus stimulated a focus which went beyond the formal to discover distinctively female modes of action based on collective shop floor culture.

The extent to which such activity can be characterized as resistance dogged the discussions, Pollert noting that 'they did give gentle nudges to authority, without in any way denting the structure of control' (1981, 154). In addition, just as previous accounts of employee recalcitrance manifested disappointment that informal practices were not the class struggle in miniature, there is concern that women workers were often colluding in rituals of romance rather than conducting the gender war: 'it is a deeply contradictory culture that women fashion: it reveals a resistant and creative attempt to overcome the stultifying aspects of the capitalist labour process – only to find this creativity has bound itself securely to an oppressive version of womanhood' (Westwood, 1984, 6). But this contradictoriness is unsurprising and runs parallel to male 'horseplay' in largely sex-segregated workplaces (Ackroyd and Crowdy, 1990; Collinson, 1992). For such skirmishes with managerial authority simultaneously disrupt industrial order and reinforce conformity to the group and its dominant identity.

Sexuality was a theme partially submerged in this period of feminist industrial sociology, but it has reappeared more strongly in recent studies. While this is the subject of Chapter 6, it is worth noting that some of the findings of earlier studies re-emerge. For example, gender-based subcultures in a Japanese auto plant enable resistance to be mobilized in response to immediate production pressures, while frequently positioning the sexes against each other rather than management (Gottfried and Graham, 1993). But the influence of post-structuralist perspectives also leads to an emphasis on discursive practices. Women workers in the auto plant, secretaries (Pringle, 1988) and betting office employees (Filby, 1992) use banter, 'bitching', and 'scolding' routines to assert their own power. Though, as in the betting shops, sexuality is an integral part of how employers want to sell services, informal practices, whether discursive or not, are a way of establishing job controls in the wage/emotional effort bargain. For all the observed limitations and contradictoriness, many women are unwilling to conform to standards of appropriate behaviour set by male managers, supervisors, fellow workers or customers.

Conclusion

This chapter has allowed us to extend and add detail to the 'mapping' process begun at the end of the previous chapter. The literatures of sociology and other disciplines contain abundant evidence of the full range of worker recalcitrance on our key themes of work, time, product and identity. But organizational misbehaviour has not been seen as a totality. The academic world has only partly unfolded the map. Understanding, at any given time, was fragmented and disjointed, reflecting special interests and particular theoretical objectives. Much employee action has been treated as a rehearsal for something else – social deviance, class struggle and other forms of oppositional or transformative behaviour. The range and understanding of misbehaviour was, therefore, often obscured. In using the label 'rebels without a cause' we are not trying to ignore, denigrate or limit employee motives. Instead we are trying to put the emphasis on presenting and understanding mis/behaviour in its own terms. Radical analysts of industrial relations (Ackers et al., 1996), organization theory (Clegg, 1989, 1990) or management (Alvesson and Willmott, 1992) have not sought to identify the extent of misbehaviour or to constitute it as a subject. Despite what seems at times to be an obsessive concern for subjectivity (Fineman, 1993; Willmott, 1989; Knights, 1990) concern has not extended to analysing the extent and variety of dissent and misbehaviour in the workplace. We return to these themes in a contemporary context in the final chapter. Meanwhile in the following chapter we take the discussion further by re-examining the theory and practice of the most traditional topic of industrial organization – the workgroup.

3 Irresponsible Autonomy – Self-organization as the Infrastructure of Misbehaviour

The research discussed in the last chapter suggests there is a range of misbehaviour to be observed in workplaces. As we have now seen, forms of misbehaviour have been written about by many groups of researchers. All of the specific forms of behaviour we suggested were possible in our initial chapter, and which we summarized in the map of forms of misbehaviour in Chapter 1 (see Figure 1.2, p. 25), have been discovered and discussed by others. The overt resistance of the recalcitrant worker and the associated tendency to work limitation has been discovered again and again in the annals we have reviewed. The related phenomena of absenteeism, sabotage and pilferage have also been repeatedly noted by researchers. Yet, despite our initial mapping, it is not clear that an adequate overall analysis and assessment of misbehaviour has yet been produced. In this chapter and the next, we develop an account of the character and dynamics of traditional patterns of misbehaviour in organizations.

Until now, few writers have considered the full range of misbehaviour, not to mention its origins and dynamics. The best available account in terms of the range of coverage is the work of Paul Edwards and Hugh Scullion (see Edwards and Scullion 1982; Edwards, 1986b). These writers discuss a commendably wide range of misbehaviour in the presentation of their research in British factories. But because they were centrally concerned with conflict, these authors do not consider very adequately any behaviour not obviously connected with this. Although Edwards, in particular, has remedied this deficiency to some extent in subsequent writing, a summary treatment of forms of behaviour is still lacking. The great virtue of the work of Edwards and Scullion, and that of some other analysts in the labour process tradition, is to point out the deep penetration of conflict into the informal social organization of workplaces. By contrast with this, perhaps the best work in terms of understanding the character of misbehaviour is that of Ditton (1977a, 1978) and Mars (1982a), who uncovered detailed processes involving the informal organization of workers. But, in a different way, neither do these writers appreciate fully the range and variety of behaviour that is possible. Their project is to account for workplace theft and fiddling, rather than to produce a satisfactory account of all misbehaviour. They show that the character of the pilferage, and the social organization necessary for it, varies systematically between different kinds of workplace and work-group; that is all.

There are, however, some signs of development in understanding. In a valuable recent work, David Collinson (1992) explores the behaviour of employees in a vehicle factory. Like Ditton and Mars, Collinson considers carefully the meanings attributed to their work and situation by workers. He uses the participative methods of investigation drawn from anthropological research, but combines this with the interest in conflict found in labour process analysis. Because of his methodological sophistication, he is able to account for a good deal of his observations in terms of overt resistance to management. As Collinson suggests also, however, there is more than this to be seen. He writes that some of the behaviour he observed could be seen as workers actively 'managing management' (1992, 49–72) not simply 'managing to resist' (pp. 127–49). Hence, Collinson challenges a common preconception about what happens in organizations, by suggesting that employees are by no means simply the passive recipients of things that are done to them, nor are they simply controlled by management. Indeed, there is a great deal of observed behaviour in these unusually detailed findings, which cannot be accounted for straightforwardly as conflict or seen as related to resistance. In this account, workers seem greatly concerned with such things as their masculinity (pp. 77–97), with joking and games (pp. 103–23) and with fantasy and self-delusion (pp. 179–204). Moreover, clearly, these preoccupations affected overt behaviour.

Creating a new explanatory framework

We propose that in order to understand the characteristic forms of misbehaviour in the workplace there is a need to appreciate that they arise from and are related to processes of self-organization. Self-organization is our label for the tendency of groups to form interests and establish identities, and to develop autonomy based on these activities. Clearly, workgroups often do develop some sort of identity which is based on informal organization. The capacity for self-organization of this kind originates from a number of sources and mediates different impulses. On the one hand, as much of the traditional industrial sociology literature rightly tells us, self-organization aims at the effective protection and extension of sectional interests, with its natural terrain being the wage-effort bargain. Given that the 'bargain' does not exist in isolation, the characteristics of much self-organization can be seen to be embedded responses to the technical division of labour.

It will surprise nobody if we suggest that groups develop distinct identities or that this is a recurrent feature of workplace organization. Nevertheless, it is our aim to develop a stronger thesis along these lines, to the effect that processes of self-organization occur in every workplace, that they involve the formation of identity, and that, furthermore, such processes usually have significance for the behaviour of the groups concerned. Self-organization also embodies aspirations that derive from social relations more generally, and so it also embodies social aspects of the division of labour. There is a considerable amount of literature that casts light on the mechanisms through which community-based values and class identities are woven into work behaviour (Dennis et al., 1956; Willis, 1977; Hebdige, 1979; Marsh et al., 1983; Hobbs, 1988). However, we want to emphasize that there are incipient tendencies for these influences to develop into something distinctive in the workplace: what emerges there involves the opening out of communal enclaves (Coleman, 1970; Zurcher, 1979). These enclaves have their own distinct characteristics, separate from other social locations. Such enclaves are not simply the result of the forces surrounding and opposing them, but represent an emergent social context which serves as a significant 'identity site' in its own right (Cohen and Taylor, 1976). Collinson (1992) argues, appropriately in our view, that much of the behaviour he discovered is related to workers' ideas about their self-identity, which is formed in distinction to the identity of other groups, and especially to the management within the firm. For Collinson, what marks the identity formation of the workgroups he studied is that they have different values, distinct from those that are officially espoused and sanctioned. His account strongly suggests that self-organization is related to this specific form of identity formation by workgroups.

Interests and identities are not opposites. They reciprocally and discursively form one another, just as the technical and social divisions of labour interact and influence each other. For us, this combination of 'self'-interest and 'self'-identity is the bedrock of employee action in the workplace. But it is a mistake to focus on behaviour to the exclusion of its infrastructure. Forms of misbehaviour such as soldiering, absenteeism or pilferage are commonly noticed. However, they must be seen to be connected to the processes of self-organization on which they rest and which make them possible. Hence it is wrong to infer that if there is no conflicting behaviour to be observed, then there is no effective organization either. As we will argue in this chapter, self-organization can, and often does, underwrite and give potency to conflict; but it need not do so. Self-organization and the impulse towards autonomy are present in all work situations, varying only in terms of the extent to which they are overt or latent.

In order to describe the expression of self-organization more adequately, we shall develop ideas contained in the best of the existing literature. First, many writers have recognized that workplace behaviour varies along a dimension from formally to informally organized. This distinction is found in the work of Edwards and Scullion (1982) amongst a large number of other sources. This is the distinction between, at one extreme, behaviour that is formally organized and regulated (one form of this is associated with trade unions) and, at the other extreme, the informally organized behaviour some of which – in the form of recalcitrance – underpins such practices as soldiering, absenteeism and other overt forms of misbehaviour. Though Edwards and Scullion have a tendency to evaluate all forms of action in the workplace by comparison with the capacity for formal organization and directed action, clearly they recognize both that informal relations exist and that they are not exclusively concerned with conflict. We think, however, that the extent and importance of informal organization has been underestimated.

Second, then, we suggest there is another important dimension on which self-organization can be assessed. The key characteristic of this dimension is that it relates to the manner of the formation of self-identity by groups, and concerns whether self-organization is directed outwards (and so commonly results in resistance to external groups) or is directed inwards (and so is concerned primarily with self-regulation). Such a distinction is present – although largely implicit – in the work of a number of writers, especially David Collinson. The tendency to self-regulation, when it is encountered by researchers, often seems to be without discernible point or direction, and so they tend to downplay or even ignore this aspect of behaviour. For example, Edwards and Scullion make a simple distinction between 'overt' conflict and 'non-directed' activities at the level of behaviour (1982, 11–12). By contrast, we suggest that there is, almost always, a tendency for groups to organize internally. What appears to be non-directed behaviour is actually, on close acquaintance, often found to be actively directed inwards – towards the behaviour of group members themselves. Thus groups may achieve identity and autonomy by different routes: either by defining themselves in distinction to groups outside themselves or by actively cultivating their own internal standards, or by a combination of these.

Understanding this pattern of self-organization is helpful in producing a general account of the misbehaviour of workgroups. It is particularly important to envisage the second identity-oriented dimension that has been distinguished here, otherwise whole areas of misbehaviour are either ignored or treated as curiosities with little relevance for behaviour at work in general. In this chapter we will be discussing, *inter alia*, ceremonial and ritualistic behaviour, which features strongly in some workgroups. Such events make little sense unless considered as examples of self-organization. Because such aspects of self-organization, when they are identified, are thought to have little point, their exploration is not often systematically undertaken.

In more general terms we argue that the pursuit of autonomy is central to self-organization and implicated in all the misbehaviour being discussed in this book. This has been inadequately recognized. True, the pursuit of autonomy is often seen, but usually only when it can be seen as being 'responsible' from a managerial point of view. Indeed responsible autonomy is a well-known concept in the labour process literature, typically associated with the behaviour of skilled workers. We take responsible autonomy to be an achieved condition of self-organization, in which there is recognition by management of the effective self-organization of employees. If the analysis introduced above is correct, however, there is a whole territory of behaviour which is equally characterized by the pursuit of autonomy, but which is either not recognized or not recognizable as being responsible. This we characterize as 'irresponsible autonomy', and we explore its character in the coming chapter. 'Irresponsible autonomy' is obviously a somewhat provocative label for much of the behaviour we shall be concerned with but its adoption here is not mere whimsy. We take it to characterize forms of self-organization and action which occupy their own space independent of management and, indeed, others in the workplace.

The recalcitrance which has featured so strongly in the literature examined in the last chapter can be located within such a framework. Though a general label in the literature, recalcitrance and its associated traditional forms of misbehaviour such as work limitation or pilferage, is distinctive in being informal and externally directed. It is usual to draw comparisons between recalcitrance and the formal, externally directed workplace action best represented in the traditional industrial relations and labour process literature. Such behaviour by groups, having structured forms of organization and being directed towards specific workplace or wider objectives, is commonly identified as 'militancy'. Formal organization may, however, be internally directed, which results in ritualistic and ceremonial activities. By contrast with both of these, when group behaviour is informal but internally directed, it is also likely to be concerned with identity formation and to manifest itself as banter, expressions of masculinity, joking and other forms of self-expression (Collinson, 1988, 1992). These kinds of behaviour cannot be connected with externally-directed conflict, but clearly do shape the identity of workgroups.

We shall now explore in detail the characteristics of these different types of autonomy and self-organization.

Responsible autonomy

The types of self-organization which are most familiar and most often examined are connected to the practices of skilled workers. Although the way they organize themselves is mainly externally directed, they also direct some of their attention inwards. So there is continuous monitoring of the work activities of group members, as well as the behaviour of non-members, supervisors and managers. In many respects the self-organization of skilled workers is not very different from that of professionals such as doctors and lawyers. Like professionals, skilled workers seek autonomy combined with the closure of labour markets and expect that employers will accept the value of their skill. But the situation of skilled workers is more likely to have been achieved in a different way: we shall consider this through analysis of Friedman's (1977) concept of 'responsible autonomy'.

To Friedman's way of thinking, the autonomy that skilled workers have is mainly to be thought about as a mechanism developed by employers through which effective control of these workers is contrived. In his view, the autonomy that skilled or 'core' workers have is not so much achieved by them as allowed or licensed by employers. The responsibility that they display is something given in return for their licence to be free of direct supervision. In effect, Friedman argues that skilled workers control themselves in ways that managers find appropriate, and this is the main thing to understand about the notion of autonomy. Responsible autonomy is presented as the main strategic alternative for management to the 'direct control' that is more likely to be applied to less skilled or peripheral groups. While there is some truth in the notion that autonomy is something which is allowed, this can lead to severe underestimation of its significance. Our argument is that autonomy of any kind should be thought of less as an outcome of managerial activity and more as something that is achieved by relentless self-organization.

Worker initiatives and managerial response are not necessarily opposed. Aspects of the self-organization of skilled workers have been recognized and indeed accepted by employers. Traditionally, not only has the self-organization of skilled workers been accepted but their formal organization has been extensively institutionalized as well. The self-organization of many workers can be, for the most part, formally constituted. The recognition of the self-organization of skilled workers, in particular, allows their activities to be more formally organized and much of their behaviour to be overt. It is also true, however, that aspects of the self-organization of these groups remain out of sight.

It is perhaps worth reminding ourselves of the extent of this recognition and acceptance of self-organization. Historically, skilled workers have co-operated with employers to develop and modify arrangements for their own recruitment and training, for example in the institution of apprenticeship. The formal existence of apprenticeship was not in itself a guarantee of the capacity to defend skills, as the box below demonstrates. But until quite recently, skilled workers in Britain maintained a tenacious grip on the organization of work in many sectors of industry, despite periodic attempts to remove it, which in turn provided support for the apprenticeship system.

Consider the position of skilled workers. They have years of tradition behind them, also five years' apprenticeship in their particular trade. The serving of an apprenticeship is in itself sufficient to form a strong prejudice for their position in industry. But whilst the skilled unions have maintained the serving of an apprenticeship as a primary condition of membership, industrial methods have been changing until the all-round mechanic, for example, is the exception and not the rule. Specialisation has progressed by leaps and bounds. Automatic machine production has vastly increased. The result is that apprenticeships are, in thousands of cases, a farce, for even supposedly skilled workers are kept on repetition work and have become a species of cheap labour . . . . So we can safely say that as historical development takes away the monopoly position of skilled workers it paves the way for the advancement of the unskilled. (Murphy, 1972, first published 1917)

The trade unions constructed by skilled workers were the first effective types of union seen in Britain, the USA and some other Western countries. The main point here is that some formal aspects of the organization of skilled workers – trade unions and apprenticeship – must be seen as coming after, and indeed being constructed on, the effective informal self-organization of workers. Until skilled groups formed an awareness of themselves and the importance of their skills to production processes, they could not have developed the institutionalized aspects of their organization. Indeed, a whole edifice of encroaching control of production and representation of worker interests was advocated as better built on the workshop organization of craft workers such as engineers, rather than the formal institutions of trade unionism (Hinton, 1973; Gallacher and Campbell, 1972; Murphy, 1972). At the same time we have to recognize that skilled workers carved out their area of relative autonomy at the expense of management and their less skilled brethren. It is no wonder that the ideologies of skilled workers – the 'aristocracy' of labour – 'have coexisted in most uneasy tension with socialist ideas' (Cockburn, 1983, 132).

The institutionalization of the organization of skilled workers, then, had its origins in the real strength of their achieved workplace organization. Discussing skilled workers, Penn suggests the following:

> skilled manual workers in mechanised factory milieux are defined by their high degree of social control over the operation and utilisation of machinery. These exclusive controls involve a double exclusion, both of the management from the direct or complete control over the labour process and of other workers who offer a potential threat to such controls. (1985, 121)

At the centre of the autonomy of skilled groups is the control of skilled workers by their own members. Only with this element included can the control over the operation and utilization of machinery be maintained. As Penn's account implies, in fact, skilled workers have achieved the continued control over the utilization of factory machinery; they have not been given it. Further it is the social control of their members which ensures that skilled workers can effectively defend themselves against potential encroachments. Penn explicitly asserts that potential limits on the control of skilled workers come from two directions: on the one hand, from management; on the other hand, from other groups of workers. A similar point is made by Cockburn (1983) in her study of skilled printers when she suggests that 'the skilled men have actively organized the subordination of their inferiors and continue to do so'. She reports one skilled respondent as saying: 'They [other workers] have got to be kept *under* us' (1983, 132; emphasis added). These sorts of arguments suggest that the status of the skilled worker is something that has to be continuously protected and defended by practical organization. Although it is infrequently observed and acknowledged, informal self-organization is nonetheless highly developed in many workplaces and involves the routine surveillance, policing and control of co-workers.

> To try to reduce demarcation we try to give shipwrights all the erecting jobs
> and fairing jobs on the berth, but try to keep all prefabrication in the sheds or
> skids for platers. But if we have two lots on the same job, we find that we also
> have two lots of labourers, one standing and letting the others work . . . . The
> tackers are supposed to help the people they work with but they don't. Any
> tradesman who wants a temporary job done should be able to do it himself.
> Even in shipbuilding a plumber can weld pipes together and do final welding,
> but this is about the only trade which can. A plater who is assembling a
> bulkhead, putting in stiffeners or tack welding has to get a tacker to do it. I
> think tackers sometimes only work a few minutes a day. (Shipyard manager
> quoted by Eldridge, 1968, 118)

It is worth noting two additional points. First, informal self-organization
and formal rules are mutually reinforcing. Job controls can be comple-
mented by regulation of internal and external labour markets, and in turn,
codified through collective bargaining agreements over what started as
'custom and practice'. These processes of consolidation have frequently
enabled workers to maintain skilled status even when some aspects of the
actual skills have been removed or diluted (Rubery, 1980). Second, powerful job controls and controls over the utilization of machinery can also be
exerted by non-craft workers (Thompson, 1989, 99, 135). When organized
with sufficient purpose and effectiveness, and in favourable labour market
conditions, the conditions for responsible autonomy can be created. A case
in point was that of some car plants in the UK from the 1940s onwards
(Friedman, 1977), where the principle of mutuality – the mutual fixing of
piece-rate prices and agreed methods by management and shop stewards –
was firmly established.

That 'frontier of control' was never likely to remain static. Employers in
Britain launched a major offensive in the early 1970s against the informal
job controls and formal bargaining mechanisms of key groups of skilled and
semi-skilled workers. Such measures undermined the basis for existing
forms of responsible autonomy. Emblematic of such a trend was the attempt
to remove the Coventry Toolroom Agreement in 1971, which had underpinned the internal and external labour market powers of craft and craft-
related workers. In a range of industries employers were anxious to replace
the piecework system which informal self-organization can exploit to create
loose rates and wage drift, with a more stable, centrally determined set of
arrangements such as 'Measured Day Work' (Coventry Machine Tool
Workers Committee, 1979). Tough employers made advances; economic
and political conditions were relatively unfavourable. As is all too familiar,
in the 1980s, backed by increased legal powers over trade unions and more
flexible labour markets, employers took back control over work and
machinery from skilled employees in some areas. The formal aspects of the
self-organization of skilled workers have been scaled down generally; and
even, in places, removed. It would also appear that apprenticeship systems
are now in terminal decline in Britain and some other countries (Gospel,

1995). However, the inability to resist general encroachment of their institutionalized powers should not be confused with the removal of the informal organization of groups in workplaces. It would be an error to assume
that taking away the institutionalized aspects of worker power is the same
thing as weakening or effectively removing workers' capacity for self-
organization.

There are a number of changes taking place at the present time affecting
the formal and informal organization of workers. Although some of these
weaken the formal organization of workers, others are likely to give very
much greater saliency to aspects of informal organization. There is, for
example, a well-established tendency towards the development of localized
bargaining in industrial relations (Terry, 1977). There is also a managerial
rhetoric which suggests that the views of employees should be taken seriously. Both of these factors are likely to encourage rather than discourage
self-organization by workgroups. We shall argue later that the traditional
pattern of organizational misbehaviour is changing – away from the familiar, traditional examples of soldiering and absenteeism and towards more
subtle kinds of behaviour that are in many ways more difficult for managers
to handle. Because the conditions for the production of responsible autonomy have now gone, it does not mean that the pursuit of autonomy will disappear. On the contrary, it is quite likely to take what will be recognized as
an irresponsible form. Although it has not been widely studied, what we can
call irresponsible autonomy is not at all uncommon.

Irresponsible autonomy

The best examples of this sort of behaviour (or the worst, depending on
your assumptions) are so unexpected that they are often taken to be untypical and even unique forms of workplace activity. Some of the examples
we shall consider are so bizarre that they invite comparisons with the rituals
and ceremonies of native peoples. This behaviour may easily be thought to
be of interest only because it is unlike anything supposedly rational people
in typical work situations might do. It seems to call for special explanations,
and it sometimes leads writers to propose them. But, in obvious ways, what
there is to see is directly comparable with the behaviour found in many work
settings. From our viewpoint, this behaviour is simply indicative of one way
in which self-organization may develop.

In a study of an American coal mine published by Vaught and Smith
(1980) it was shown that groups of workers gang up on some of their own
members, subjecting particular individuals to extreme punishments and
degradations. One example is quoted in the extract on p. 62, but there were
many others. Among other things, dirtying the genitalia of fellow workers
seemed to be a commonplace occurrence.

However, in case there is any thought of dismissing such behaviour as
likely to be limited to remote or geographically isolated locations, similar

---

The hanging of Short Ruby

One night, Short Ruby . . . stretched out in the bucket of the scoop and went to sleep. The mechanics, mad because he had gone to sleep on their unit . . . decided to 'hang' him. After binding him from head to foot with electrical tape, they raised the bucket of the scoop, tied a length of shooting wire to his penis, secured the other end to a roof bolt overhead and then lowered the bucket until the wire was stretched tight. The men then sat in a semi-circle before the scoop bucket and tossed small rocks at the shooting wire. Each time a rock found its mark, the men were rewarded by an 'ooh' from Short Ruby. When Short Ruby began to worry aloud about what would happen if the hydraulics bled off the scoop, allowing the bucket to drop, one of the men suggested that: 'Maybe we'll have to change your name to Long Ruby'.
(Vaught and Smith, 1980, 174)

---

activities can be found closer to home. In a detailed study of the workgroups in an English slaughterhouse, for example, very similar tendencies were found. In this research, a young and inexperienced worker, who was set to work at the end of a short production line, was harassed and attacked. The new man was subjected to ill-treatment that built up over several days and weeks. Each day the slaughtering gang deliberately caused work to build up at his station, leaving a good deal for him to clear before he could take any break. More often than not, he had to continue working without a break to clear a backlog of work. Yet he stoically carried on, ignoring the efforts of other workers to make life hard for him. This only seemed to make matters worse. One day, in addition to being harassed in this way, some of the workers began to amuse themselves by making the recruit the target of missiles – full sheep bladders and the like – thrown across the shop. On one occasion, a sheep carcass was pushed hard along an unpowered 'siding', catching him in the back and knocking him over into the blood and offal on the slaughter-house floor. This caused general hilarity. Events culminated in the man being 'baptized': he was summarily grabbed and held upside down by the gang with his head in a tub of blood (see also Ackroyd and Crowdy, 1990).

It might still be objected that both mine and slaughterhouse are unusual kinds of workplace. It is true that they are both dirty and dangerous, and that these features have undoubtedly had something to do with the extreme behaviour observed in them. However, the fact is that events very much like these have been seen in careful studies conducted in many locations. Factories of all kinds are rife with such events. In his book, David Collinson (1992) describes behaviour very much like that recorded in the slaughter-house and mine. He asserts, as do Vaught and Smith and many others, that learners and novices are given particular attention by workgroups. From a variety of such reports, it seems that defiling other workers is a common accompaniment of self-organization. It appears in factories and machine shops as well as more exotic locations. Such degradations shade into defiling 'practical jokes', which take place almost everywhere – amongst office workers as well as manual employees. A report of another study based on

---

Greasing the apprentices

Pancake Tuesday was celebrated by 'greasing the bollocks' of the apprentices
with emulsion and then 'locking them in the shithouse, bollock naked'. . . .
Having graduated through degradation ceremonies [apprentice lads] would
be recognised as mature men worthy of participating in shop floor banter.
That is, if they could take the daily practical jokes, for which their lack of
knowledge made them ideal victims . . . (Collinson, 1988, 189)

---

long-term observation, this time in a small machine shop, cites some good
examples. Boland and Hoffman (1983) record a miscellany of practical jokes
played on fellow workers: 'A new worker will have jokes played on him so
that he learns his place. The ambiguity of self confirmed by humour allows
for movement through established hierarchies' (Boland and Hoffman, 1983,
193).

Clearly humour has always been an important feature of self-organization
in the workplace. We suggest here that it is a vital ingredient in the punitive
and protective aspects of self-organization we described at the start of this
chapter. Forms of joking behaviour at work are also changing. As we argue
in Chapter 5, joking behaviour is becoming more subtle and corrosive,
changing from a phenomenon which sustains a similar outlook amongst
employees, to a satirical and distanced evaluation of the activities of managers and the polices of companies.

The rite stuff

An explanation for much of the behaviour described above is that these
rites and ceremonies are functional for the groups in which they occur.
Where there is potentially lethal machinery in operation and/or unpredictable work conditions, it is argued, it is necessary for workers to watch
out for each other and develop a high level of practical awareness and solidarity (Dennis et al., 1956; Fitzpatrick, 1980). In these circumstances, ego-
centric and self-serving behaviour may be positively dangerous for others
and tends to be sanctioned. In addition, where management presence is
likely to be remote or impractical, it is valuable if operatives can learn to

---

More practical jokes

'Blueing' is a popular trick in which an indelible marking ink is rubbed on the
handles and knobs of a machine. This is especially funny if the individual
touches his face after having grabbed the blued knob or handle . . . . In a
similar vein, the hose which sprays a fine stream of coolant over the raw steel
as it is being machined can be adjusted to spray at high pressure directly onto
the machine operator. Other machine jokes involve removing gears or fuses
from a machine or reversing the direction in which the machine rotates.
(Boland and Hoffman, 1983, 191)

---

trust in each other's judgement, and rely implicitly on each other's support. Buttressing arguments of this kind, it is also true that social anthropologists think rites and rituals magnify the meaning of shared events and so develop group identification and solidarity.

For these sorts of reasons it is argued that, in the context of the mine or the slaughterhouse, events such as some of those that have been described above, which clearly do have ritualistic qualities, are functional for the groups in which they occur. Such events as hanging obviously would impress members with the power of the group, and it is plausible to see this as developing group identity. However, Vaught and Smith go further. They write:

> The sexual themes and dramatic performances . . . may be viewed as perverse, brutal and degrading, *if abstracted from the situated milieu in which they occur.* Within context . . . however, they are a powerfully integrating force for the group. (1980, 180; emphasis added)

These authors have fallen into a simple but fairly fundamental error: because repeated practices may have identifiable social effects, it is not correct to say this is their cause. Nor is it a reason for suspending judgement on them. There should be no equivocation about such matters. The greasing described by Collinson and the harassments in the slaughterhouse are degradations of those to whom they are applied. The treatment meted out to some of the miners which was described by Vaught and Smith was (and presumably still is) indefensible. Clearly, rites may be morally wrong. At the very least we need to ask why solidarity must be achieved at the cost of individual degradation. Groups are often strongly integrated by quite other means – the allocation of mutual esteem and regard found amongst some professionals is an obvious case in point. Given the coercion that is involved in these situations, the view that is also commonly developed, that group members enjoy special freedoms, seems questionable from an external point of view. We shall return to this issue.

But the main objection to such explanations of behaviour is not moralistic. The fact is that these explanations attribute singular importance to events that are not unique, merely extreme examples of a particular class of behaviour. Events such as these have a very punitive character, but in other respects they are not remarkable, and there seems no reason to take their alleged functionality seriously. As the next box helps to corroborate, the punitive tendency of workers towards their own membership is common. Much of it is associated with the creation of informal hierarchies. What we are looking at in the degradations of workers so far described, then, are extreme manifestations of the capacity for self-organization. The punitive tendency in the development of group autonomy is not the only kind, but it is common and in these forms is easy to identify. We suggest that, because of physical isolation, and the dangerous circumstances in which they work, not to mention remote or disengaged management, some groups have developed a distinctive kind of autonomy. However, the tendency to

---

Group solidarity and the individual

Give them an inch and they'll put on you viciously, the bloody swine!
(respondent quoted by Dennis et al., 1956, 129)

Never show weakness . . . I only hope nothing happens to me. If I lost a leg,
they'd laugh for a week, then follow me to the canteen doing Long-John
Silver impressions. (respondent reported by Linstead, 1985, 750)

You've got to give it out or go under. It's a form of survival, you insult before
they get one back. The more you get embarrassed, the more they do it. So
you have to fight back. (respondent quoted by Collinson, 1988, 188)

---

develop autonomy is not unique to these examples. Similar tendencies are
noted in other situations with remarkable frequency.

The micro-politics of groups

It cannot be argued that events similar to the 'baptism' of the slaughterman
or the 'greasing' of factory workers are widespread. However, much of this
behaviour has at least two aspects, which appear simultaneously, and these
are recurrent features of the processes associated with the micro-politics of
groups. Groups develop informal hierarchies and, around this, some kind of
identity for themselves. 'Hanging' differs from 'greasing' and 'blueing'
mainly in the extent of the defilement of members and the violence
employed to perpetrate it. However, there are milder and less overtly aggressive ways in which groups are constructed by their members. Everyday
experience at work (even in the senior common room) suggests that
assertiveness, sarcasm, barbed wit, parody, mimicry, general 'kidding' and
the like, not to mention organized practical jokes, are ubiquitous. These, and
the gossiping by which people test, react to and attempt to alter accounts of
events or their own reputations and those of colleagues, are the currency of
social control in all kinds of work settings (Noon and Delbridge, 1993). What
these events have in common with more violent and overtly manipulative
forms of self-organization are that they are mechanisms by which informal
hierarchies and group identities are developed and sustained.

The development of identity and control is present in even the most rudi-
mentary groups. In a pioneering paper written in 1958, Donald Roy reports
on a very small group of unskilled workers engaged 'in repetitive manual
work'. He records the way in which the working day was divided by the group
into a series of intervals demarcated by specific 'times'. Thus, 'peach time'
marked one break from work followed by 'banana time', 'Coke time', 'fish
time' and so on, the intervals being named after the kind of refreshment
taken at each interval. Roy argues that these designated 'times' broke up
long periods of extremely tedious work, providing intervals of rest and diversion. They therefore helped to 'kill the beast of monotony'. But this designating of 'times' is not simply a matter of marking the passage of time. The

---

Daily banana time

Each morning after making the snatch, Ike would call out 'banana time!' and
proceed to down his prize, while Sammy made futile protests and
denunciations. George (the charge hand) would join in with mild
remonstrances, sometimes scolding Sammy for making so much fuss. The
banana Sammy had brought for his own consumption at lunch time. He never
did get to eat his banana, but kept bringing one for his lunch. At first the
daily theft startled and amazed me. Then I grew to look forward to the daily
seizure and the verbal interaction which followed. (Roy, 1958, 159)

---

interludes are also given meaning by their association with particular events.
Clearly too these meanings are intertwined with the creation and re-creation
of group relationships. The 'banana time', which provides the title of Roy's
paper, is not simply a regular break time defined by members eating bananas.
In fact, it is a relatively arbitrary time interval marked by the pilferage and
consumption of a banana belonging to one worker by another. According to
Roy, each and every day, a worker called Ike would steal and consume a
banana belonging to a co-worker called Sammy.

The continued daily provision of the banana must have been to some
extent a voluntary matter for Sammy. The banana must be regarded as some
kind of quasi-voluntary tribute or gift, perpetually provided and perpetually 'stolen'. However, its summary but, after a few occasions, entirely predictable, seizure clearly defined relative positions in the group, as well as
providing entertainment and diversion. In this way, the banana theft has
some of the same attributes as some of the other behaviour we looked at in
the last section. Like the 'baptism' or the 'greasing' noted by researchers,
the theft of the banana was not reciprocal. Though, like those other events,
it would possibly have been represented as a 'joke' if some sort of account
of it were required, like them it is not an equal exchange and not really very
funny, even though it may be connived in by the victim.

Roy's report is interesting because he shows that, even in a very mundane
work situation, subtle processes of self-regulation and group formation exist.
Roy manages to observe and describe events which, although they are not
physically threatening, can be seen to be as puzzling as the defiling and
aggressive events which other research reports have featured. When they are
fully analysed, these processes are revealed to work in similar ways to the
more extreme and obvious processes found elsewhere. On the basis of the
sort of careful observational work that Roy has undertaken, it seems likely
that self-organization is usually milder and less blatant than in the violent
examples we have so far considered. However, such reports also show that
some form of self-organization – featuring group identity and hierarchy – is
usually present. In its central features, informal self-organization differs little
from the extreme examples. In many ways it is the latent potential of group
identification and mobilization that is exhibited.

In many situations, the punitive aspects of informal self-organization are
not very developed or obvious to the casual observer. Yet they are usually

there in some form. For this reason it is an interesting paradox that, even when the effects of self-organization are likely to be seen as extreme by any external assessors, they are not experienced as being remarkable by participants, despite their sometimes violent and punitive character. On the contrary, as several commentators have found, self-organized groups are generally seen by their members as free of coercion and control. Collinson (1992) goes so far as to suggest that his factory hands experience their work as occupying 'free space'. This is despite the fact that these workers are to a considerable degree both controlled by the management from the outside and by definite internal and self-created hierarchies from the inside. But events like 'greasing' and 'blueing', which we have argued enforce informal hierarchies, are usually accepted by those who are the victims of these practices. Even the 'hanging' of Short Ruby was not seen as extraordinary but part of the order of things by those who participated.

If this is correct, one question for us must be as follows: what is it about our own typical patterns of organization, which our own assumptions lead us to accept as normal, that with different assumptions from our own, could be seen as strange and even bizarre? The subject matter being studied here, as we have demonstrated, merges imperceptibly into the micro-politics of groups. That there is politics in the factory or office is the nearest we usually get to the direct perception of the processes of self-organization in which we ourselves are continuously engaged.

Not all irresponsible autonomy is inwardly directed and ceremonial in nature. Some forms, as we shall see below, are both recalcitrant and aimed at management and its systems.

Irresponsible autonomy and the effort bargain

Seeing informal organization as an inadequate kind of formal organization calls attention away from the need for consideration of the phenomenon in its own right. The assumptions of scholars in the field of industrial relations certainly lead them to overlook and to devalue the organization that necessarily underpins forms of misbehaviour. It can hardly be otherwise when they define this behaviour in terms of its lack of organization. However, it should be clear that, in many circumstances, it has been the potency of informal organization that has given organized actions their moral charge or economic effectiveness. In some circumstances the capacity for self-organization has considerable output in the form of overtly militant and formally organized actions in the sphere of the effort bargain. When formal and informal organization are aligned, the effects of informal organization on formal action can be considerable. Yet, in the right conditions, the politics of quite small groups can be highly recalcitrant and have considerable impact on organized industrial relations.

We want to explore this through the case study research into events at Plessey Telecommunications in Liverpool involving one of the authors (Thompson and Bannon, 1985). There was, in this company, a combination of scarce labour and full order books. There was also a long and strong tradition of informal organization in the community plus weak management. However, this example shows graphically the way in which self-organization pulls apart as much as it unites the groups involved.

At the end of the 1970s, the Plessey Company was experiencing some competition in the labour market in Liverpool, particularly in the market for some types of skilled worker. It was suspected by managers that the reason for excessive labour turnover was that wage rates were uncompetitive. The Company was also experiencing escalating wage drift and training costs. To deal with this, management decided not to replace the existing payment system with something new, but to attempt to reconstruct the old one. Accordingly, all the jobs in the factory were to be reassessed and retimed and the resulting rates applied to whole departments. What was proposed was in fact a very conventional productivity deal which linked a basic wage to a fairly low level of output as established by time study, but offered premium payments for progressively higher levels of output. To deal with the problem of labour turnover, the idea was to be relatively generous to certain skilled grades, and to those whose work was central to production tasks. What the company reckoned without was the effectiveness of the informal organization of the different groups of workers, even amongst the relatively unskilled.

All groups exercised what work limitation they could in the job-timing process, but had different degrees of success. In one large department (no. 15) there were broadly three groups of workers. The skilled and central tasks (those of the functioneers, inspection and relay adjusters) were located at the end of the shop, whilst unskilled assembly work was located at the opposite end, at which the production sequence began. About halfway along the flow line were the 'wiring track groups' whose work required a mid-range of skill. After the retiming exercise, during which the work of all groups was rerated, the skilled workers made no secret of their capacity to achieve high levels of wages in very short periods of time. The unskilled workers had made some progress in getting good timings for their jobs, but the contrast between their new level of earnings and that of other groups was not immediately apparent because of the careful response of the middle group of wiring track workers. The middle groups were among the last in the factory to be measured. This was mainly due to the activity of their shop steward, who not only helped to ensure that good timings were secured by her people, but also sensibly restrained them from exploiting the relatively loose timings that resulted too soon. Thus, after the wiring tracks received their new rates, production was deliberately restricted, to ensure that work study would have no cause for remeasurement.

During the period of continued output restriction, the average bonus paid to the wiring tracks was at or about the standard performance. Thus the wiring track workers, who were still restricting their production, acted as a buffer between the unskilled workers of department 15, who had achieved little from the retiming exercise, and the high flyers whose earnings were now very high indeed. After a month or so of continued deliberate output

---

Subbuteo and industrial relations

To encourage the 'high flyers' to stay in the plant, the management allowed them to play games. The poker schools would have bigger pots than some of the gambling clubs in the city. . . .

John Smith the senior steward remembers some of the negotiations . . . . 'When they were playing subbuteo they had a league going with a big following. You would get them all round the tables cheering away. When a goal was scored they would jump up and down wildly. You can imagine the effect that this had on people sitting there working for bum cash. You can imagine the reaction from the Post Office when they brought visitors around. After that the management tried to cut the games out. They called in the high flying stewards to negotiate. When they opened the door and invited us in, the stewards all ran in, in a single file humming the music from *Match of the Day*. It was supposed to be a serious meeting and the management were serious. That was the funniest thing – management were serious.

So management tried to negotiate what games would be played. They said, 'All you can play is dominoes, draughts and chess, but no game that accommodates spectators.' Whilst this was being argued, one of the stewards said: 'Come on, you'll have to make this quick, I'm in the final after.' And it was true, they were all waiting for him outside the door to play.

The senior steward of the ETU also remembers the negotiations:

'We negotiated that they could play subbuteo but couldn't move from their own benches and they couldn't have a referee. So the lads were saying "How can we play subbuteo without a referee?" It ended by mutual agreement that they could still play subbuteo but with restrictions on spectators'.

(Thompson and Bannon, 1985, 42–55)

---

restriction, the wiring track workers finally relaxed their voluntary restriction of output and their earnings also moved ahead sharply.

This is an instructive example, because it demonstrates both the extent and the effectiveness of self-organization and the limits of general solidarity. All groups in the factory are informally organized, but the extent to which this achieves effective expression depends on subtle differences of personnel, management policy and outlook and other circumstances. The high flying section's informal organization was highly effective. Some workers in this group were producing enough in two days to obtain very high levels of wages; and they flaunted their privileges. In the middle of the shop the self-organization was largely internally directed and more carefully hidden. At the other end of the shop the self-organization of workers was also mainly latent. The huge tensions in department 15, which eventually found expression, make little sense unless these groups and their boundaries are recognized. It was the developing informal organization of the unskilled workers – which found support from the workers' trade union – which was the source of pressure for change.

Surprising though it may seem, these problems were only confronted by senior managers after quite a long time, and the motivation to do so was actually placed on them by groups of the workers. Their first response was to negotiate an arrangement which, instead of dealing with the anomalies of the payment system at source, brought forward a scheme to compensate the low earners with a proportion of the bonus of the high earners. This satisfied nobody. A strike by the lower paid workers was necessary before the steps were taken that eventually resulted in a more adequate solution. In between, however, the advantaged workgroups in the new pay regime took many steps to capitalize on their advantages. A lot of antagonism resulted between the groups in the department.

As these processes were working themselves towards a conclusion and tensions in department 15 were rising, the highly skilled groups were allowed to play games during the time when they had completed their work. This was to prevent them, having earned maximum possible bonus well before the normal finishing time, simply going home. However, their behaviour while playing games was disruptive, and this caused added antagonism. Other employees in department 15 were still working while the games were going on, for much less money. Obviously such a situation could not long continue. The surprise is only that it took a strike by the low paid groups to bring this conclusion forcefully to the attention of the managers.

The compensation scheme by which the high flyers recompensed the low paid soon collapsed – at considerable cost to the company in unrecoverable compensation payments. Overall the company had failed to shift the effort bargain in its direction, its attempts foundering on the rock of irresponsible autonomy. The situation proved extremely difficult for either the management or trade union officials to rectify and the factory ended up 'split into many factions, each pursuing its own course of action for attack or indeed defence in the battle for wages and conditions' (Thompson and Bannon, 1985, 55).

Connections reconsidered

Having considered some developed forms of self-organization in some detail, it is instructive to look again briefly at some of the assumptions discussed in the literature reviewed in Chapter 2 about what has been labelled 'the recalcitrant worker'. As we suggested there, a common theme of a great deal of this literature involves the discovery of nonconforming behaviour combined with more or less overt resistance to management. This behaviour has the properties of being both externally directed and informally organized. What we have to emphasize now is that recalcitrance also has considerable informal organization associated with it. This may not be as extensive as the self-organization that is evidently present in the rituals and degradations we described in the extreme forms of irresponsible autonomy considered in this chapter. But for resisting behaviour to be undertaken at all requires some informal organization. Although this 'organization' may not be obvious, consisting of little more than the tacit understandings of participants, it nonetheless exists and has effects.

In most forms, self-organization is extremely difficult to manage. Recalcitrance depends on a shared outlook of opposition, including detailed conceptions of reasonable levels of working effort, ideas about appropriate kinds of non-work activity and of 'reasonable' amounts of work effort or completed production. There is also often substantial tacit agreement on effective practices and norms governing the conduct of group members, especially in their relations with company officials – rate fixers, supervisors and others with authority. Such practices obviously involve a developed complicity between the individual members of groups of employees. Organization in this sense is a continuous activity, and the processes involved are subtle. They involve groups developing their identity and, inevitably, there are shifts of alliances and relationships going along with this. In sum, the conduct of recalcitrant work limitation – including supposedly fundamentally individual behaviour such as soldiering, absenteeism and pilferage – depends on mutually adjusted and other-regarding activity. The best research on workgroups and their practices of work limitation, from Lupton (1963) and Cunnison (1964) to Burawoy (1979) and Collinson (1992), shows how dependent work limitation is on group complicity.

The forms of action associated with the recalcitrant worker should not be confused with solidarity; especially not plant-wide solidarity and still less class-wide solidarity. When we shift to consider the more general concept of irresponsible autonomy the point hardly needs making at all. Yet, if our analysis is correct, these two are closely connected. An analysis of the patterns of self-organization in terms of autonomy suggests in fact that group identification is usually not strongly solidaristic – even at the level of the small group. Considered in this way, the self-organization of small groups is, more often than not, highly restrictive in its identification of means and ends (see box).

Self-organization is even less likely to be confused with class-wide militancy or political commitment, but surprisingly often it develops various forms of practical effectiveness. As Thompson and Bannon (1985) point out, the most recalcitrant groups in the Plessey plant, the ones that gave management most trouble, were the least likely to show any interest in broader trade unionism and conventional strike action. In a way, this modesty and lack of potential is a key to understanding the effectiveness of self-organization. It often achieves little more than marginally altering conduct into compliance with group norms. Management is, nevertheless, often frustrated by its development as we shall argue more fully in our next chapter. Management is certainly disposed to allow such self-organization

---

Informal organization and workers' solidarity

What is noticeable throughout the affair [events surrounding the introduction of a productivity agreement] is that the solidarity of the cement workers caved in whenever it came under pressure. Each time groups saw a short-run advantage for themselves they were willing to forget the consequences for their workmates. In the event, most of these short-run advantages turned out to be very short-run indeed or completely illusory. (Peter Armstrong in Nichols and Armstrong, 1976, 125)

to develop, partly because it does not fully identify the behaviour for what it is, and partly because the costs of correcting it, beyond an early point, would be considerable. Unable or unwilling to remove these practices at their beginnings, management very often increasingly works around the misbehaviour associated with them as they develop. Thus the groundwork for the toleration of such things as work limitation, absenteeism and pilferage is imperceptibly secured.

To argue in this way is to shift the emphasis in the analysis in different directions to those who see this sort of behaviour as lacking organization and as a less effective version of industrial militancy. If they recognize the self-organization in workplace behaviour at all, it is habitual for industrial relations specialists to see it as unorganized conflict and, as such, an inadequate approximation to organized conflict. Hyman argues that, in some circumstances, unorganized conflict may function as a proxy for formally organized events (see 1972, 53–6). If for some reason, he argues, access to formally organized action is blocked and the expression of discontent frustrated, then it may find expression in unorganized action. As we have seen in our discussion of Thompson and Bannon, this can be true; but the importance of self-organization is by no means restricted to this sort of potentiality. The causation is more the other way round, in that self-organization may in some circumstances develop into formal organization and action. At the least, those with an interest in industrial relations should now be prepared to recognize that what they tend to identify as unorganized behaviour in the workplace is only formally unorganized. Informal organization is typically both extensive and varied, and while it is sometimes congruent with formal organization and capable of pushing in the same direction, often it is not.

This is not the place to debate the relationship between organized and unorganized conflict, a topic that has been given remarkably little consideration in the literature (Bean, 1975). However, it is worth asking whether the emphasis on formal organization and organized action is always appropriate. Even when Britain had a high strike rate, strikes occurred in only a minority of workplaces. In addition, traditionally more than 95 per cent of strikes were unofficial in the sense that they were not recognized by trade unions (Crouch, 1982). At the height of their institutionalized power, trade unions still had to cope with the divergent interests of different groups in organizations before workforces could be effectively represented (see Nichols and Armstrong, 1976; Nichols and Beynon, 1977). Most importantly, attempts to formalize practices and organization have often failed. The most prominent example was the Donovan Report in 1968, whose clear target was the potency of informal organization and bargaining in many large British workplaces. The goal was to persuade management to develop formal, factory-level agreements and incorporate the shop stewards into formal bargaining and structures. But as Terry (1977) demonstrates, the preference of employees and management for informal practices and rules, which both thought they could manipulate to their own advantage, meant that 'significant groups within such factories have not chosen to use the new agreements to eliminate informal practice' (1977, 76). For some analytical purposes, the time has come to re-evaluate the relative importance of formal and informal organization and their relation to patterns of conflict.

Conclusion

We have argued that autonomy is habitually sought and it is, to some degree, achieved by groups of employees. But such an idea has to be appropriately understood. Self-organization is often deeply hidden and sometimes not very fully developed. It is the potentiality for rapid development that is often as important as the actual presence of such organization. Self-organization can be and often is distinctly opportunistic. Yet self-organization is typically shaped by and can be seen to be a response to the structures of the formal organization in which it is contained. Clearly, there is informal organization within managerially defined workgroups and teams, as well as other occupational categories. Indeed, new self-organization is capable of forming and reforming very rapidly around these imposed divisions – in response to new contingencies and initiatives. Hence, although it is always in some way related to formal organizational structures, self-organization cannot be reduced to or replaced by formal organization. This is, in part, because self-organization is the capacity to form identities in contradistinction to those imposed by formal hierarchies.

This last point is important because theorists have sought the explanation for self-organization solely in its instrumentality. The rational pursuit of higher wages, the adjustment of the effort bargain and the extension of *de facto* control over the labour process, of course, are likely to involve a degree of self-organization. Informal organization is useful for (and invariably implicated in) purposive action by workgroups: such things as avoiding direct control by management and/or developing a group's economic interests. Because of this too, self-organization is likely to be regarded as potentially if not actually 'irresponsible' from a managerial point of view. Nor is it surprising that the behaviour sustained by self-organization can come under attack by management. Terry's (1977) judgement on the experience of the Donovan reforms – that a degree of informal regulation was inevitable – gives some support to our view that self-organization is active and growing. However, a number of influential commentators do not agree, seeing in contemporary forms of management and organization the successful squeezing out of informal controls and the elimination of that 'free space' identified by Collinson. These issues will be addressed in our final chapter, but, before that, we want to take a look at attempts to manage misbehaviour, and to consider the interaction of the forces we have considered in this chapter with the activities of managers.

4 Management and Misbehaviour

In the last chapter we dwelt in some detail on the self-organization of employees. This was for two reasons. First, it is essential to establish the idea that people at work are not inert or passive. They actively engage with their work, developing identification with workmates and the activities they undertake. They adapt their conduct to what they experience. These tendencies have been recognized by a good deal of research and writing about work, as we have seen. It is suggested here, then, that self-organization is active everywhere. Second, because of this, self-organization continues to be of enormous importance to the experience of work and to the effect of management initiatives. People at work can and do make innovations in self-organization, both in response to what management does and independently. The behaviour of workgroups develops and produces new patterns of behaviour to which management, in its turn, often feels it has to respond. In later chapters, then, it will be argued that there are currently some new developments in workplace behaviour that are difficult to understand unless the capacity for innovation is recognized.

What makes the processes we were examining in the last chapter different to those which we shall consider now, is that previously we were deliberately laying emphasis on the pursuit of autonomy by employees. We suggested that the tendency to seek autonomy is endemic and, when achieved, it is often beyond the perception – not to mention the control – of management. We were concerned to draw attention to behaviour which would continue to exist in the same form only if it escapes the attention of managers.

In this chapter we shall shift our attention to focus more centrally on management and its activities, and the way that this bears on the self-organization of workers. Managers often act unknowingly on existing patterns of self-organization; and, even when they do have some perception of what exists, this is usually far from being accurate and complete. In this discussion it will become clear that we are not talking about the activities of management as formal functions, but focusing on the issue of manageability. The processes we shall identify implicate a variety of workplace actors. In other words, we shall be considering what kinds of action create 'trouble' in organizations, what determines whether and how it is responded to by managers, and what form those responses take.

The pursuit of autonomy is central to misbehaviour, but it cannot be adequately discussed without reference to management in the sense identified above. Misbehaviour has to be noticed as such, and it is management that has the power and discretion to define behaviour as acceptable or unacceptable and to devise categories and procedures for their identification. Indeed, it is the pursuit of manageability through the manipulation of categories and procedures which leads directly to the production of specific forms of organizational misbehaviour. This perspective takes us beyond the mistaken view that the common forms of misbehaviour in organizations – low working effort, absenteeism and pilferage – are explained simply by the dispositions of individuals. It is, equally, the active identification, monitoring, categorization and labelling of activities which produce organizational misbehaviour. In an obvious sense, distinct forms of misbehaviour are the characteristic artefacts of distinct managerial regimes.

In considering the complex relations between management and misbehaviour in more detail, this chapter utilizes the concept of managerial regime to set out some of the systematic patterns of initiative and response. Using the concept of a 'regime' leads us to look for characteristic artefacts: such things as categories of conduct, rules and procedures by which such things are to be identified, and policy formation related to these. It also leads us to think in terms of the costs and limits of regimes. Recognition of practical and other limits of regimes has caused a number of writers to identify the 'frontier of control' between management and employees using the concept of Goodrich (1975) who first developed the idea in 1920. The delimitation of a number of distinct behaviours – 'absenteeism', 'pilferage' and 'soldiering' – is indicative of the existence of specific regulatory regimes producing particular categories of 'misbehaviour'.

We shall return to the definition of regimes later. However, it needs to be underlined at this point that there is no attempt in the following account to provide a historical narrative of regimes. The idea of a line of development can never capture the variety of forms and social relations that require consideration. Hence, in our account we will combine an emphasis on the appropriation of time, product and the restriction of working effort with a focused and intensive examination of the dynamics of highly regulated managerial regimes. As is common in this field, a central reference point will be Taylorism. Our contribution concerns the way that Taylorism and similar regimes featuring direct control interact with the capacity for self-organization to produce distinctive patterns of misbehaviour.

The events we shall consider here are the subject matter of the classic studies of the appropriation of time and product reviewed in Chapter 2. As we argued in Chapter 1, three of the distinctive directions that misbehaviour can take are effort limitation, appropriation of time and appropriation of product. We shall suggest here that management is implicated in the production of these different forms of misbehaviour and argue against the idea, which common sense suggests, that they are simply the product of an individual's disposition and motivation. Misbehaviour is produced by the organization and by the way impulses to control behaviour initiated and

directed by managers interact with self-organization. To make this fundamental point, let us consider the production of absenteeism.

Defining and producing misbehaviour: the case of absenteeism

The identification of absenteeism, which suggests unexcused and perhaps
habitual absence from work, does require employees who occasionally do
not attend work when they are expected to. But absenteeism is also actively
produced by a particular sort of regime of control. How so? The production
of absenteeism typically works something like this: if an employee does not
clock on, then he or she does not get paid, and a note is made of a potential unauthorized absence to be recorded as an instance of absenteeism. In
many firms, absentee records will be automatically made in this sort of way.
Unless the employee makes efforts to show that a particular absence was
allowable – let us say for jury service or attendance at a funeral – it is
recorded as an instance of absenteeism. Compare this with what happens
with managers or university teachers – there is apparently no absenteeism
amongst these groups. But, on consideration, it is actually more accurate to
say that there is no close monitoring of what managers and professors are
doing with their time, no records of when they are not present, and thus no
possibility of any calculation of their 'absenteeism'. This is quite different
from the idea that managers do not take time off from their work for their
own purposes. Managers work under quite different conditions than other
employees. So far as the use of time is concerned, they may be said to work
under a time perk rather than a time penalty system – if a manager is not
to be found it is assumed that there is a good reason for it. If a shop floor
worker is absent it is assumed there is (or perhaps that there can be) no
good reason for it.

In this way we must see the recording of problematic misbehaviour as a
product of controlling regimes as well as the behaviour of individuals and
groups. In essence, what is regarded as misbehaviour arises from the close
scrutiny of behaviour from a particular point of view, and the mobilization

---

What is absenteeism?

Without the organization and its concept of attendance, absence has no
meaning. Absence exists only as it is defined by the organization and its
relationship to the employee. (Mark Fincham in Goodman et al., 1984, 17)

We want to ask a more fundamental question: why is it interesting to discuss
something called absenteeism, a concept that is laden with guilt and
accusation? Absenteeism is a concept which may be more descriptive of the
managerial need and longing for control than of individual behaviour.
(Arvedson and Hedberg, 1986, 561–2)

of an array of procedures and arrangements to note, record, measure and attempt to deal with it. The managerial regimes that produce absenteeism keep detailed records of attendance, monitor attendance by reviewing and assessing such records, and act on the data by selecting out for attention individuals whose records transgress given standards. All this implies a regime of management which involves not only the routine keeping of attendance records, but the review and comparison of absence records, the establishment of norms of acceptable attendance and the attempt to control behaviour by 'policing' transgression of norms. Obviously recording procedures used to compile records, and what is done with them, vary a good deal. For this reason it is extremely ill advised to compare absenteeism between plants without careful consideration of the way recording systems have been set up to monitor absences and control behaviour. In one plant in which one of the authors conducted research, a senior manager had been sacked because of, among other things, an incorrigibly high level of absenteeism in his factory. However, research later showed that peculiarities in the methods used to calculate absence in that site had grossly inflated recorded rates. When absence rates were recalculated using standard procedures, absence in the company was found to be not significantly different from the average for plants of comparable size.

To underline the point about the importance of managerial practices, let us consider the case of the car production plants of North Italy, in which recording absenteeism was entirely given up for a period in the 1970s. In Italy at the time, absence from work was assuming epidemic proportions (see box). Managements often responded to employees taking time off from work by allowing it to happen subject to loss of earnings. This did not affect large firms as much as might be expected. Because of the scale of activities and the stability of rates of absence, the demand for labour could be met by employing more people. All that was required to make this system work was an increase in employee willingness to be moved from job to job. As a result of this policy, among other things, time and attention was saved from

---

Presentisimo

Further evidence suggests that absenteeism is truly a problem of international concern . . . . In Italy, for example, absenteeism has become so institutionalized that many organizations cannot cope with those rare days – usually twice a month on pay-day – when everyone shows up. This problem is serious enough to merit its own name, presentisimo, and results because many Italian manufacturers must hire between 8 and 14 per cent more workers just to get the work out. When everybody attends to get their paycheck, there is not sufficient work (or work space) to go around. The situation in Italy reached some sort of peak in 1982, when police began arresting some of the more serious absentees, charging them with fraud for hours not worked. Even so, a high level commission impanelled to study the problem made little progress; its first meeting had to be cancelled because of poor attendance! (Steers and Rhodes, 1984, 230)

the costs of routine surveillance of records and policing of attendance. The firms effectively abolished the functional problem caused by absence from work – that there might not be enough people for the available for work to continue effectively – which is usually the real basis of managerial concern about absences.

But the Italian firms did not entirely avoid trouble: problems now arose when too many employees felt the need for increased earnings at the same time, say, in the run up to a public holiday. In this sort of instance it was too much attendance which produced waste, in that there were, now and then, too many employees in attendance for the available work. It is not clear how long this system survived, and for us it is sufficient to note that while it was in place it removed absenteeism from the list of managerial concerns. No doubt too the moral tone of this regime was different from the traditional outlook – which is that it is the fecklessness of individuals which causes problems.

The complicity of management

The previous discussion draws attention to the fact that, although it is management's own rules which define problems, they are also often, to a remarkable degree, complicit in the toleration of misbehaviour. This section explores further the dynamics of this complicity.

Managers and supervisors have often been prepared to make many concessions towards accepting misbehaviour. This is for a variety of reasons – lack of care for example, or because these practices apparently do not threaten their central concerns with the productiveness of work itself. As a result of concessions, however, they become further implicated in the production of misbehaviour and rule-breaking. Paradoxical though it may seem, there are some benefits in the practice of allowing misbehaviour. For example, it enables the correction of misbehaviour to be a powerful and effective control device which can be periodically used. It also allows the possibility that habitual practice may be redefined as unauthorized or even criminal periodically, as management decides. Thus when workers have become used to earning premium wages by forms of misbehaviour, it is sometimes useful to reaffirm, or to threaten to reaffirm, that they are actually illegal. For workers, rule-bending becomes expected and has to be undertaken as part of the process of making a living. Seeing how far the rules will bend becomes habitual behaviour for the worker. Allowing degrees of rule-bending by managements is also a recurrent pattern, in which the manager and the supervisor become complicit conspirators.

As an example of this, Jason Ditton has analysed the management of a bakery, in which fiddling and pilferage by bread sales staff were well known to supervisors, who did not always disapprove of it (1977a, 1978). Indeed as Ditton suggests, pilferage (from customers) was actually unofficially fostered. One might well wonder what possible advantage there could be in this for management. From their point of view, given that pilferage is likely to occur among workers who are responsible for goods and who spend a good deal of time out of sight, it might be argued that the costs of eliminating fiddling outweigh the advantages of allowing it to occur within well-defined boundaries. Ditton argues that by allowing pilferage and fiddling; or, more accurately, by encouraging it to take customary forms, management acquires a powerful control device. The basic point to note is that such 'pilferage' might, at any time, be redefined by managers as unacceptable 'theft' and not only subject to official sanctions but to criminal proceedings as well. It is behaviour that is potentially treated as criminal, but habitually ignored. This allows a very powerful if complicated form of control to arise around the toleration of pilferage and fiddling as allowed/disallowed forms of misbehaviour. Although this is a blatant example, involving routinely threatening employees with the weight of the criminal law, something similar is habitually done when managements crack down on a particular form of misbehaviour which has become habitual. In these circumstances complicity between management and workers over forms of misbehaviour breaks down because of managerial withdrawal from cooperation.

By such means it is often possible for managers to check misbehaviour that has existed for long periods. It is clear, however, that there are consequences of such policies, in the form of innovations of new forms of misbehaviour, the storing of grudges and the like. One thing that any reasonably conscientious review of the history of management suggests is that it has not built up a record of trustworthiness, on which employees can rely. On the contrary, the opposite seems to be the case. What we have described here as complicity involves a very limited degree of trust. Roughly speaking, management can be relied on to be less punitive than perhaps it could be some of the time. But the experience of the periodic withdrawal of customary complicity must

---

Every man is born to do something in life, and my function is to manage. Now take an example. As far as I can see any man who takes on the job of shop steward wants his ego boosting. But you have got to boost his ego in the proper manner . . . .

Now take an example of a man who is perpetually late.

Now I'm the manager and it is my function to manage. It is my function to discipline this particular man. But I also have to deal with the steward. So, what do I do? I take the shop steward aside and tell him that in half an hour's time this man, Smith, is going to walk into the room. I tell him that I am going to stamp and bang the table, and tell the man I am going to put him out onto the road.

Then, I'll say to the steward, 'And what you can do is intervene at this time. Make a case for the man. And we'll agree to let the man off with a caution.'

Now the man comes in and the steward says, 'Come on Mr. Brown. Couldn't you give him one more chance?' I relent. The shop steward gets out of the meeting with the man and says to him: 'I've got you off this time, but don't expect me to do it again.' You see the shop steward gets his ego boosted. He gets what he wants, and I get what I want. That's what good management is about. (Nichols and Beynon, 1977, 122)

lead to some – rationally grounded – cynicism about the policies and general intentions of managers. Indeed, such cynicism not only exists but tends to be deeply ingrained. For many it is an axiom that vigilance about managerial behaviour is always required. For this reason, also, self-organization is much more likely to be mobilized in an oppositional mode than a cooperative one.

Complicating the problem of complicity and manageability is the probability that managers also misbehave. One of the reasons why managers have so many problems with misbehaviour is that they are frequently implicated themselves. Managers may be the agents of capital or part of the line of command in public sector organizations, but they are also individuals with their own goals and needs, not to mention representatives of professional and other interest groups. Managerial misbehaviour (Punch, 1996) is a significant problem in organizations for several reasons, not least because managers are the people responsible for defining and policing the formal or informal rules governing acceptable behaviour. Any 'lapses' by managers therefore may threaten the legitimacy of the overall regime, because such misbehaviour is extremely vulnerable to employee dissatisfaction.

Managerial misbehaviour may matter less when it is an integral part of a wider set of practices. For example fiddling of expense claims may be mutually tolerated in a situation where 'everyone is at it'. Indeed management may initiate or organize such activity. But such action is dangerous because managers have to take action if others overstep the boundaries. The consequences can be escaped by using intermediaries such as shop stewards to pull back dangerous behaviour. But it is not always possible. An educational organization known to one of the authors faced problems caused by a number of embarrassing incidents among staff of sexual misbehaviour, including two individuals caught in the act on a table by a cleaner. The vice-principal was designated to chair a sub-committee to draw up a code of ethics. One problem with this was that the same individual was a notorious womanizer whose rapid turnover of secretaries was legendary. No code of ethics ever emerged.

Misbehaviour cannot be allowed to become too visible up the line of command. This is not normally a moral matter. Few organizations are run by a Ross Perot who bans adulterers, gays or men with facial hair. It is more a case of management having to be seen to work within 'the rules' or at least not bending them too far. Power is a double-edged sword. Managers have greater available resources to misbehave and they frequently abuse that access. But to usurp such resources while making or calling for economies elsewhere simply creates tensions and enables other employees to rationalize their own existing or potential misbehaviour.

Manageability and the context of action

Complicity, toleration and managerial involvement cannot explain fully what happens in all or even most circumstances in which organizational misbehaviour becomes a significant concern for managers. This is because there are a number of contingent but nonetheless key issues which influence whether specific misbehaviour is made into an object of action for management. These factors affect the judgements managers make about the appropriateness and likely effectiveness of taking action against specific instances of potential misbehaviour. These are as follows:

- the need to maintain a degree of cooperation and consent from employees;
- the extent to which the behaviour is functional to efficiency, profitability or 'good order';
- whether action would cost more in time and resources than toleration or accommodation;
- the degree of moral legitimacy available to challenge the unwanted behaviour.

Managerial discretion: the case of pilferage

Such considerations help to emphasize the fact that there is a large area of discretion in decisions about the way to respond to misbehaviour. In some areas the extent of discretion is obvious. In many ways, the case of pilferage brings out very clearly the discretion available to managers. It illustrates the fact that, so far as misbehaviour is concerned, management is explicitly or implicitly involved in a recurrent cost–benefit analysis on whether, when and how to act much of the time. Zeitlin (1985) gives a clear example of the president of a US company who kept an office manager on despite his dipping into the petty cash to the extent of $2,000 a year – because he was in the judgement of the president worth at least an additional $15,000!

The topic of pilferage is an illuminating one, for this is an activity which is endemic in organizations, but often ignored by managers and shamefully neglected in the academic and managerial literatures. That it is largely ignored is reflected in the comment by Anderton and Keily, who carried out one of the few serious academic studies. They state that the analysis of employee theft suffers from 'a lamentable lack of evidence' (1988, 37). Despite the frequent absence of hard data, that it is a significant problem is not in doubt. For example, figures compiled by the British Retail Consortium estimated that in 1993 shoppers had to pay an extra £120 a year to compensate for theft by shoplifters and staff. Interestingly staff theft, estimated at 32 per cent, ran only slightly behind the proportion taken by 'real thieves' at 34 per cent. Yet the extent to which it is tolerated can be seen in the creation of a variety of euphemisms to describe this theft of corporate resources, from pilferage itself to more ridiculous terms such as 'stock shrinkage' or 'product leakage'.

Though we want to focus on appropriation of products, this is a grey area and attention is increasingly being focused on theft of resources and time, including misbehaviour such as use of the phone for private purposes. A desire to acquire some of the products of work for personal use is a recurrent feature of organizational life. It is said that it was in fact the desire to set limits on appropriation of materials which, in considerable measure, often motivated the formation of the first factories (Marglin, 1974). This occurred in the following way: some of the earliest forms of machine production were in textiles which were produced in the homes of operatives on their own looms. The business person – called the 'putter out' – used to provide materials and instructions, which weavers would then make up. A number of practices – sometimes called embezzlement – involved the weavers using fewer materials than were needed, and in other ways fiddling to increase their share of the rewards from their work. The result was for the entrepreneur to group the machines together so that he could oversee the use of materials more economically and effectively. Contemporary work organizations, with their greater complexity and access to resources, allow far greater potential for product appropriation. Increased sophistication of monitoring devices also facilitates increased managerial intervention. Below we describe the broad range of options open to manage pilferage. A similar range of options can also be discerned for other kinds of misbehaviour.

Punitive action/criminalization

Historically employers had a tendency to criminalize pilferage. Even today, when an employee pilfers and is discovered, prosecution is a likely consequence. This is particularly the case where organizations rely on discipline and enforced obedience to rules and hierarchy for their basic operation, such as the police or the army. Other organizations whose reputation relies on public trust, such as banks, will tend to sack rather than prosecute, precisely because of that vulnerability. A remarkably large number of organizations act on a reputational basis and prefer to cover up staff dishonesty. In a large retail chain where a relative of one of the authors was a manager, staff theft was widespread. Senior management only took action when the amounts taken 'crossed the line' and could be identified with a particular group of early morning cleaners. They set a trap using their own security guards and nabbed the cleaners as they came out of the store considerably fatter than when they went in. However, the cleaners were sacked rather than prosecuted. When you see the sign SHOPLIFTERS WILL BE PROSECUTED that is likely to mean shoppers, not those on the inside. It is, however, a choice. Not all organizations have a policy of sensitivity. Woolworths have used a monthly crime bulletin to discourage pilferage and were involved in a notorious case in 1997 when they sacked a pair of shopgirls for eating two sweets – a Mr Blobby Jelly and a Fizzy Cola Bottle – which had fallen on the floor and were about to be thrown in the bin.

Monitoring and enhanced surveillance

Using supervisors or supervisory systems to monitor employee activity is a simple and less draconian alternative. But traditional 'physical' systems such as 'clocking on' are relatively easily evaded by any determined informal network, and in the words of one food industry manager, routine pilferage is not easily identifiable, 'unless you keep a close watch on people. Then it is counter-productive in most cases because it reduces efficiency' (Anderton and Keily, 1988, 40). True, companies now have at their disposal an array of electronic systems. Running an entertaining 'Big Brother is on the loose' story, one British newspaper referred to US industrial security experts who talked of employees who were 'untrustworthy and lazy. Their sole motive is to rip off the company. They are the scourge of every modern American workplace and have a new name: "Time thieves"' (*Independent on Sunday*, 14 April 1994). The article conjured up images of soaring sales of sophisticated surveillance equipment, including smart-cards and keys, Active Badge Systems which emit infrared signals every 10 seconds, and keystroke monitoring. Talking to employees does not confirm that we have arrived at a *1984*-style dystopia yet, though paranoia over managerial monitoring of emails and use of the Internet is definitely observable.

One practice that appears to be on the increase is monitoring of phone calls, but this is more likely to be in order to enforce work norms than eliminate time theft. For example, the article in the *Independent on Sunday* quoted above, referred to the sacking by British Telecom of an operator whose average call time was 73 seconds instead of the recommended 60 seconds. But technological capacity is not an indication of actual usage. Almost all large organizations have the machinery to monitor employee phone calls, as well as restricting access to certain numbers. Though organizations frequently impose some kind of hierarchy of access by rank of staff and time of day, it is surprising how few controls are placed and how infrequently 'abuse' is punished. But we shouldn't be too surprised if we consider the factors raised earlier in the chapter: bosses are almost certainly

---

Pilferage limitation tactics

What managements do is to structure hotel situations to limit fiddle opportunities rather than aim to eradicate them. One of the ways is to employ checkers. Another is to structure an opposition of the interests of Head Waiters and Chefs. Chefs are responsible for buying as well as cooking the food consumed in a hotel, and for accounting. Frequently they are given a 'percentage' for extra production out of a given stock, and this, therefore, gives them a strong incentive to work closely with the checker to limit fiddles. These controls can on occasion, however, provide a two-edged weapon for management. In one hotel, the Chef and the female checker were believed to be in an alliance for their own benefit and were known as 'Bonnie and Clyde'. (Mars, 1973, 205)

doing it themselves and surveillance would reveal their own wrongdoing, the costs of operationalizing and enforcement are likely to be greater than any savings, and loss of employee goodwill is highly likely to follow. While pilferage of any highly expensive or visible resources is likely to provoke action, staff consumption of everyday corporate resources continues to be regarded by all and sundry as a perk of the job.

Institutionalized perks

It is also possible to provide, usually as a supplementary addition to wages, restricted access to the product of labour on a formal or informal basis as 'perks' of the job. Many retail employees such as those of Marks and Spencer are allowed cheap access to unsold goods at the end of the trading day, while in vehicle production there are usually discounts and special purchase schemes for employees. When Britain had a mining industry every miner used to have an allowance of 'free' coal. Similarly in much of the meat trade there are allowances of meat for long-standing employees. But such provision does not reduce the desire for meat amongst those employees that are denied access. Nor does it eliminate unofficial removal of meat. Pilfered meat is known universally as 'duck'. The examples could be multiplied. These days employers are seeing the motivational and other benefits that flow from allowing some sort of preferential access to the products of work and even from a share in the ownership of the organization.

Encouragement

This appears to be extremely unlikely, but it is not impossible. While 'encourage' may not be exactly the right word, stories from sales situations, particularly bar work, abound of managers who 'tip a wink' to staff to engage in low level fiddles in order that they may avoid paying higher wages. The best example comes from the work of Jason Ditton, referred to in the previous section. He comments that in the firm he studied: 'the . . . management do not merely accept or tolerate occupational crime by their employees; in effect, they demand it! The firm's entry and training procedures are explicitly geared to teaching recruits how to rob the customers regularly and invisibly' (1977a, 34). The ostensible reason for such a policy was that it removed the uncertainty arising from potential mistakes in the sales transaction. It is better for the staff to be 'taught' how to fiddle the customer than 'come in short', or rob the firm. He quotes a senior supervisor: 'It's best if the supervisor tells him there's a fiddle; it's a bad thing if the man finds out for himself' (ibid.). But this is merely wishful thinking. The salesmen became extremely adept at topping up their wages through fiddling, so much so that eventually this was transformed into fiercely guarded perks.

The last example indicates that our categories for action are likely to overlap. We have little hard research evidence on what management actually do and why. In Anderton and Keily's (1988) study of five printing, food and retail companies, they also found considerable common ground in responses. The commonality arose from the treatment of fiddling expenses and pilferage of small items as 'legitimate' and/or not cost-effective to deal with. Employers in the printing industry were particularly aware of the potential damage to industrial relations in a highly unionized sector. While they all had a formal or informal line when action – normally grievance procedures followed by dismissal – was invoked against 'serious' theft, it would be difficult to grace the policies with the term strategy. But this, in part, reflects the sensitive and difficult nature of this form of misbehaviour. If we broaden the discussion, especially to the work terrain, it is possible to identify clearer patterns of action.

Managerial regimes and their strategies

Writers on the workplace have become ever more interested in identifying the strategic options and practices that management have for dealing with employees. Indeed conventional OB has undertaken some consideration of these issues. However, discussion of alternative management strategies is often undertaken in very unrealistic ways. Social scientists are apt to discuss the adoption of strategies in terms of the completely free choice that may be made by managers. The work of Douglas McGregor (1960), whose ideas concerning different kinds of management style are very well known, is a case in point. McGregor developed a distinction between two different types of general approach to the managerial task. On the one hand we have theory X, which assumes that employees do not like work, that they will avoid work if they can, and will behave badly at every opportunity if forced to work, and so on. On the other hand, we have theory Y, which supposedly takes a more enlightened attitude. This is that people do like work and are naturally active and creative. Hence, they can be allowed to decide for themselves how to order their own work and to be responsible so that they will work without supervision.

Similar distinctions are made by many other commentators. It is common for broad comparisons to be made between the controlling ambitions of the approach adopted by 'scientific management' and its derivatives, beginning with F.W. Taylor (1947), and the outlook of the human relations school beginning with the findings of the Hawthorne research and the work of Elton Mayo (1933). Clearly, human relations and theory Y are more humane. If they are likely to be found both more congenial and more effective as well, why management does not adopt these approaches all the time is a mystery. The fact is, however, that the direct control stance towards labour is much the most common and in one shape or another is adopted far more consistently. Except for the control of managers, professionals and some skilled workers, theory Y and human relations have, in the past, seldom been implemented in sustained or complete ways so far as ordinary employees are concerned. In reality the kinds of autonomy realized by skilled workers are a long way from the idealistic notions of Mayo and McGregor, have to be recurrently fought for and may be lost.

In contrast, much critical research, often informed by a labour process analysis, has tended towards the view that direct control of work is the habitual practice of management, and the outlook of recalcitrance and mis-behaviour the habitual attitude of employees. It also begins from the constraints in which management operates. It is a basic function of capitalistic enterprise, for which management is held responsible, to make profitable returns on investments. Without this, capital will be withdrawn and the enterprise will fail. This means it is imperative that firms remain competitive in product markets, producing at least as cheaply and efficiently as their competitors. In turn, managers are constrained to adopt efficient techniques for production, which typically means making things in as large batches as possible with long production runs, the use of standardized components, the utilization where possible of cheap, unskilled labour and so on. Thus, in the exercise of managerial discretion over such misbehaviour as absenteeism, pilferage and work limitation, the usual recourse is to be punitive and controlling and to seek to put in place effective procedures for improved surveillance, with only occasional interest being generated in relaxing controls if they are effective.

Of course, managerial efforts are geared towards all the concerns of profitable organization, towards what has sometimes been called the 'full circuit of capital' rather than just being concerned with the regulation of labour, but the latter sphere is a significant and legitimate focus of interest. The direct control of labour, in which employees are allowed very little discretion as to how to complete simple and repetitive tasks has been, to a considerable degree, part of the basic character of capitalist enterprise. However, it would be wrong to say that management does not have any choice in regard to policies. Making choices, within a range of parameters, is actually central to the managerial role. What we have to note, is that what is appropriate to do in order to remain profitable will vary from time to time and place to place.

This is not the place to undertake a sustained analysis of management and the reasons that periodic changes in policies are seen. (For a discussion of the relevant work here see Storey, 1983, 1989; Friedman, 1987; Willmott, 1987; Thompson and McHugh, 1995.) But we can illustrate some of the issues with reference to a much used distinction regarding management: that offered by Andrew Friedman (1977). Friedman distinguishes broadly between two distinct kinds of strategy towards labour. As Friedman originally formulated this distinction, he wrote about management adopting either the strategy of 'direct control' or, alternatively, what he calls 'responsible autonomy'. This distinction has some similarities with the polarity offered by McGregor; though the more humanistic policy is not hopelessly idealistic as is McGregor's. Direct control and responsible autonomy are now often thought about as different ideal types of strategy that may be adopted by management. Clearly, we have been influenced by Friedman's analysis in this book, in particular when contrasting the idea of responsible autonomy with what we have called irresponsible autonomy in the previous chapter. We have, however, been using the notion of responsible autonomy in a rather different way from Friedman. We tend to see this not so much as a strategy of control, but as the product of a disposition to act and a policy adopted by management. The degree of autonomy which skilled workers have is something that has been effectively defended by them and not simply a means of control chosen by management.

We prefer to situate the idea of managerial strategy within the concept of managerial regime. While we have no problem with the general idea that management can act strategically, we want to move the discussion away from a top-down approach and to focus on the broader patterns of manageability. 'Managerial' therefore refers to a process involving a variety of workplace actors, rather than a property of management. What, then, are the general characteristics of a managerial regime looked at in this way? A regime refers to a pattern of control based on systematic attempts to regulate and/or accommodate to specific forms of misbehaviour. Both aspects are important. While management always seeks to regulate activity, other than in exceptional circumstances, it can only do so through a policy of partial accommodation of the self-organization of workgroups. But to do so allows management to maintain that degree of cooperation and interdependence that enables organizations to function. In this sense a managerial regime is based on mutually understood rules, both informal and formal. The regime will necessarily have economic and normative dimensions. The former refer to structures and practices geared towards minimizing the disruptive costs of misbehaviour in the effort bargain. The latter refer to those means of moral regulation and ideological persuasion that are used to justify the core practices of a regime and persuade members of the organization to comply with it.

Although we do not wish to present models of managerial regimes, we suggest that it is helpful to describe them using two dimensions. Adapting the ideas of Alan Fox (1974), we suggest that there are such things as low trust and high trust managerial regimes. The former are distinguished by a generalized attitude of suspicion about the motives and actions of employees, and are often also associated with a perceived need to exert continuous surveillance over many aspects of employee behaviour. Such regimes are also very commonly associated with a dynamic process towards the development of high levels of regulation. We shall examine some of the processes of change in regimes later in the chapter. At this point it is important to establish simply that the degree to which managerial regimes seek to regulate the conduct and performance of employees may also vary.

Combining the dimension of high trust/low trust with the dimension of high regulation gives us four types of managerial regime (see Figure 4.1).

While our use of regime generally is intended to designate a combination of practices to adopt to regulate a range of misbehaviours, it can in some circumstances refer to arrangements to deal with a specific class of actions

	High regulation	**Low regulation**
Low trust	Relcalitrance/militancy (Direct control)	Indulgency pattern (Irresponsible autonomy)
High trust	Controlled autonomy	Responsible autonomy

Figure 4.1   **Types of managerial regime**

such as work limitation. Indeed, it is possible that the degree of trust and regulation applied to different forms of misbehaviour may pull in different directions. The value of identifying differences of managerial strategy is to consider them in combination with the different conditions of workgroup organization which were set out in the last chapter. These types of managerial strategy tend to be found in association with different kinds of responses, as depicted in Figure 4.1.

All of them feature a characteristic accommodation of the pursuit of autonomy and the characteristics of the managerial regime. The highly distinctive pattern of low trust/high regulation regime – in the top left box – has been noted many times by analysts. This combination, which is very common, is associated with the policy of direct control. We argue that it interacts with the self-organization of workgroups to produce recalcitrance and industrial militancy. This combination is often associated with a dynamic process in which attempts to exert control become reinforced by the responses of employees and intensify. The end result is that management and labour are continuously organized to confront each other over a range of practical issues. In the low trust/high regulation regime, the orientation of management is often matched and reciprocated by the attitude of 'making out' (as Roy calls it) against management opposition. As Burawoy has pointed out, employees become psychologically engaged by the process

---

Close supervision

In a legal dispute in the 1920s, an overman (foreman) in a Scottish mine was called on to testify as to whether a certain worker did his work properly. The cross-examination, as reported by Goodrich (1975, 137), went as follows:

Overman: I never saw him work.
Magistrate: But isn't it your duty under the Mines Act to visit each working place twice each day?
Overman: Yes.
Magistrate: Don't you do it?
Overman: Yes.
Magistrate: Then why didn't you ever see him work?
Overman: They always stop work when they see an overman coming, and sit down and wait till he's gone – even take out their pipes in a mine free from gas. They won't let anyone watch them.

of grappling with management. Working the system or making out – that is, being preoccupied with gaining marginal advantages in the process of earning a wage – becomes habitual.

Management can share the same sort of habitual outlook. However, the hidden costs of this sort of regime are considerable. The price paid by management for control is the need for continuous vigilance concerning innovatory initiatives that might be taken by employees, there is a perceived need to devise counter-moves to any initiatives taken, and the need to anticipate the effects of actions on the potentially fragile industrial relations in such plants. Low trust management is conventionally big management: bureaucratized, rule bound, introspective and a slave to its history. Low trust regimes breed a generalized reluctance to cooperate with managements and to exploit any lapses that occur. The term we use to describe this attitude is 'recalcitrance' and we judge it to be an extremely common basic attitude to management. It is associated with a wide range of innovations in misbehaviour as low trust dynamics take hold. Fox has, we think rightly, seen this as the dominant attitude in industrial relations in Britain (Fox, 1974).

However, the analysis of Figure 4.1. sets up the possibility of other types of managerial regime than the low trust/high regulation regime. We suggest that the low trust/low regulation regime is that in which the pattern of self-organization we described in Chapter 3 as irresponsible autonomy can really flourish. By contrast with this it is in the context of a high trust/low regulation regime that responsible autonomy will exist.

Finally there is the possibility of a highly regulated regime, in which high trust of employees is also exhibited. Whether this is practically viable for many companies is not at all clear. The possibility that employees will mistake high regulation for lack of trust, so that such regimes tend to degenerate into the more familiar type of low trust regime, is obviously present. However, in the past 15 years, both mainstream and radical analysts have argued for the success of such policies, using the concept of corporate culture (Bate, 1994; Ray, 1986). It has been argued that there are a growing number of workplaces in which significant levels of task autonomy have been ceded to employees. The examples cited are often highly skilled technical staff, but they work within a framework of increased normative rules and specifications of values and behaviour. 'Controlled autonomy' is, we believe, an appropriate term for such regimes, and we shall consider them in the final chapter. Suffice it to say here that both the extent and efficacy of managerial policy aiming at controlled autonomy can be exaggerated

Efforts to regulate are always contestable and often contested. This tends to produce lack of trust. The endemic tendency to self-organization by employees tends to collide with the authority of management, producing what Goodrich has identified as the 'frontier of control'. Goodrich's (1975) concept is useful because it acknowledges limitations to the extent of the control. Concern about absenteeism, for example, reflects the desire of management to restrict absences from work, but equally, it also indicates that employees do gain limited access to time away from work by being absent. Both regulation and accommodation are clearly present in these kinds of behaviour. Partly because there is resistance to regulation, there are periodic changes in management policies towards employees, though the action of people at work is only one source of motivation for such changes.

The broad dynamics within regimes reflect two fundamental pressures. First, there is a dialectic of innovation in terms of regulation and misbehaviour in which rival groups seek to assert their interests and identities. Secondly, there is an implicit or explicit cost–benefit analysis undertaken by management in which they assess the potential and requirements for action. When the sedimented practical effects of misbehaviour build up to a point where accommodation or toleration is no longer feasible, some attempt at a qualitative break can often be made. That does not tell us which new form of regulation will be adopted. For example, in the course of such reviews it is sometimes noted that attempts to regulate behaviour through new apparatus of evaluation and recording can add greatly to costs, and that perhaps a different policy approach should be considered. At such times, the sense of extending to groups of workers some degree of autonomy or self-regulation may be perceived.

It is useful at this point to move from a broader consideration of the dynamics of managerial regimes to a consideration of the dynamics of the most historically prevalent type of workplace social relations.

The dynamics of direct control regimes

For the last hundred years or more, the central issue for management has been that of how hard employees work, the question of effort intensity, as it is sometimes called (Baldamus, 1961). During much of the nineteenth century, the key issue between owners and workers had been how much time was spent at work (Thompson, 1968). Surprising though it may seem, until then almost everybody assumed that the longer time spent at work, the more work would be done. Since the end of the nineteenth century, however, the issue has been more to do with how hard people work while in the workplace. Before 1900, management produced the means to control the effort made by workers in factories, in the shape of incentive payment systems. These involved the payment of bonuses for production above standard amounts. However, these often did not seem to be very effective in enabling managers to make people work harder.

In retrospect this failure can be understood as effective resistance to management. Incentives did not result in more efforts because employees largely decided how to organize work without reference to management. Thus, any short cuts devised or special techniques developed to make production easier were a saving to employees, allowing them to produce more without increased effort. Employees thus had quite high control over their earnings, even with incentives. Managers soon came to believe that they would have to take over the design and allocation of work tasks themselves if they were to achieve control of the intensity of work. One of the key pioneers of this line of thought, of course, was F.W. Taylor, who discovered what he took to be a systematic tendency to effort limitation amongst factory hands which he called 'soldiering'. Soldiering and its importance have been considered in Chapter 2.

Taylor went on to devise an elaborate system of practical action which managers could adopt. This he called 'scientific management'. The aim of this was to wrest control of the effort expended in work from employees. Among other things, Taylor and his successors began the modern practices of work study. Taylor was amongst the first to articulate the strategy of direct control; before this the emphasis was to allow traditional autonomy in the allocation of work. Effectively from this time on – 1900 or so – new groups of professional managers were increasingly taking the view that they should decide the content of jobs, determining who should be employed, what they should do at work down to the smallest detail, and the amount employees would be paid for performing as required. Thus, the practice of job design was initiated, as was the conscious selection of employees according to their suitability for particular jobs. Some managers saw the need for extensively developing the managerial role in the ways Taylor suggested.

There is a massive literature on the characteristics and extent of diffusion of Taylorism and its impact on different industries and countries (Littler, 1982; Thompson, 1989). Although some of Taylor's prescriptions for management practice were not fully taken up, even in his native United States, his approach is symptomatic of a much more directive attitude which set the pattern in much of the Western world. From this time many managers assumed, as Taylor suggested, that work should be simplified and reconstructed so that relatively unskilled workers could do most tasks. Such workers could then be rewarded strictly in accordance with the work done, and costs kept to a minimum.

In short, the strategy of direct control was adopted as the basic one. However, a number of qualifying points should be made. First, following our argument, the soldiering Taylor and others first observed was not, as Taylor himself seemed to think, simply a product of a natural or systematic indolence. Soldiering must be seen, in considerable measure, as a response to an earlier but less developed kind of management. Before Taylorism and scientific management, long hours of work were required without very effective or close supervision. Keeping the level of effort low was one obvious way of dealing with demands for long hours of work for low wages. Second, changes to work in terms of content and pay as envisaged by scientific management were not easy to impose on people – especially skilled and organized workers. The systematic use of Taylorism was limited in Britain, for example, because of the continuing formal and informal organization of workers. Only when recession hit hard and unions were weak, were there sustained attempts to introduce systems of scientific management (Littler, 1982). In many industries in Britain, the retention of craft autonomy by employees was common. Skilled workers, in particular, retained considerable autonomy.

Taylorism and the strategy of direct control initiated a protracted guerrilla war in many workplaces. 'Scientific management' did not eliminate soldiering quickly or easily: ways of actively undermining the direct controls that were put in place were sustained continuously over the decades to come. Resisting misbehaviour, deriving from the strategy of direct control can still be identified in industry today. Regimes of managerial control after Taylor were very much more elaborate in the lengths to which they went to plan, allocate and supervise work. One of the key findings of detailed studies of managerial regimes in factories using piecework, such as that by Burawoy (1979), is the way in which piecework incentives engage the worker in all sorts of stratagems to subvert or overcome them. Burawoy, and several writers before him (Cunnison, Lupton, Roy) identify the game-like features of the encounters between supervisors and production workers in piecework payment systems. No sooner is a rate set for a particular job than the operatives try to find ways of doing it quicker and so earning extra wages for small additional effort. All kinds of rules and checks on the behaviour of workers are necessary in order to make the system work. What is known as 'wage drift' in which incentives form a larger and larger proportion of wages becomes a problem for administration. In such regimes too, quality soon becomes an issue, for workers are only concerned with producing units as quickly as possible. This has often led managers to employ other workers to inspect the work done. At the least, close and detailed supervision of workers is required, minute by minute as well as hour by hour. This is not achieved without cost.

In the early period of direct control through the use of job design and

---

The normality of direct control

'No manager would be worth his salt who did not endeavour ceaselessly to make his labour bill per unit of output lower. To call this scientific management is simply to give a high-sounding title to an old and well-understood thing . . . . It is an ordinary doctrine of works management that better methods must be adopted as soon as they present themselves. It is scientific of course, but to call it scientific is like speaking of the common pump as a philosophical instrument.' (Respondent quoted by Levine in Brown, 1977, 158)

For many years works jobs have been closely studied, workmen have been carefully selected, detailed instructions for doing work have been given, tools and appliances have been standardized, and even functional foremen, notably inspectors have been used . . . . The novelty of scientific management lies not in the fact that these principles have been set to work, but that they have now achieved consciousness. (Renold, 1914, 122)

piece rates, attempts to exert control over one aspect of work behaviour – say the amount of work completed per hour by the introduction of a piece-work payment system – did not simply have the expected effects. It may have led to increased effort, but it also resulted in the redirection of behaviour. If the introduction of incentives means that higher pay may be achieved with less time spent at work, there is the possibility of people absenting themselves from the workplace when they have earned what they think is enough. Once a connection of this sort is established, the choice for managers then becomes more complicated. They may continue to attempt to produce more output performance as before – and to institute new controls over absence. Alternatively, they can persist with attempts to increase performance at the expense of occasional absences, or revert to looser controls of work performance and better attendance.

By such processes regimes of control can become routinized and typical patterns of misbehaviour become recurrent and endemic. Edwards and Scullion (1982) in their important study of forms of control and resistance in different kinds of factories, argue such a case. They suggest that the detailed study of particular plants reveals that there is a clear correspondence between arrangements for control of work and the forms of misbehaviour that can be observed in the workplace. Although in this study too there are some quite marked differences in the extent of effective worker organization for resistance to managerial control, the overwhelming impression is that managerial regimes are closely associated with distinctive patterns of misbehaviour. They argue that if certain devices of managerial control are present, then so too will be certain forms of misbehaviour. If absenteeism, for example, is endemic to a particular plant, as opposed to, say, working to rule or striking, this is mainly explained by the way in which the managerial regime is organized.

As distinct from Edwards and Scullion, we have argued that there are

---

Capturing the piecework system

For many workers piecework was an unpopular system, associated with greater work intensity and increased exploitation. This was certainly the case in the engineering industries where piecework seems to have made the biggest strides. But . . . [in the 1960s and 1970s] there has been a fundamental change of attitude – piecework has become popular with many workers and unpopular with many managers – because as Cliff has put it it has been 'turned back on its maker'. It was the years of affluence – the nineteen fifties and sixties that piecework seems to have been finally 'captured' by the workers. In the years of post-war economic boom, with buoyant labour and product markets many managers were willing to pay fairly generously for . . . extra output – and . . . shop stewards located their ability to force the pace through piecework bargaining – the conditions were such that the agreement was transformed from something which had allowed employers to cut rates to being something that enabled workers to jack up rates . . . . (Cliff, 1974, quoted by Brown, 1977, 314)

some dynamic processes to the changes of managerial strategies that have been significant historically. One is that the intensification of direct control does not lead to elimination of misbehaviour, merely to its deflection and adaptation. In fact it is typical for regimes to become locked into the perpetuation of particular forms of misbehaviour, and to promote and consolidate distinctive (and often frankly resistive and uncooperative) ways of thinking and acting by employees at work. Many of the characteristic responses to contemporary managerial regimes that are familiar today have clear similarities and continuities with earlier managerial regimes. Even where apparently new systems of remuneration have been worked out, such as measured day work, where incentives are paid to groups rather than individuals, levels of pay are still systematically related to levels of actual output based on time studies, and the expected levels of production are calculated and assessed in basically the same ways as Taylor and his successors thought necessary. And the guerrilla warfare continues.

Once set on the policy of attempting to control work behaviour, management is also set on an inexorable course towards growth in the scale of its activities, as it tries to establish control. Without assuming more than that working people will conform to new managerial controls to some degree, but also shift their behaviour to preserve, as best they can, their customary levels of effort, it is possible to see typical sequences of events associated with the management strategy of direct control. Increases in the scale of management and decline in trust between managers and workers are two obvious and recurrent features of these processes. A highly stylized account of the kind of sequence we have in mind is set out in Figure 4.2.

A variety of trajectories of development are possible, as are considerable differences of time scale. In Figure 4.2 it is assumed at the outset that labour is organizing its own work, including traditional levels of effort expenditure. Management decides that soldiering is going on and starts to measure the amount of work actually done. Measurement seems to provide evidence of work limitation and closer supervision is introduced. Workers continue to produce at their customary level, but still seem not to be working very hard or very long, because they have innovated some effort-saving procedures. Management then decides that soldiering is extensive, and something must be done to control it. Close monitoring of individual output is a common response, sometimes linked with more refined piecework incentives. Workers respond by trying to defend customary levels of effort and earnings. They do this by a variety of expedients, and the range of possibilities is not restricted to work limitation; it can include time indiscipline and or pilfergage and destructiveness as well.

Pretending to work is one obvious thing to do, which can easily exacerbate suspicion on the part of supervisors. Another expedient is to establish informal output quotas, in which employees collude to produce only a specific number of finished products. This is effective precisely because it subverts the point of individual records and individual incentives. In the circumstances, management may well decide that pretending to work and

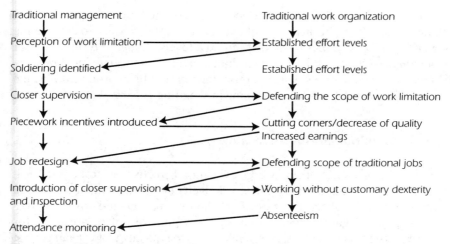

Figure 4.2 **The production/amplification of misbehaviour by control**

quotering output provides definite evidence of soldiering, and form the view that jobs will have to be more comprehensively redesigned and piece-work rates more carefully set. Workers respond with more innovations – in the first place simply to maintain customary levels of effort – such as cutting corners in production cycles. In addition, however, they may inno-vate quite new forms of misbehaviour – absenting themselves from work on a casual basis more frequently (absenteeism), perhaps, or causing machines to break down when they encounter piece rates that do not pay well (utilitarian sabotage), and so on. The strategy of direct control, in short, gives relevance to a posture of suspicion and defensiveness that becomes deeply ingrained. In some economic circumstances, this can lead to dramatic changes in the utility of the high cost procedures associated with direct control.

In such a sequence we can identify two effects which tend to intensify the impulse to control. The first is a measurement effect. By this is meant that management identifies a potentially damaging practice in use – initially in the above example, what it takes to be soldiering. Systematic attention is then paid to the phenomenon and various measures of it are introduced. This usually not only confirms that the behaviour exists, but gives definite grounds for concern. Though no change at all in the traditional behaviour of employ-ees may have occurred, measurement alone reinforces an initial judgement that something needs to be done. If the action taken by management is ineffective, as it often is initially, this will show up in subsequent measuring. But, as a second effect, it is probable that increased managerial attention will cause behavioural innovation – activity is directed to new kinds of work limi-tation behaviour. This may be simply shifting things around as old patterns of behaviour come under scrutiny, or are subjected to control. Sooner or later such changes will be spotted by the closer surveillance now being under-taken, giving more evidence of the untrustworthy work-limiting tendencies of the workforce. This second effect to be identified, then, we may label an innovation effect. In this chain of events, it is not necessary to assume that working effort declines from its traditional levels, though it is often thought obvious that it does. It is only clear that, as a result of the activity of management, a great deal of evidence of misbehaviour has been produced. The evidence will be the basis for continuing in the same general direction.

Conclusion: humanistic alternatives

Regulation does not take place in a vacuum. Effective control of labour is, to a considerable and often unacknowledged degree, dependent on external conditions. The characteristics of the labour market and forms of state financial and legal intervention in economy and workplace are often formative external conditions. But regulation also typically works against existing patterns of self-organization and helps to provoke and to shape new patterns of behaviour. Reviewing the history of managerial regimes it is clear that recalcitrance and resistance to management has been everywhere and continuous. Direct control within a high regulation/low trust framework, was aimed originally at increasing the amount of work done, and it achieves this to a considerable extent. But despite the consistent pursuit of those objectives through job design, piecework incentives, close supervision and the like, management has found these have given rise to a range of strategies of practical subversion, which have helped to undermine their effectiveness. Even with constant vigilance, employees innovate new forms of behaviour which exploit any weaknesses of managerial control.

Given such continuous erosion, management is obliged to respond with a search for new means of regulation. It is not unrealistic to talk of a vicious circle of control building up, in which the desire to establish greater control over employees leads to responses by them that are interpreted as implying, if not actually requiring, a need to exert yet more control. We have described traditional regimes as ones in which the emphasis is on a mixture of direction and adaptation to forms of collective employee misbehaviour. Controlling or adapting to misbehaviour involves an essentially passive attitude to the phenomenon itself, while using sanctions, rewards and rules to set the parameters of acceptability. The historic alternatives to traditional, scientific regimes derive from the human relations tradition. Such alternatives attempt to anticipate and deal with what is believed to be the behavioural causes of misbehaviour in the drives and dispositions of employees.

The volume by Giacalone and Greenberg (1997) on 'antisocial behaviour in organizations', which we discussed in Chapter 1, is full of recommendations on how to alter the climate of organizations so that outcomes can be modified to 'reduce deviant behaviour'. In one chapter, by Boye and Jones, the authors refer to an employer study that found 10 organizational values that were related to lowering counter-productive workplace behaviour. They were fairness, caring and empathy, empowerment, career-enriching opportunities, equitable pay and benefits, inter-personal cooperation, accurate job–person matching, honesty and ethics, safe working conditions and job security. Similarly Analoui and Kakabadse (1993, 60) include in their list of desirable managerial actions 'enabling practitioners to deal with unconventional practices' and managing conflict more effectively. The antidote to the consequences of irresponsible autonomy is high trust behaviour by management.

What employee would not want to be treated in this way? But those who devise such 'motherhood and apple pie' formulas seldom put as much effort into considering why organizations so seldom resemble anything remotely like their own policy utopias, or how realistic their prescriptions are for dealing with the deep-rooted conflicts in interest and identity found in the workplace. If the general strategy of 'being nice' does not work, managers can always use the other historic human relations device of identifying and eliminating individual deviants – before they can do any damage. In conformity with this, contributors to Giacalone and Greenberg (1997) discuss a variety of psychological tests and personnel selection methods. These are designed to identify miscreants and to screen out unreliable employees. These procedures include the use of organizational surveys, 'to determine if their employees do possess counter-productive values and high levels of job stress' (Boye and Jones, 1997, 182). Such procedures and programmes can be seen as the contemporary successors to the 'counselling programme' carried out at the Hawthorne Works by the Harvard researchers under the direction of Elton Mayo nearly 70 years previously (Ackroyd, 1976).

Even ignoring the internal contradictions of the arguments, their practical impact has to be seen in the context of somewhat optimistic and exaggerated expectations of whether and how employers will use them. Lip-service is often paid to the need to develop new ways of incorporating labour, to the necessity of developing high trust relations, the need to develop self-regulation amongst employees and so on, but in practice attempts to do this are rather rare, and, where they exist, they only partially conform to the theory. Nevertheless, despite a wealth of evidence (see Milkman, 1998; Warhurst and Thompson, 1998) about the limited take-up and ineffectiveness of such approaches, many academic and popular managerial writers continue to herald a supposed shift away from authoritarian regimes – as we see the emergence of 'new organizations'. For some commentators the idea that we have moved decisively away from the direct control and direction associated with Taylorism and Fordism is to be understood in terms of an evolutionary sequence in the character of managerial regimes. The disappearance of overt conflict and forms of misbehaviour is thus to be sought in the disappearance of confrontational politics within the firm.

We do not deal with such arguments here for the simple reason that they are discussed in the concluding chapter, where we pick up again the story of the development of contemporary managerial regimes. The dominant academic argument is that contemporary regimes are shifting, albeit slowly and unevenly, towards forms of regulation whose goal is to eliminate rather than direct misbehaviour. In the space of less than a decade, the employment relationship has allegedly been transformed through a series of strategies and devices – social and technological – into a qualitatively new kind of attachment in which misbehaviour of any kind is seldom seen. Contemporary theory emphasizes that the elicitation of employee commitment has always been relatively low on the managerial agenda. Now, this has become a central theme of human resource management and corporate culture theories. They speak of organizations that are value rather than control driven.

But this is leaping ahead of our account of the nature and growth of misbehaviour. Even while managerial regimes were of the relatively traditional type, there were always different, often partly 'hidden' territories of misbehaviour. Mostly these were concerned with management and self-organization and the production of identity. In the next two chapters we want to explore issues of workplace humour and sexuality, both to uncover what has often been previously marginalized and to provide a link to our concluding chapter where issues of culture and identity have been placed central stage by current organizational theorists.

5 Only Joking? From Subculture to Counter-culture in Organizational Relations

Our analysis so far has been concerned with giving a better account of misbehaviour as it has expressed itself in the past, and the historical role of management in shaping and redirecting it. However, there is a second part to what we have to say about misbehaviour. This concerns the present and the future. In this chapter and the next, we redirect our attention to look more carefully at the contemporary situation to consider what is happening to organizational misbehaviour today. We begin by suggesting that although there is, undoubtedly, significant continuity with the past in workplaces, and the old repertoire from absenteeism to sabotage continues, there are reasons why such things are less in evidence than might be expected. Organizations are in a period of significant change, and this is marked by considerable innovation in the form and content of the misbehaviour expressed in them.

Joking is very common in organizations. In the next chapter we look at sexual misbehaviour at work. Both, we argue, show great historical continuity. The presence and importance of forms of practical joking has already been indicated, and in the next chapter it will be demonstrated that social scientists have shown that sexual misconduct has traditionally been common in organizations. Certainly, workplace humour and joking relationships have been recognized as significant kinds of behaviour at least since the 1950s (Bradney, 1957; Sykes, 1966). Collinson (1988) notes 15 papers describing joking behaviour in a wide variety of workplaces. In the first serious attempt to analyse industry as a cultural system, Turner specifically noted the importance of joking in this setting (Turner, 1971, 42–6). Almost every careful ethnographic study of work organization and behaviour has revealed joking practices and joking relationships (Roy, 1958; Lupton, 1963; Collinson, 1988). Joking at work is clearly not a proclivity that has arisen overnight. But although neither joking nor sexual misbehaviour is new, both have acquired a new significance.

It is not being claimed that as joking and sexual misbehaviour are becoming more important, so the traditional forms of misbehaviour – from work limitation to sabotage – have withered away and disappeared. Not enough is known to assert this with certainty. Some commentators, especially management consultants, do claim that absenteeism and pilferage have declined in recent years in a similar manner to the decline of reported strikes. It is true that the persistently high unemployment we have experienced in Britain makes it likely that forms of misbehaviour are in remission as well as organized industrial action. However, whether traditional forms of misbehaviour have really declined, as opposed to become less significant managerial concerns, is debatable. Even for the measurable kinds of behaviour there are only incomplete and inadequate records. Absenteeism can be measured precisely, for example, but since recorded figures vary greatly according to the assumptions and conventions used to compile them, and even for individual companies long-term data sets are not abundant, there is in fact little definite evidence for long-term decline. Finding reliable evidence for misbehaviour has never been an easy task, if only because the tendency to misbehave is usually hidden. In addition, as we have shown, attempting to measure and control it distorts the activities themselves and creates new problems.

Although the evidence for the decline of traditional forms of misbehaviour is doubtful, we do think that organizations have entered a period of significant change in the last quarter of the twentieth century. Both groups of employees and their managers have changed their expectations about work to some degree and, for this reason, the organizational behaviour (and misbehaviour) to be observed is also changing.

A struggle for the appropriation of identity

The workplace is an arena in which the struggle over the appropriation of identity is becoming more prevalent. It has been recognized for many years that work experience contributes to the formation of identity (Goffman, 1963, 1969; Turner, 1971; Clark et al., 1994). It follows from this that social and organizational change are likely to have effects on conceptions of identity (Collinson, 1992; DuGay, 1996). Whilst such effects are difficult to gauge and can be exaggerated, there is some evidence for change in the new patterns of workplace resistance of the kind that we are now going to consider. The increased saliency of joking behaviour, and the innovation of new forms of such behaviour, are evidence of a shift in emphasis away from the traditional sites of contestation between employees and their managers. Struggle at work was, until recently, centrally concerned with material issues, with amounts of work done and the reappropriation of time and materials by workers as the principal matters of dispute. These days, struggle is more centrally concerned with the matter of identity. Collinson suggests that this was so even amongst his respondents in the factory, and that joking was central to it. He writes: 'Concerned to show that they are "big enough" to laugh at themselves, the men insist that joking reflects the essential nature of the person.' (Collinson, 1992, 107).

There is a good deal about the present situation and the increased importance of joking that is explicable in conventional terms. We live in interesting times so far as management is concerned. Until the last 20 years, the circumstances in which management worked varied between times of economic growth (when sales are high and labour relatively powerful) and recession (where product markets are weak and labour on the defensive). Greater competition in the domestic economy, however, has changed these ground rules. These days, because of greatly increased trade in goods across the world and the easing of trading restrictions, profits from business are under pressure. Companies face severe competition in domestic markets, even in the upturn of the business cycle. The need for sales means that the quality of goods and services has become much more important. If, because of competition, production alone is not sufficient to secure sales, management is forced to rethink its attitude towards quality. The behaviour of employees is crucial here. Hence, employers are, in turn, forced to rethink their priorities regarding labour. This is the source of much of the interest in employee-centred management that is given lip-service today.

The paradox of this situation for managers is that they have greatly increased powers: being able to threaten redundancy is potent in view of continuing high levels of unemployment. At the same time, however, managers still have to produce high quality goods or supply high quality services, which implies obtaining high levels of conscientiousness and commitment from employees. Misbehaviour poses an acute threat to the quantity and quality of production. For these reasons, management has developed an interest in obtaining a higher level of involvement and commitment, even though employment is scarce.

Management has an interest, at least rhetorically, in taking a different attitude towards employees. But this point must be balanced by another of perhaps more importance: employees also have an active interest in personal involvement in, and social reward from, their work. The historical tendency to secure autonomy, which we have examined in earlier chapters is, in many instances, being extended. Now there is an interesting overlap – and apparent congruity – in the attitude and policy of employers and that increasingly adopted by employees. As a result of these two motivations, significant change in attachment to work is developing, and new relationships at work are being negotiated. A realignment is taking place between companies and their demands on the attention of employees and the personal attachments of people. The boundary between the private sphere (the firm, the market place) and the public sphere (the home, the family and the community) is being redrawn.

However, the area of agreement about what is happening is much more apparent than real. On the one hand, employers have a commercial motive to try to appropriate and control the sentiments of their employees (Hochschild, 1983). On the other hand, employees have an interest in obtaining social rewards and recognition at work, as they always did; but they also recognize new opportunities in the current context. These sound much the same; but are not. In many ways the motivations are, in fact, directly contradictory. Management is interested in manipulating identity, whilst employees have an interest in expressing and exploring it.

Employers these days may take the line that they wish employees to express themselves and explore their potential, but actually they are interested in this sort of capacity only in so far as it is conducive to the benefit of the organization. They tend to have preconceived ideas about how much and what kind of individuality is needed. They do not, in fact, wish to find too much variation from their ideas in this area; nor do they want dissent concerning their favoured policies. Despite an apparent openness, therefore, there are things employers are definitely unwilling to countenance or indeed listen to. This is, in many ways, highly unsatisfactory from the point of view of employees, who wish to develop their own judgements and to express *themselves*. Joking is appropriate in these circumstances. It is a way employees can give voice (Hirschman, 1970) to dissenting and unacceptable points of view. Given the unavailability of the other options postulated by Hirschman, 'exit' (which often remains costly) and 'loyalty' (which often remains untenable); and given that more potent forms of voice such as trade union representation have been denied, there is an active search for effective voice. We will see later that dissenting voice, formulated as joking, is made more potent precisely because of the structural imbalance between employers and employees. Joking is a mode of discourse that stands in contradistinction to serious discourse, and which is excused from the normal conventions. Joking is, for this reason, perfectly appropriate when a group with power is espousing a willingness to be intimate, but is still incapable of admitting equality. It is in this sort of situation that joking becomes a useful tool.

There is a point to be made here about the impertinence of employers with regard to employee attitudes. Managements have for decades treated the creativity and capacity for independent thought of working people as of negligible import – something that should be ignored, if not treated with open disrespect. The implication of Taylorism and similar forms of management policy which have dominated thinking for decades is that the mentality of the employee is not worth considering, still less worth taking seriously. The motivations and attitudes of working people have been assumed to be at best irrelevant to good organizational performance. For some considerable time, it has been assumed that employees can be adequately managed without consultation and adequately motivated by marginal incentives in cash. This sort of treatment has made its contribution to the consolidation of a set of values which is very robust and insular; amongst other things, being deeply and incorrigibly cynical about management motivations and objectives. Despite this, it has now become fashionable to ignore this history. Employers now glibly persuade themselves that it would be a good idea to change tack, and to decide to 'mine the gold in the workers' heads' (Peters and Waterman, 1982, 102). Almost overnight in historical terms, it is now assumed that the ideas of the employee (obviously) will be placed at the service of the company. The assumption that such a volte-face will be met with enthusiastic acceptance by employees is surprising. It should not be puzzling that employees generally do not take such claims seriously.

In a nutshell, our argument is this. Ironic, sardonic and satirical commentary on managerial initiatives, which have been endemic in Britain, have become, in the current context, significant forms of misbehaviour. Management today has an interest in trying to incorporate the sentiments of its employees and to harness their goodwill by doing so. In conformity with such policy, management often either makes promises or implies special treatment for employees which it has been unable to fulfil, or will be unlikely to fulfil. But yet it also adopts an open attitude towards employees. While managerial rhetoric suggests that the opinions of employees matter, have to be listened to and should be acted upon, all parties also know that very little can or will be done to change the basic situation of employees. In these circumstances, management is likely to continue to receive unfavourable comment on its initiatives and innovations – which it is now constrained to listen to and is often unable to answer. Hence, a good deal of contemporary joking at work features cynical comment on the validity of managerial claims and the actions and motives of managers. It is no exaggeration to say that it constitutes a continuous undercurrent of satirical debunking of management pretensions. As we express it in the title to this chapter, the distinctive subculture of employees is becoming a more pointedly critical and overtly satirical counter-culture.

Analysing workplace humour

Joking is common in workplaces, but few have seen it as deeply subversive or even potentially so. Numerous studies have shown that joking is almost as prevalent as the normal discourse without which business could not be continued. Organizations are full of jokes and humour. Humorous talk has been shown to be an almost continuous accompaniment of the serious talk undertaken in business and commerce. Thus, it can be asserted with some conviction that if you do not see constant badinage in your organization, you are not seeing the relationships as they really are so far as the majority of the participants are concerned. Such behaviour is not confined to ordinary employees. Barsoux (1993) and Lawrence (1996) have argued that joking is a national characteristic of managers in Britain. Different groups within the same organization are often not sharing the same meanings in their joking: managerial joking themes do not connect with those found on the shop floor. Distinctive joking conventions demarcate employee values.

Among the many important observations made by Michael Mulkay's rich and valuable book, *On Humour* (1988), are ideas which help to explain the ubiquity of humour in the workplace. A basic point is to recognize that humorous discourse is an alternative type of discourse to the dominant or 'serious' mode, which has a different character and to which different implicit rules apply. For Mulkay, the humorous mode of discourse is a permanently available alternative form of expression, one in which the imagination is allowed more scope, and which is drawn on by participants to direct and redirect conversations, to recontextualize them, and to retain a sense of perspective. Mulkay argues that taking humorous 'turns' in conversations is often facilitative, helping to deal with problems that arise in practical discussions, but which cannot easily be solved by purely rational means. There have certainly been some fascinating detailed studies of joking which show that in practice the humorous and the serious 'modes of discourse' are intimately related, and that people move between them with great facility and awareness (Drew, 1987). Thus, humour provides devices and short cuts which help serious discourse along. For Mulkay, to be able to joke is a highly skilled and often helpful social accomplishment. As such it has obvious applications in the workplace. However, his view is that humour is a subordinate and facilitative mode of discourse, and therefore does not fundamentally challenge anything.

Viewed in this sort of way there seems little to object to in the use of humour at work. Some forms of it may waste a good deal of time, but there is little here to support any suggestion that it can become a significant form of misbehaviour. Indeed there are numerous management pundits who have a much more positive view about the role of joking than Mulkay. For these writers, humour in the workplace can make a very positive contribution. Joking allegedly has the following valuable effects: it reduces tensions between groups, forges strong relationships and allows participants to cope with stress. For these and other reasons it is not infrequently claimed that joking and humour can be useful managerial tools (Duncan and Feisal, 1989; Barsoux, 1993). Although, as we shall see, there are particular dangers for people in authority in the use of humour, clearly the phenomenon has positive qualities that could, conceivably, help the social integration of organizations and boost their cooperative qualities. If this is true, joking and humour are unlikely candidates for consideration as significant forms of misbehaviour. It is a large step from claiming that joking at work is commonplace, and even that the majority of people participate in it, to suggesting that joking at work is a significant kind of misbehaviour.

However, general discussion of the possible roles of humour overlooks the extent to which joking by ordinary people, as opposed to set-piece jokes or comedy routines, is strongly related to the context in which the joking occurs. Mulkay also makes a useful distinction between pure and applied humour. Here a line is drawn between jokes that seem to be motivated by nothing other than joyous delight in having fun, and those that are obviously aimed and targeted in particular ways. Applied humour makes certain points about situations, groups and classes of people and has definite effects in mind. The difference between having fun with an idea, and making fun of somebody, is broadly the distinction. Applied humour is often serious commentary, masquerading as joking, but, like pure humour, is exempted from the normal rules of social discourse. Genuinely clever and original jokes are relatively rare; and for these reasons we rightly value comic talent. In practice, of course, much joking involves the re-use of old jokes and entails a good deal of repeated or recycled and stereotyped content. Moreover, particular situations conventionally evoke and sustain particular kinds of joking commentary, in which familiar jokes are recycled, and messages are restated. But humour is also dynamic to some extent, in that old jokes fail to amuse, and new ideas are constantly invented.

Workplace joking certainly tends to have applied characteristics. It is often crude and is usually targeted in very obvious ways. It also features particular themes but these themes are embroidered and developed. How jokes are applied and made to work is a complicated subject, which will recur in this chapter. A high proportion of jokes have both butts (whom the joke is about) and audiences (whom the joke aims to amuse and influence) (Davies, 1982). Butts and audiences are seldom the same, and the joker ridicules the butt for the benefit of the audience. In ethnic jokes, for example, the butt of a joke is the supposedly inadequate group the joke describes (if you are English, the Irish; if you are French, the Belgians and so on), whilst the audience is the receiving group (whose self-esteem or sense of insecurity is massaged) (Davies, 1982). In this sort of observation we see some evidence for a much-repeated idea about humour: that it is double-edged (Malone, 1980). Applied humour aims to bolster or reassure one party, at the expense of another. Comedians and script-writers must try to deal in pure humour to some extent, lest they offend significant sections of their audience. But comedians, and still more so the characters in sitcoms, have recognizable points of view which can be inferred from the kind of jokes they tell, and therefore they do make use of applied humour. In the workplace, by contrast, the attempt to apply humour, to make it work, is the dominant impulse.

At this point it will be helpful to focus on examples of workplace humour which, along with joking, has always been underestimated as an indicator of dissent from authority. Traditionally, workplace humour has constituted a distinct set of values which are espoused by employees, to such an extent, we suggest, that there is often a distinct organizational subculture. Because joking is a central constituent in this, most of the forms of joking are effective dissenting acts. On this general theme, Collinson suggest that the behaviour of shop floor employees was one of the characteristic ways they defined their identity as distinct from that of others and especially of the white collar denizens of the offices and of the management. Thus:

> The uncompromising banter on the shop floor, which was permeated by uninhibited swearing, mutual ridicule, displays of sexuality and 'pranks', was contrasted, elevated and exaggerated above the more restrained demeanour of the offices. Ironically, when compared to others, the subordinated world of the shop floor came to be seen as free space in which the 'true self' could be expressed. (Collinson, 1988, 186)

Specifically, joking was seen as a core activity in the creation of 'free space', Collinson's workers actually defining themselves as a 'community of comedians' whose outlook is very distinct from that of the company as a whole.

We suggest that there are three kinds of joking that are commonplace at work, and which we shall now consider in more detail. These are: clowning, teasing and satire. The distinctions are in fact difficult to make in a hard and fast way, but all of them are examples of joking in the workplace which contain and express distinct identities and dissent from authority. However, whereas clowning and teasing express an anti-managerial subculture, in which emphasis on difference and dissent are the predominant motifs, satire represents a development with a more serious and sustained critical intellectual element, which can be seen as something qualitatively new. Satire is different from traditional forms of workplace joking, which are themselves often rather more critical and corrosive than is believed. Satire springs from a critical counter-culture within organizations rather than a traditional dissenting subculture.

Our use of the terms 'subculture' and 'counter-culture' is distinctive. We are working with an inclusive and heterogeneous idea of culture, in which cultures as complex patterns of meaning are assumed to allow dissent as well as conformity (Smircich, 1983; Wright, 1994). Even the characteristic beliefs of classes, organizations and groups are seen as variations on those of the main culture and allow different degrees of critical content and reforming potential. Subcultures are distinguished by the articulation of distinctive values within the main value system, whereas counter-cultures are social movements in which there is active espousal of alternative values.

Bring on the clowns

Clowning, in which people make fools of themselves (i.e. become the butt of their own jokes) for the amusement of others, is amongst the most elementary forms of humour. Clowning is extremely common at work. As in the circus, it is publicly playing the fool. Clowning appeals generally because we see in it not only stupid behaviour, but also a lack of concern about the consequences of stupidity. Clowning ignores the conventions of prudent conduct, and it is funny because it is somebody else, and not us, bearing the consequences. Although clowning is very common at work, it is one of the least acceptable forms of humour in the workplace from the management point of view. The clown wastes time and resources, breaks the rhythms of work and diverts people's concentration. In these ways, the clown provides a poor example. A key point is that clowning involves an explicit rejection of disciplined and even ordered behaviour. Because of this clowns in the workplace voluntarily but invariably blight their chances of promotion. In a similar way, the behaviour of the medieval court jester was tolerated and even valued, but such a person was not promoted to high offices of state.

If clowns jeopardize their own situation in the official hierarchy, it might well be asked why clowns and clowning are so common at work. The answer to this is complex. But a key part of the answer draws on our earlier argument concerning self-organization and its importance. Identity is formed and defined in opposition to the formal organization and its values, and deliberate clowning is a radical departure from the responsible behaviour that is required at work. Also important is the realization that, in many cases, clowns escape from the – sometimes very uncomfortable – position of being the butt of the joking of others. By becoming a clown one chooses the circumstances in which and the way one becomes a butt. More positively, the clown may come to stand for something. There is the possibility of becoming a local (anti) hero by becoming a celebrated clown. Clowns at work, challenge assumptions by refusing to be bound by conventions, and thus they are, in obvious ways, both subversive and potentially heroic. Clowning can be a clear symbolic statement by people who neither expect nor want preferment from management.

Management usually judges other forms of humour to be more acceptable than clowning, even though they may be more partisan and applied. For example, one form of joking which has been widely reported in the literature, but which seems to pass largely without comment or sanction by management, is widely referred to as 'teasing'. Various commentators have noted examples of teasing at work, and there have been several attempts to describe and analyse it (Bradney, 1957; Sykes, 1966; Emerson, 1969; Fox, 1990). The ideas of the anthropologist, A.R. Radcliffe-Brown, who published a study of primitive joking relationships as long ago as 1940, have been influential. Radcliffe-Brown writes that he considers the joking relationship to be: 'a relation between two persons in which one is by custom permitted, and in some circumstances required, to tease or make fun of the other, who is in turn required to take no offence' (1952, 90). He then distinguishes between symmetrical relationships (in which both individuals tease each other to the same degree) and asymmetrical relationships (in which one party teases much more than the other). Radcliffe-Brown argues that the teasing is in some way required by the system of relationships in which some primitive people find themselves, and the joking relationship contributes to the integration of the society concerned (see also Wilson, 1979). According to this view, the study of joking relationships will show how the joking relations are produced and how they contribute to social integration. In this sort of way, Bradney (1957) argued in an early British study of the joking relations in a department store, that they were required by features of the organization of the store (such as the physical layout and the management structure), and that they contributed to organization by dissolving potential tensions.

Please don't tease

The kind of analysis undertaken by Bradney, based on the functional analysis of Radcliffe-Brown (1952), glosses over some significant differences in the relationships found in primitive societies and modern workplaces. For example, teasing in industry is sometimes very aggressive indeed. It often shades into behaviour that is best described as systematic demoralization of its targets. In fact it is not easy to classify this teasing by any of the criteria suggested by Radcliffe-Brown. From ethnographic studies of modern work, there is a problem about both the symmetricality of teasing relationships in work, and the toleration of them by participants (Boland and Hoffman, 1983; Ackroyd and Crowdy, 1990; Collinson, 1988, 1992). These are the very features Radcliffe-Brown used to define such relationships. On the shop floor and in many work settings, teasing is not restricted to relations between specific pairs of individuals. There is usually asymmetry, in that some individuals are teased much more frequently than others; but the most outstanding feature of such behaviour is that it is ubiquitous. Teasing is not restricted to specific partners.

Anyone and everyone is a likely target of the tease from time to time. Further, far from being obviously functional there are, very frequently, huge problems arising from teasing. Teasing often results in bitter resentment and semi-permanent feuds. Many individuals definitely do not tolerate teasing very well; and some of them will not tolerate it at all. Collinson (1992) notes that teasing is often met by intolerance. This he calls 'snapping' and 'losing your rag'. One of the most common complaints about individuals who snap in the manner described by Collinson is that they have denied reciprocity in joking. 'He wants to give it out, but won't take it back', as respondents will say. There seem to be few rules governing the limits of teasing or the toleration of teasing; or at least fewer and less meticulously observed rules than are claimed for primitive societies. One of the few rules that people recognize is that there is a distinction between normal badinage at work and more serious personal affront. In the factory Collinson studied, workers distinguished between normal (and tolerable) 'piss-taking' and abnormal and unacceptable 'malicious piss-taking'.

The worker ignores malicious teasing at his or her peril. This is because the character of this teasing is not found in a comparison with primitive behaviour – where teasing helps to consolidate and perpetuate existing relationships. On the contrary, it is appropriate to think of this behaviour as attempts to change the informal hierarchy of self-organized groups. Teasing tests the vulnerability of individuals to subordination: if they accept too much of it they move down in status; if they snap effectively, they do not. It is, in fact, behaviour that is related to the processes of self-organization that were discussed in Chapter 3. A key question that is lurking behind this sort of discussion of teasing is the following: if teasing is indicative of intra-group negotiation and contention, surely it cannot also be regarded as a significant form of collective solidarity and resistance? To make sense of this we must point back to the findings of Chapter 3. Even though it may not be consistently directed against management, and so is far from being solidaristic in classic understanding of the term, this behaviour is also far from being manageable or supportive of management.

Fred's finger

Fred was a seasoned operator of one of the large fruit pie machines at ELS Amalgamated Bakery . . . . The operator was expected to keep his machine running, liaise with the fruit and dough mixers upstairs, supervise the other two people who worked on the machine and train any newcomers . . . .

On one particular shift, a mixing of fruit was proving difficult for the fruit depositing mechanism to handle. In attempting to clear the obstruction, Fred, against all he knew to be good practice, inserted his hand into the unguarded mouth of the depositor and lost the end of his middle finger. Fred was treated, but no-one could tell where the finger end was, and approximately 4,000 pies, being suspected, were thrown away.

The incident stimulated much discussion and comment . . . .

A supervisor is reported to have said: 'Fetch quality, and get me a deviation recipe for meat and apple.'

Another comment was: 'They were going to get some "finger hunter" stickers made and pack them 4,000 pies.' (Promotion boxes usually bore a sticker marked 'Bargain Hunter'.)

Or yet again:

Operator 1: 'Fred's walking straight back into a warning when he comes back.'

Operator 2: 'How's tha' mean?'

Operator 1: 'Well they found his finger tha' knows.'

Operator 2: 'Did they?'

Operator 1: 'Aye but t' Health Inspector says his finger nail were dirty . . . .'

(Linstead, 1985, 752–4)

Individuals at work often suffer from the teasing we have described. Sometimes they do so acutely; but they are not, as a result, disposed to see what happens to them as unjustifiable oppression. On the contrary, the opportunity to participate in banter is often seen as a significant and valuable freedom. The ability to participate effectively in such activities is taken to be a basic part of the self-image of the worker. In Collinson's study, for example, he reports that workers remorselessly teased their workmates. In some instances, people were deliberately pushed into emotional breakdown by teasing, whilst it was actively denied that this was a matter for regret. Collinson writes:

> In the case of 'Deaf Dave', the joking resulted in his total emotional breakdown . . . . Dave had his leg pulled and took the pain like a man on a daily basis in the axle department. But his disability made him an easy target . . . and one day the men went too far . . . Dave broke down . . . . After the incident, although he continued to claim 'it's a good job I can take it', he received only unsympathetic replies such as 'you've fucking got to mate!' (Collinson, 1992, 118)

Yet these workers also gave out very positive evaluations of the benefits of being in their workgroup, and cast the opportunity to engage in teasing in terms of personal freedom. They saw their willingness to participate in aggressive teasing as 'having a laff', which capacity was very important to

---

From a factory wall: supervisors and bums

When the body was first made, all the parts wanted to be SUPERVISORS.

The Brain insisted: 'Since I control everything and do all the thinking, I should be Supervisor.'

The Feet said: 'Since we carry man where he wants to go, we should be Supervisors.'

The Hands said: 'Since we do all the work and earn all the money to keep the rest of you going, we should be Supervisors.'

The Eyes too staked their claim: 'Since we must watch out for all of you, we should be Supervisors.'

So it went on: the Heart, the Ears and, finally . . . the Bum. How all the other parts laughed to think the Bum should be the Supervisor!

Thus the Bum became mad and refused to function. The Brain became feverish: the Eyes crossed and ached. The Legs got wobbly and the Stomach went sick.

All pleaded with the Brain to relent and let the Bum be Supervisor. And so it came to be, that all the parts did their work and the Bum simply supervised and passed a load of crap.

MORAL: YOU DON'T HAVE TO BE A BRAIN TO BE A
SUPERVISOR – ONLY A BUM

---

their self-image. Indeed it is not an exaggeration to say that workers tended to define their identity in terms of the freedom to express themselves by just this 'having a laff'. The apparent paradox of this behaviour is resolved by recognition of the structure of teasing. Because it is an applied joke it involves a butt and an audience: the teaser draws attention to their own importance in the eyes of their audience, by diminishing the standing of the teased. The joker appeals to the sentiments of the group, which highly values individual potency.

We take teasing to be strong evidence for the existence of a dissenting subculture within many organizations. This emphasizes differences between the values of the group and that of the management and the organization as a whole. Those managers and managerial advisers who think that organizational cultures can be easily identified and manipulated should read this kind of account closely. There is little to support the notion that groups equipped with such values will be readily incorporated into a dominant set of values controlled by the management. The point about this notion of identity is that it defines itself against the dominant values which those in authority promote. Indeed, there is reason to think that, as the attempt to incorporate the sentiments of employees becomes more concerted, so the defence of an opposing position becomes more entrenched. As we shall see, there is some evidence of a broadening and deepening of the critical attitude towards managers that is consistent with an ironical, and even satirical, detachment from the concerns of managers.

Satire – from the Latin *satura,* to stuff

It would be wrong to conclude, and Collinson (1988, 1992) certainly does not, that the kind of aggressive teasing considered above indicates that the behaviour of workgroups is simply individualistic. Another apparently paradoxical aspect of this joking is that, although it features distinct elements of individualism, in that it is usually one individual picking on and trying to belittle another, these nonetheless embody a group sentiment. A robust sense of the individual self, which is defended and promoted by teasing, is not incompatible either with a cynical attitude towards management or significant degrees of agreement between workers about the appropriateness of cynicism. The teasing we have described shades into and overlaps with another type of joking, which has more direction and serious intellectual content. This is appropriately described as satire because it involves a systematic cynicism. Satire engages in mimicry and mockery (from irony, through sarcasm and distortion to insult) which is used to expose the foolishness, partisanship and/or hypocrisy of its target. Teasing has some of these qualities, in that employees pick on some of the supposed attributes of their workmates to mock and lampoon.

Mockery and lampoonery can of course be readily turned on management and supervision, a common and recognizable target which the audience readily accepts as fair game. When the management is satirically criticized, by the use of similar sorts of behaviour as that which are involved in individual teasing, it can generate a degree of solidarity between workers. As with teasing, in workplaces where such satirical traditions are well entrenched, there is competition between satirists to develop their informal status by being effective critics of management.

Jokes are often designed by their users to communicate serious messages. It is often noted in studies of humour how closely joking and serious discourse are interwoven (Mulkay, 1988; Drew, 1987). Even in professional comedy, it is often not clear when the serious mode is being employed, or when a parody of it is in use, for jokes invoke the contrast between the serious world as we know it to be constituted, and the world as the humorist suggests it might be. The value of the humorous mode is that suggestions can be framed that otherwise cannot be mentioned in serious discourse, and which can nevertheless be disavowed as a joke, should they not be acceptable. It is often noted that joking suggestions are often met with serious responses, not another joke. Emerson (1969) has analysed the interactions of nurses and patients in a hospital, in terms of the way jokes are used to disguise tentative requests for information or reassurance, which are usually met by the required serious information. In a similar way, joking interactions, however apparently innocuous, should be seen as also involving negotiations. Consider the following real fragment of dialogue: An employee (female) asks a supervisor (male) in mocking tone: 'What, here again?' Which evokes the straight response:

The lotus is a fragile flower

At Northern Plant, consultants had been brought into the plant to
(re)introduce Kaizen as a means of 'driving forward N-Gineering's
Continuous Improvement Philosophy'. The re-timing and re-ordering of
existing machining procedures, working practices and arrangements,
involving the close supervision of Kaizen consultant team, had resulted in a
marked increase in output during the two week period when the consultants
had remained in the cell. Following their departure to other cells, production
immediately fell to its previous level. During feedback presentation, the drop
in production was ascribed by a consultant to a 'disciplinary problem' which
the company would 'need to deal with' if Kaizen was to succeed. One of the
workers attending this session invited the consultant to recall how, in his
initial presentation of the philosophy of Kaizen, he had emphasised that the
success of the initiative was dependent on the development of a blame free
culture of mutual management–worker support for a 'search for continuous
improvement.' The consultant was also reminded that he had described
Kaizen as a concept that was very much like a flower, that needed to be
watered and nurtured and that patience was needed to make it grow. To the
considerable amusement of both the workers and the middle management
present at the session the consultant was asked: '. . . if my flowers in the
garden at home don't grow straight away when I water them, should I carry
on watering and wait for them to grow, or hit them with the watering can?'
(Worthington et al., 1997, 15–16)

'But I haven't been here since this morning.' This is met with a meaningful look at the huge clock suspended over the entry to the shop which is
standing at 12.30, and is followed by the comment: 'I see, you don't want
to trust me, you want to marry me.' All this is apparently trifling but, in
context, the layers of negotiation are numerous. The management has
announced a 'trust programme', in which employees have been promised
new freedoms from direct supervision in return for set quotas of work. But
the joking also involves ironic references to the lack of trust in marriage,
and the gender of the supervisor.

The most blatant form of satire is that in which there is consistent and
persistent expression of scepticism about all managerial assumptions and
suggestions. It depends on (and sustains) a lack of emotional identification
with the problems of managers. The basic attitude is referred to by David
Collinson (1992, 1994) as 'resistance through distance'. The 'distancing'
referred to is symbolic rather than physical and is well illustrated by the
joking patterns discovered by Frank Worthington (1997) in a plant which
he has studied for several years. In much the same way as stories about
Fred's finger (see box) became the theme of a whole series of jokes, in a
bakery reported on by Linstead (1985), management practices can become
the subject of sustained satirical comment. The hypocrisy of managers who
will undoubtedly profit personally from proposed changes in work organization, but who fail to acknowledge that increased productivity will only be
sustained by the progressive intensification of the work of employees, can
easily become the subject of much cynical commentary. Worthington notes

willingness and ability to turn management rhetoric back on the managers themselves in humorous ways. Feeding back to Kaizen consultants their own initial rhetoric (see box) is another example of this. In this plant, the suggestions to a supervisor that he might like to look over some new manning schedules during a tea break met with the counter-suggestion that the consultant might like to look over the pages of the racing paper, *Sporting Life*, and proffer some suggestions about the form of the runners on the afternoon card.

Satire can be relentless and seemingly petty; but nonetheless can be effective at conveying messages. A recurrent message of satire is: we do not have sympathy for your projects or ideas. Trivial dissent is as effective at conveying this message as is disagreement over large points of principle. An example might help to show this. At one time the office telephones in the plant studied by Worthington were sabotaged by leaving them connected to telephone chat lines all night, running up bills of several thousand pounds. This caused outpourings of indignation from management about the costs of this carelessness. One worker, another member of the racing fraternity at the plant, was heard to comment that he regularly lost a fortune at the races, but didn't come moaning to the company about it or expect sympathy from them. Following the telephone sabotage, one can well imagine the jokes about telephones which proliferated: shouts of 'It's not for yooou!' (echoing the advertising slogan of British Telecom) to greet managers appearing on the shop floor; gratuitous statements, like 'It's good to talk', being interpolated into conversations and so on. At a briefing, in which managers were complaining to members of the shop floor about the cost involved in having to scrap and redesign a component, one employee remarked that it did not seem very much money to lose for a company that made such good profits. He is reported to have finished by remarking: 'It's not much – hardly the cost of a phone call to you – is it, really?' In view of the sensitivity of the issue, the man was suspended.

The view that satire is a prevalent form of anti-managerial joking comes up against some major objections. One is that the account does not fit the observed patterns of joking. For example, it is a finding of several studies where joking activity has been quantified, that the majority of jokes are voiced by high status people with lower status people as their butts. If this is so, there is a problem for the argument that jokes are effective forms of dissent. If this observation is accurate – and there is something to be said for it, as we do see teasing as establishing and reinforcing informal hierarchies – it can be argued that this approach confuses frequency of joking with its perceived importance and effectiveness. People in authority do find joking easy – there is every possibility that they will be politely applauded and little likelihood of listeners snapping. In some circumstances too, it is tempting to them to use joking as a way of improving their standing. But joking is a complex process and authority is easily undermined by the familiarity required by it (Malone, 1980). Jokes can, all too easily, backfire on people in authority.

A joke that misfired

Possibly the most expensive joke of all time was told by Gerald Ratner in 1991. At the time, he was the CEO of Ratner's, the largest retail jewellery chain in the world. At a prestigious business lunch organized by the Institute of Directors in April 1991, Ratner joked that many of the goods sold in his jewellery stores cost as little, and would probably last as long, as a high quality sandwich. The joke was picked up by the reporters present and publicized in the mass circulation newspapers bought by large numbers of the customers of Ratner's shops. The result was plummeting jewellery sales. The downturn in the company's sales was compounded by a developing recession in retailing. The price of the ordinary shares in the company tumbled from £4 to 25p. Just over a year later, Ratner accepted the inevitable and resigned from the board. Thus, it can be argued that, in addition to a substantial loss of shareholder value, this joke cost Gerald Ratner personally his £600,000 a year job (not to mention the use of the company helicopter and various other perks). Eventually, the chain was sold off and renamed before it returned to profitable sales.

Because jokes are double-edged and can be outright subversive, managers often instinctively avoid the temptation to try to develop their status by joking. Periodically, management pundits discover humour and recommend its use to managers. But there are probably almost as many management papers which suggest caution.

(For a recent report refering to the Ratner episode, see the *Daily Mail*, 12 February 1998)

Jokes as subversion

Some writers think that humour is inherently ineffective as a means of communication. Mulkay (1988) is quite consistent in taking this point of view. He writes at length, at the very end of his book, of what he alleges is 'the mute voice of humour'. In addition to the suggestion that because it is a non-serious mode of discourse, humorous communication will always be discounted by comparison with serious messages, Mulkay also puts forward some more basic propositions to account for the ineffectiveness of joking. In evolutionary terms, he argues, humour probably has its origins in appeasement gestures. Like appeasement gestures amongst animals, humour has the tendency to limit and defuse conflict, and to leave relationships precisely where they are. To find biological arguments of this kind underpinning the work of a sociologist in this way is surprising. Mulkay's thesis is also open to the criticism that it insufficiently acknowledges that the effects of humour may vary greatly according to their social context. His analysis does not give sufficient consideration to the way joking may be situated. Acts of communication and attempted communication are likely to have very different effects in different circumstances.

In many contexts, the contemporary workplace being one, humorous and satirical utterances may be the only safe way of expressing an alternative point of view. In the absence of respect for democracy, of course, satire is not necessarily safe, as the critics of the Nazis found out. But satirical utterances may be effective where there is a degree of tolerance. At the least, satire keeps dissent alive and sustains the independence of those disposed to be critical. Satire provides an alternative evaluation of official courses of action. These are also reasons why satire is often not acceptable to those in authority. There is a recurrent impulse to use power to stifle dissent. Indeed, if this form of humour is really an appeasement gesture, it is remarkable how often it is read as aggression; and how often it achieves the opposite of appeasement. Certainly, satire does not inure the butts of satirists nor their audiences to their situation. An intriguing comparison here is with persistent joking against aspects of the communist regimes of Eastern Europe and Russia. Nobody would pretend that joking was what brought them down; but the popularity of jokes against these regimes is an index of covert distancing from established authority by the population.

Jokes in general contradict expectations and pose alternative patterns to those which everybody expects, and so are subversive of established patterns of linguistic and social order. Jokes, in fact, lend themselves to critical uses. Indeed some analysts of joking have made symbolic subversiveness the central characteristic of joking. Analysts of humour have observed, for example, that being funny often depends on paradox, unexpected contrast and inversions. Humour identifies, plays on and uses contradictions. Mary Douglas argues that:

> A joke is a play upon form. It brings into relation disparate elements in such a way that one accepted pattern is challenged by the appearance of another in some way hidden in the first . . . any recognisable joke falls into this joke pattern which needs two elements, the juxtaposition of control against that which is controlled, this juxtaposition being that the latter triumphs. Needless to say, a successful subversion of one form by another ends the joke, for it changes the balance of power. (1975, 96)

Douglas goes further to suggest that jokes often work well because they express or somehow mimic contradictions in the social structure in which they arise. Although humour and joking need not do this, it is undeniable that such contradictions are a potent source of what we find funny in humorous situations. The examples of joking that we have discussed suggest that, among other things, joking identifies strengths and plays on weaknesses. The weaknesses and vulnerability of social organization are an obvious target and source of humour.

Reversing the hierarchy: the cultured employee

Irish labourer: I've come about the foreman's job, guvner.
Manager: Any qualifications?
Irish labourer: No, but you can ask me anything you want.
Manager: What's the difference between a Girder and a Joist?
Irish labourer: That's easy sir, Goethe wrote *Faust* and Joyce wrote *Ulysses*.
(quoted by Linstead, 1985, 745)

Joking is a particular class of reflective and discursive comment on social relations, which can be used systematically to draw out contradictions and to express dissent. Humour is used constantly to explore social and individual fault lines. Hence its importance to organizational researchers is methodological as well as theoretical. We should ask: what is it about relations in a particular organization that the jokes found there illustrate? What forms of relationship and interaction do they facilitate, mask, deter? In general, humour has precisely the subtlety of exploring and expressing and delineating informal social structures. It is the essence of humour that it can express, question and explore aspects of relationships. As such it is an invaluable potential guide to organizing as a practical activity. Rather than a marginal phenomenon of limited significance, the use of humour in organizations turns out to be an extremely important diagnostic device. More than this, however, since organizations are full of paradoxes and contradictions jokes can resonate and play on them. Because of this, humour has potential for subversion and resistance. This possibility itself should be enough to lead to an interest in humour and joking as a submerged and overlooked seam of radicalism. Humour, undoubtedly, can be subversive; and, in the current context, can be a potent tool.

Deconstructing Dilbert

Management's words and deeds, or the gap between them, has always been the target of employee humour and occasional mockery from within the ranks. In the current context, where all sorts of untried and unlikely innovations are being undertaken by managers in the attempt to retain profitability, it is an obvious and effective resource. Many of these innovations are palpably against the interests of employees, but introduced with a rhetoric of participation, and communal benefit. Hence, the spread of managerial fads and fashions is providing fertile and seemingly ever-expanding source material for satirical jokes and themes. One indicator of the popularity of satire is the fame of Scott Adams's character 'Dilbert', who features in the comic strip of the same name. Dilbert is a put-upon engineer employed in a large organization who suffers daily from the new policies of management. Remarkably, Adams's book *The Dilbert Principle* (1996) which features a commentary on a collection of the strips, has topped the bestseller lists for non-fiction in the UK and other countries.

The cartoons and accompanying text are an explicit attack on managerial fads and other new ideas and practices. Everything which contemporary popular management theory holds dear – mission statements, quality, teams, downsizing, re-engineering – is held up to ridicule in a wonderful 'best-practice in reverse' mode. All the main managerial functions and their self-interested appropriation of the latest fads get it in the neck, from marketing and sales to Ratbert the consultant and Catbert the brutal Human Resources director. The hierarchy-driven, status-obsessed reality of organizational life

Figure 5.1

is laid bare through a clear view from below. In sharp contrast to the 'great lies of management' and the associated images of the supposedly egalitarian character of post-bureaucratic structures, we are presented with a view of the illogicality and absurdity of many contemporary managerial practices.

Conventional objections to the limits of workplace humour certainly apply here. Though we pick up tips on how to misbehave to good effect, the best that these cartoon characters achieve is simply to survive; and many of them do not manage even this, being regularly expelled from their organizations in palpably unfair ways for ludicrous reasons. They don't resist, at least not in any effective way. Indeed, one strip shows Dilbert and fellow workers being fitted with attachable spines before they consider joining a union. But the eponymous hero and his band of co-workers typically experience, without much comment, more and more unlikely examples of managerial action. Indications of surprise or shock are often minimal. The permanent questioning curl of Dilbert's necktie is sometimes the only indication of the manifest absurdity of the management practices featured. But, arguably, lack of explicit or extended comment is often more effective than elaborate debunking might be.

Nor are we given any tools to understand the rise and spread of management fads and fashions. The best Scott Adams can do in the text of *The Dilbert Principle* (1996) is to suggest that, as the world becomes more complex, its inhabitants become more idiotic. Everyone is implicated in this organizational dumbing down: employees as well as managers are subjects and subject to 'nitwititis'. But to focus on the limitations of any explanation misses the point about the popularity of Dilbert. It's not so much the resources Adams gives us, but the way we use Dilbert as a resource. It is common to find the cartoons posted up in factories, shops and offices. In central Scotland, where the strip has been run for years in Glasgow's evening paper, workers and managers alike send their friends and colleagues examples of the latest comment on what they are experiencing in some organizational change programme. In doing this, they are paralleling what is happening in the production of the books. Adams gets over 200 emails a day from employees detailing the unfortunately all-too-believable actions of their own senior management, often reproducing them alongside the cartoon strips. Taken with each other it is never clear whether art is imitating life, or organizational life is increasingly becoming some ridiculous theatre of the absurd in its own right.

Limits of satirical effectiveness

For some who write about the behaviour found in contemporary workplaces, it is not that the satirical attitude does not find much expression, but that this, and almost any critical voice, has been effectively eliminated by managerial action. There are two different positions here. On the one hand, there is the contention that employees are so cowed by managerial power that, although they would like to express dissent, there is seen to be no point. Ogbonna and Wilkinson (1990) have a concept to describe this, which they label 'resigned behavioural compliance' with managerial expectations. By contrast, there is the view that managerial control is so complete that even the tendency to criticize has gone. It is not simply that there is no opportunity to do other than comply with the requirements of the job, and little opportunity to meet with colleagues in order to express dissent. True, deviations from what is expected would be difficult because of constraints on time (task requirements are exactly specified, and there is no time to do other than fulfil them) and opportunity (there are few face to face encounters with supervisors and others) but the main impediment is that workers have accepted that the goals, policies and objectives of their employers are right, and their place is not to question, merely to comply. There are many who take this point of view. (See for example Ray, 1986; Knights and Willmott, 1989; Webster and Robbins, 1993; Willmott, 1993.)

In making a case for the elimination of dissent, the ordinary plant or office situation is pointedly ignored. To make these arguments it is common to draw on the experiences of the employees found in a small number of untypical case study firms. The work of Alvesson (1987, 1991), who studied work in a computer consultancy, and of Kunda (1995), who studied a large American IT house, has been very influential. These case studies do not show that critical impulses do not exist, but something more subtle. At least two points are usually made by writers with these views about the muting of dissent in such organizations: that critical impulses are voluntarily restrained by employees; and more seriously, that criticizm is readily accepted and assimilated by the ideological (they say cultural) sophistication of the managers. However, satire becomes an effective critique by being sustained and unforgiving. Satire works only so long as the perpetrators are unwilling to compromise with their ostensible targets. The engineers and other professional white collar employees of Kunda's 'Tech', and similar establishments, have their radicalism blunted by their willingness to be incorporated by the management. Knowing that preferment in career terms has as its price acceptance of the management outlook (Kunda refers to this as the managerial culture) the extent of employee cynicism, and even more so the consistent formulation and expression of a critical view, is likely to be severely blunted. There is nothing mysterious or new about this: acceptance of office within organizational structures usually means, in public pronouncements at any rate, toeing the party line and evincing acceptance of an official company point of view. What is different here is the identification of the managerial position as culture, implying a hegemonic character to these beliefs which is inaccurate and potentially misleading.

The second line of argument is that the sophistication of the cultural defences makes serious dissent impossible. Such is the development of the cultural apparatus that the company deploys, which includes the idea that self-reflection on performances and critical comment on policies are permissible, that it somehow encompasses and renders neutral any satirical intent. Kunda writes:

> Members evaluate each other on their ability to express embracement and distancing and to know when to stop. By structuring and defining as playful those occasions when commonsense alternatives to the formal ideology are pronounced . . . real dissent is preempted. Moreover, a particular kind of communitas between members is fostered . . . the communions of self-aware and talented actors commenting on their roles and performances . . . . Consequently, within the very broad boundaries delineated by those incidents where deviance is openly suppressed, contradicting or escaping an adherence to normative demands is often difficult if not impossible. Participants become mired ever deeper in a paradoxical normative trap within which whatever one does, thinks or feels can be – and often is – interpreted as confirmation of ideological reality claims. (Kunda, 1995, 158)

But if we examine this complex language closely, this is not an argument to the effect that disagreement and joking are accepted to such a degree that criticism has little power. There is an admission that extreme forms of dissent are sanctioned and suppressed. Hence it is not being claimed that there is no place that a critic can stand, but that the expression of criticism is limited – often voluntarily – and the motivations of critics are ambivalent. It is interesting and significant that, as with Dilbert, common sense is opposed as the obvious alternative to managerial ideas and policies. Thus, one ingredient of effective satire is present – a contrast between managerial policy and other standards and ideas about good or reasonable practice. But there is no disguising the fact that another crucial requirement for satire is absent. This is the uncompromising opposition of the critic. The engineers at 'Tech' and similar establishments have their ideological commitment to criticism fatally blunted by their acceptance of the salary and the promises of preferment which are main rewards of employment for the middle class.

For the majority of the working population, as opposed to the well-paid and reasonably secure consultant or engineer working at 'Tech' and similar organizations, satire is likely to hold more appeal. For those whose pay is low, whose promise of promotion remote or non-existent, or whose dependency on managerial preferment limited, the corrosive bite of satire is likely to have more appeal. The continuous testing of the claims and promises of managers, which cannot be fulfilled, actually leads to widening of the differences between employers and employees, not their diminishment. In the final chapter of this book we will directly criticize those who have argued that the present policy of managers, which attempts to incorporate employees by controlling their sentiments and beliefs, is effective. We think it does not work in the manner that it is expected to; and indeed, because of the vigour of the counter-culture in organizations, actually has little prospect of success. Realistic consideration of joking behaviour against the background of the history and sociology of misbehaviour indicates why this is so. The vitality of joking at the expense of managers indicates a continued recognition of the differences of the interests of employers and employees. It is also a measure of the distance between them.

6 Ruling Passions: Sexual Misconduct at Work

> The ruling passion, be it what it will
> The ruling passion conquers reason still.
>
> Alexander Pope, 'Moral Essays', III

This chapter is about sexual misbehaviour, 'mating manoeuvres on company time', as Roy (1974, 44) memorably described it in one of the few early studies. For such phenomena to be identified and discussed, sexuality has to be seen as part of organizational life. From the frequency with which office politics is intertwined with sexual politics in a variety of high profile court cases, it would appear that it is. A recent case of a Royal Navy officer, who wore novelty musical underpants (which played 'Jingle Bells') and who chased a teenage Wren around a warship while wearing a Santa Claus hat, made the headlines. He was cleared of eight charges of sexual harassment, but found guilty of 'conduct prejudicial to good order and naval discipline' ... 'by engaging in a sexually explicit conversation with a female rating during an anti-submarine warfare exercise' (*Guardian*, 10 January 1998). The court also heard that sexual banter and bawdy humour were commonplace. This echoed a previous case where an industrial tribunal heard that a regional branch of the Child Support Agency in the Midlands was described as a 'hotbed of sexual activity'.

Yet such activity has created few academic ripples. Traditionally, sex has reared its head mostly in terms of its relevance to the division of labour: the sex structuring of the workforce (Mills and Tancred, 1992, 16). *Organizational* sexuality appears to be a contradiction in terms, except for a specialist sub-group of sexual organizations. A similar absence can be noted in industrial sociology: 'Sex is a commonly overlooked aspect of informal social organization in the lower reaches of factory life' (Roy, 1974, 44). On the surface this is strange because we know that the workplace is a site of romantic and sexual contact, if only because of the oft-quoted surveys showing that this is where most affairs start and that it is where a sizeable minority of people meet their partners (Hearn and Parkin, 1987, 14).

But is this just incidental – the private crossing the path of the public? For we are also told that organization man is dedicated to the job, embracing the rational and excluding the personal. It does not appear to be a concern for managers. The Institute of Personnel Managers claims to get more requests for advice on how to deal with substance abuse than workplace romance (*Independent*, 4 September 1993). As we shall see later, this may be changing.

But what *do* we know? Our problem is that there is a distinct shortage of empirical data on sex at work. Before the recent spate of contributions, and overlooking for the moment the neglected piece by Roy, 'Coping with Cupid' by Robert Quinn was one of the few sources of information, he managed to make it unintelligible in the characteristic style of organization behaviour – 'The organizational romance is perceived as an exchange or transaction between two people' (1977, 44). Despite the increased recent attention, ethnographic, empirical case studies are rare. What we do have is an emergent debate, which this chapter draws on, about the importance of sexual misconduct as an emerging form of misbehaviour.

Organizational analysis and sexuality

As much contemporary writing has shown, the idea of sexless organizations is compatible with the dominant reading of Weber's analysis of the rise of bureaucracy and instrumental rationality: 'Organization theory portrayed organizations as formal hierarchies with definable rules and procedures, peopled by employees who were not only without gender identity but also devoid of sexuality, a bundle of only specifiable functions and skills' (Cockburn, 1991, 147). Sexuality is seen as part of what is or should be a private realm. In fact any tainting of rational-legal authority by what Weber called patrimonial privileges is tantamount to misbehaviour; hence the traditional rules in many organizations barring someone being in a position of authority over anyone to whom they are married or with whom they have other close personal ties. Organization man becomes the bearer of rationality, with women sometimes excluded from jobs on the basis of their supposed emotional nature (Ramsay and Parker, 1992). But both sexes are ultimately implicated because emotions are dangerous to efficiency and people in love irrational. Or as an article on managing romance put it, 'At the beginning of an affair, a woman, like a man, is in a state of heightened sensual awareness, loses critical faculties, and almost willingly gives up judgement and reason' (Collins, 1983, 148). Furthermore, the suppression of the libido through the desexualization of labour has been a necessary precondition of goal-directed behaviour and profitable production (Burrell, 1992). For all their emphasis on informal organization and the 'human factor', this feature of classical theory has not, despite appearances, been challenged by the human relations tradition.

In fact some contemporary organizational writers, including liberal feminists such as Kanter (1977), are keen to extend the Weberian framework by presenting manifestations of sex and gender such as the boss–secretary relationship and managers obsessed with masculinity and potency as surviving relics of patrimony and personal relations. Redistribute power by making bureaucracies truly rational and sexuality will disappear, perhaps to be replaced by the androgynous organization in which masculine and

I was told to wear more make-up and shorten my skirt. I was horrified. This was from a male assistant director. He was genuinely trying to help. He didn't actually say 'look sexier', but the role model he picked was astonishing: the kind of person who sat so you could see her stocking tops. Sort of Sharon Stone with knickers . . . .' Kate is not a model or an actress, but a banker . . . . She never thought her looks were relevant: bright and direct, she is more Jodie Foster than Sharon Stone. She has now moved jobs to become an analyst with an American investment bank. There, she finds male colleagues more respectful, but reports that for women in the firm, appearance still counts.

For women, starting to work in the City can be very similar to boarding at a boys' school . . . they can expect to be wolf-whistled, jeered and marked out of 10 on their looks and dress on the trading floor. 'My first day on the dealing floor', Harriet remembers, 'I was told all the traders thought I was a stupid bimbo because I had long blonde hair . . . . At first, I was reduced to tears most days'. In fact she got away comparatively lightly. 'Apparently a girl at an American bank was called a cunt for her first six months on a dealing floor and nothing else'. Among City men, opinion seems divided. David, for example, a 24-year-old money market dealer, was genuinely nonplussed by tales of rampant chauvinism. 'You wouldn't get that here', he said. 'You get a lot of dealing room banter, but if anything, it falls less heavily on the women' . . . . But when pressed, he conceded that: 'The dealing room only invites a certain type of woman: they have to have passed the test on both looks and character'. (Rosanna de Lisle on 'Women in the City', *Independent on Sunday*, 13 February 1982)

feminine styles can be blended in balanced coexistence (Sargent, 1983). In this sense some feminists have seen organizations as 'over-sexualized' and women workers as benefiting from organizational arrangements where what matters is skill and ability – a non-sexual meritocracy. This has been heavily criticized by more radical writers (Witz and Savage, 1992; Pringle, 1988) for the naive belief that structurally embedded gender relations can so easily be set aside. In fact, for Pringle, the boss–secretary relationship is not marginal but paradigmatic of contemporary organizational power in which male-defined sexuality underpins bureaucratic control.

The theoretical trend is therefore towards a rediscovery of sexuality. According to Witz and Savage (1992) this rediscovery takes two main forms. Some (e.g. Burrell) want to 'add on' an account of organizational sexuality; accepting that instrumental rationality has been dominant, but wanting to reveal a pervasive sexual 'underlife'. This is additionally dubbed 're-eroticizing the organization' by Brewis and Grey (1994) on the grounds that Burrell wants to encourage sexuality and eroticism in order to subvert relations of power and managerialist attempts to assimilate the pleasure principle. Others (e.g. Hearn and Parkin, Pringle) want to 'add in' an analysis by projecting a view that 'sexuality is everywhere', a fundamental structuring principle of organizational life reproduced in physical displays, verbal exchanges and social relations. The latter perspective parallels and draws from a Foucauldian analysis of power, because by revealing one – by making it visible – you reveal the other. Indeed the concentration of goods and services in large corporations created new public patriarchies, 'new hierarchies for men to occupy and new sites for the formation of public masculinities' (Hearn, 1992, 98). But regardless of the entry point, the effect is similar: the reality of a male-dominated organizational sexuality is uncovered.

Even in supposedly 'desexualized' organizations the rules are still made by men, as Sheppard illustrates in her study of how women managers have to constantly manage their appearance and behaviour in order to achieve a credible status fit. 'Blending in' is the most frequently used strategy and must be carefully exercised in order not to appear threateningly assertive: 'One woman described in considerable detail how she has learned to change her body language when doing presentations to groups of men so that she no longer paces, uses a pointer or puts her hands in her skirt or pocket (all of which she cites as characteristic of men and as connoting personal authority)' (1989, 149). Other evidence shows that men in authority offer job 'favours' in return for sex and that women are the most likely to be removed if relationships go wrong or create problems for management (Gutek, 1985; Collins, 1983; Cockburn, 1991); that women managers and power holders constitute threats to male sexual self-image (Sargent, 1983). A good worker who fails to conform to ascribed femininity may be perceived as sexually suspect (Breakwell, 1986, 71) and the 'bad woman' accused of sleeping her way to the top (Collinson and Collinson, 1989). Much of male power is unspoken, but can be identified in the sexually saturated language of business: markets are penetrated, policies thrust and the outcomes of competitive struggles are seen in terms of people being fucked or screwed, of being wankers or wimps (Hearn and Parkin, 1987, 147–8). The biggest insult one worker could think of for colleagues who have bought the company's strong culture was that they would 'bust their balls' (Kunda, 1995, 2). A report to a Women and Psychology conference documented the treatment of female employees on the dealing floor in the city (Brooks-Gordon, 1995). Women were divided by their male colleagues along a spectrum of 'babes', 'mums', 'lesbians', 'dragons' and 'one-of-the-boys'.

A further route to the discovery of organizational sexuality has been the literature on emotional labour which details the bureaucratization of feelings in service and other occupations (Fineman, 1993; Taylor, 1998), which was stimulated by Hochschild's (1983) pioneering study. Drawing primarily on the experience of flight attendants, she showed how corporate social engineering was leading to demands on employees to manage their feelings to enhance the 'quality' of the service encounter. While this process was by no means confined to sexuality, where women were concerned a crucial dimension of visual display and projection of personality involves eroticizing the task; a trend confirmed in other studies discussed in this chapter (Filby, 1992; Adkins, 1992).

Where does this leave sexual misbehaviour?

If we accept that sexual behaviour at work is extensive, what would sexual misbehaviour consist of? In some ways the misbehaviour in previous chapters can be seen as an expression of opposing or contrasting rationalities, with employee attempts to appropriate time and product frequently clashing with managerial efforts to specify work performance. This is also a useful way of understanding the issues in this chapter. Sexuality is a central means of shaping and affirming our identities, and masculinity and femininity are affirmed in part through workplace rituals and practices which can, like other forms of misbehaviour, disrupt the industrial order and pose problems for management. Some central participants in the debate (Hearn, 1985; Hearn and Parkin, 1987) try to make such links, arguing that sexuality and emotions are also alienated and objectified in capitalist work relations. Lack of control in the labour process is therefore the backcloth to responses as varied as mutual sexuality which 'cocks a snook' at authoritarian work regimes, pornography as an escape from boredom and expressive macho behaviour compensating for redundant skills or jobs; while even harassment can be seen as a means by which workers seek to create a perverse form of human contact.

Not surprisingly these arguments have come in for some fierce criticism. Adkins (1992) rightly observes that Hearn and Parkin work within a framework that can only explain sexuality and male sexual misbehaviour as a product of capitalism, to say nothing of the strange argument that apparently it is only men that suffer from and react to alienation. Like most writers in this field Adkins sees sexuality and identity less in terms of relations between labour and capital, than as an expression of the primacy of gendered power. More mainstream feminist research tends to support this view. The concept of 'sex role spillover' is used by Gutek (1985) and others to reinforce this argument and explain the pattern of workplace sexuality. She argues that expectations arising from the female role of subordinate sex object and male role of dominant aggressor are carried into work. Cockburn (1991, 143) notes one aspect of this process: 'Men's power in the extra-organizational world, in the family, the state and civil society, enters the workplace with them and gives even the most junior man a degree of sexual authority relative even to senior women.' Once this point has been recognized, it becomes impossible to operate with the concept of separate public and private spheres.

In general theory and empirical study, sexual misbehaviour is thus primarily about what men do to women and is constructed around the object of sexual harassment. Indeed, 'the issue of sexuality in the workplace became visible and was brought to public attention in the form of sexual harassment' (Gutek, 1985, 5). This emphasis on the 'negative' side of sexual misbehaviour is supported by reference to the considerable body of survey evidence showing the extent of such activity (TUCRIC, 1983; Gutek, 1985; Robertson et al., 1988; Di Tomaso, 1989; IRS, 1992). Though the quality of the information and numbers of people reporting a problem varies, definitions differ and the range of practices, from cleavage gazing to assault, is immense, there can be no doubt that harassment constitutes a serious potential work hazard for women. Harassment is just an aspect of a wider set of individual and collective male 'power plays' designed for or having the effect of making life uncomfortable for women and keeping them in their 'proper' subordinate place (Di Tomaso, 1989, 72). The relationship to power is indicated by research that demonstrates that the subject of harassment is more likely to be young and unmarried (Stockdale, 1996), or a temporary worker (Rogers and Henson, 1997).

This emphasis is important but becomes distorted when such practices are held to be the norm of male–female relationships. Some commentators promote the view that it is impossible to separate out a discrete area of special or specific behaviour, quoting with approval respondents who, for example, retrospectively redefine all their previous sexual interactions as harassment (Thomas and Kitzinger, 1994, 155). Stanko argues that 'Most harassers are not behaving in "aberrant ways", but in a manner typical of men's treatment of women in a heterosexual encounter' (1988, 99). This is a version of the widely held view that organizations are governed by a compulsory heterosexuality in which non-coercive relations are impossible and which squeeze out any other form of sexuality (MacKinnon, 1979; Adkins, 1992). For Ramazanoglu, 'The exercise and experience of violence in academic life is part of the general need for men to control women' (1987, 64). She asks rhetorically how many academic men have had their knee patted while discussing departmental affairs or had the size and desirability of their bottom publicly discussed by colleagues. Such arguments construct a version of organizational life in which men and women have entirely different sexual experiences. Using her research into the UK tourist industry, Adkins claims that because looking good and acting nicely was part of the job for women but not for men in the leisure park and hotel, the two groups, 'participated in different relations of production . . . women did sexual work and men did not' (1992, 226).

From this perspective, there is little or no space for jointly created, consensual sexual misbehaviour by men and women. Gutek admits that, 'There is little systematic description of non-harassing sexual behaviour at work' (1989, 57). This absence is recognized and remedied empirically by other contributors to the debate. Influenced by post-structuralist perspectives, Pringle's study of secretaries locates sexuality as a more complex phenomenon. Just as power is everywhere, so is sexuality; and such activity is constituted in a relational manner with women as active subjects, as resisters. Using her material, which we shall return to later, she argues that, 'It is by no means clear that women are yanked screaming into compulsory heterosexuality. Most actively seek it out and find pleasure in it' (1988, 95). Office humour uses parody to imitate, exaggerate and ridicule existing stereotypes. 'Talking back' was also a big feature of women employed in the betting shops studied by Filby (1992). Though pressured into using their sexuality to sell the service, the women responded with joking and scolding routines replete with outrageous sexual references. Reflecting on her case studies of equal opportunity policies, Cockburn supports the argument that women can and must seek out their own paths to pleasure at work: 'What needs to change is not the sexiness of women but the vulnerability of women' (1991, 159). Such themes have affinities with the critique made by a new generation of 'victim feminism'. Naomi Wolf comments that 'power feminism' is 'unapologetically sexual; understands that good pleasures make good politics' (1993, 149).

Arguments that heterosexuality is potentially negotiable and pleasurable and that opposition to harassment is only a component of workplace sexual politics have produced a predictably critical response from those pursuing a radical feminist agenda (see Adkins, 1992, 210–13). But the critique of workplace sexuality simply as compulsion is surely correct. The latter view leads inexorably to treating women as victims or passive objects, Yet that is quite unlike real life, where women are more assertive and confident sexually and do not spend all their time confronting masculinity (Segal, 1987, 153–4). To return to Ramazanoglu's rhetorical question: anyone who has not experienced women (academic and otherwise) discussing men's bottoms and other bits of their anatomy has led a very sheltered life. Though women are constructed as 'theoretical' victims the practice is often revealed to be different in their own studies. For example, Adkins notes that 'women *enjoyed* some of their sexualised interactions with men and found the rest annoying rather than threatening' (1992, 224; original emphasis). Such contrary findings are often either ignored, treated as a form of false consciousness, or attributed to the effect of 'structural mechanisms'. The latter is a handy catch-all category. Ramazanoglu manages to implicate male academia in violence because violence is defined as any action or structure that diminishes another human being (1987, 65). Alternatively, when no evidence of harassment is reported, it may be assumed to take place anyway (Di Tomaso, 1989, 81).

There is a need for a multi-dimensional explanation of organizational sexuality; one that can identify the negative and positive practices, the differences and similarities between and within the experiences of women and men. Treating men as a 'universal world gender class' (Hearn, 1992, 229) simply sets up a sophisticated form of guilt by association where what matters is not individual men's participation in coercive sexuality, but that the reservoir of practices is available for all (Hearn and Parkin, 1987, 95), that all benefit (Ramazanoglu, 1987, 73) or that few intervene to stop it (Stanko, 1988, 97). It is important that no occupation or relationship, such as boss–secretary, is regarded as 'paradigmatic'. Reading much of the literature it sometimes feels as if the organizational world is populated primarily by cocktail waitresses and their sex-crazed customers. We need an account of the full range of occupations, rather than an over-emphasis on the more sexualized sphere of personal services, despite the previously discussed insights on emotional labour.

If we can break out of the straitjacket of one-dimensional conceptions of sexual behaviour and misbehaviour, we can understand the latter more effectively. In their earlier work Burrell, and Hearn and Parkin were right to try to make links between the capitalist labour process and sexual misbehaviour. Unfortunately the latter undermined their own case by failing to disentangle the complex elements which shape and comprise workplace sexuality and compounded the error by overlaying their analysis with clumsy attempts to apply Marxist terminology, notably the awful women as 'a reserve of sexual labour' (1987, 85). However, Burrell is subject to some odd criticism from Brewis and Grey who, without any apparent reason, extend the territory of re-eroticizing the organization to sado-masochistic practices: 'the celebration of violent eroticism has the potential to legitimate the distinctly unplayful use of the apparatus of torture: the power drill, electric cattle prod and scalpel which can be the real life counterparts to postmodern irony' (1994, 81). Writing about sex is clearly a dangerous activity in its own right.

In practice, the complex influences which derive from capitalist, patriarchal and other social relations produce varied effects. One stream, for which there is considerable evidence, some of which we will examine later, is that masculinities and femininities are means through which employees respond to workplace realities and changes. A recurrent vehicle is the homosocial ritual. Though often defined in terms of seeking out and preferring the company of the same sex (Morgan, 1981, 102), the practice is relational and frequently concerned with defending identity and territory; 'Masculine identity attempts to drive out the feminine but does not exist without it' (Pringle, 1988, 89). A recent study of gender subcultures in a Japanese assembly plant in the US utilizes the concept of sex games in which male

---

Harry spoke of the night that Ed had stayed out without going home at all. He was with one of the girls from the plant and went back to work with her for the three o'clock shift. His wife was alarmed in the morning and called Harry's wife. Harry had tried to cover up for Ed by saying that he probably had to work overtime, but Mrs Grover phoned the plant to find out that Ed did not work overtime . . . .

Harry spoke of Ed's interest in feeling the girl's legs after he had had a beer or two. Hank spoke of the way Ed's mouth used to be smeared with lipstick by morning after a night of drinking. Hank told with a laugh of the time Ed got sore at him when he [Ed] was kissing a girl in the booth while Hank was running his hand up and down her leg.

Roger's behaviour next came up for discussion, and comments were made on his crudeness in asking a girl for sexual favours as soon as the group sat down to drink . . . Hank told of the time that he was with Roger in the Grill, and the blonde feeder walked out on Roger at the start of the evening . . . Roger swore he hadn't said anything out of the way . . . Hank said he knew better than that; he knew that Roger had insulted her . . . Harry remarked that girls expected a few drinks before you started to get familiar and that even then the matter could be handled more politely.

Hank remarked that he had never seen such a place where the girls went for the fellows like they did at Finished Board. He made the comment that everyone was 'fixed up' with a girl there but Chuck Dashiell. (excerpt from field notes showing two workers discussing the activities of fellow 'oldsters', Ed and Roger: Roy, 1974, 53–4)

and female workers 'adopt different social rituals to constitute their gender identities' (Gottfried and Graham, 1993, 615).

While the practices and their meaning are less innovatory than the latter authors believe, the concept is useful because it calls attention to the informal rules and internal logics which structure interactions. We have already referred to sexual harassment as power plays. But if heterosexuality is not always compulsion, then the workplace can be seen also as a site of love, lust, affection and romantic friendship, a point made in a different context by Burrell (1992, 77). We can therefore refer to a final set of games and associated misbehaviour that returns us to our opening sentence about mating manoeuvres on company time. For these games can be seen as a form of 'making out' which appropriates time and identity. With respect to the former, Pringle noted that, 'It is undoubtedly true that for both men and women sexual fantasies and interactions are a way of killing time, of giving a sense of adventure, of livening up an otherwise boring day' (1988, 90). Whether it be the fiddling of flexitime by secretive lovers noted by Collinson and Collinson (1989), the long lunches taken as part of courtship rituals, or the regular flirtations where employees can practise their own form of safe sex; it adds up to a lot of time not working. Or as a co-researcher of Roy commented, 'it looks like all they make in that factory is each other' (1974, 48).

As for the latter, sexual encounters affirm desirability and reinforce key aspects of the varied identities that employees carry with them from the private to the public sphere. But in different ways, all the forms of sex games we have referred to are concerned to appropriate identity and the associated practices may bring them into conflict with managerial attempts to regulate the workplace as a public sphere. None of the sex games are new. Roy's unique account of sex in a 1950s American factory observes that, 'The factory provides a place for working class people to meet each other, to develop ties of friendship or courtship' (1974, 53). But social changes have opened up the space for an increased range of making-out behaviour.

Workers' playtime: realigning the public and private

As one study noted, 'organizational life has not always been known for its close personal relations' (Collins, 1983, 142). In fact it is widely recognized (Walby, 1986; Hearn, 1992) that in the nineteenth century the workplace was structured so as to segregate, marginalize and suppress sexuality. Prominent instances include the moral panics concerning sexual contact in mixed workplaces. Though the most publicized site of controversy about possible promiscuous sexual contact was the mines, concern about this issue led to the exclusion of women (and children) from many types of employment through the Factory Acts and other industrial legislation. The imagery of weak-willed women falling prey to the uncontrollable urges of men was applied to office and white collar work. One employer told a government commission, 'No doubt there are dangers, in a moral point of view, in having the two sexes working together. We however are always on the spot ourselves and see that all is right' (quoted in Cockburn, 1983, 184). The best that could be said of mixed workplaces was that they may have had a civilizing effect on men, a curious echo of a current argument against single-sex education. More contemporary rhetoric, marshalled to rationalize the exclusion of women from the military in the US, also trades on images of woman the temptress who will distract men by her presence and divert them from their instrumental duties.

As the twentieth century progressed, extreme demarcation became more rare, but widespread practices such as the marriage bar minimized opportunities for interaction. Even in clerical work, where women were taking up jobs, grades, tasks and even supervisory responsibilities, they were in watertight compartments (Hearn, 1992, 158). With women rhetorically and practically assigned to the realm of the household, the public–private split appeared to be reinforced. Sex was not much encouraged in private and certainly not in the public sphere of organizations:

> Sexual respectability was considered very important in many office jobs like banking and insurance, and if there was any evidence of sexual misconduct a young man or woman's career prospects could be ruined. The police or vigilante patrols arrested people who became too amorous in public places. Social workers had the power to place 'promiscuous' girls in institutional care. (Humphries, 1988, 19)

However, we are returned to a recurrent problem – how much do we actually know about what was going on in the workplace? Too many of the above accounts were written with a distinct class bias concerning the deleterious consequences of unrestrained lower class sexuality, or by reformers and religious obsessives motivated by defence of the moral order.

First hand accounts are rare and a different picture can emerge. From interviews for the study *A Secret World of Sex*, Humphries shows that the workplace was often a finishing school for sex education. Admittedly, the initiation ceremonies were alarming and the banter and teasing sometimes crude, but the factory and to a lesser extent the office 'provided a preferable alternative to the sexual secrecy of home and school' (1988, 62).

I went to work in the factory and there were loads of women there and me being the only boy there, one day they says to me, 'Go down the cellar and get something'. I went down and next thing they all jumped on me, got me down, got me trousers down, played with it, in fact I didn't know what was happening I thought I was in a new world. They all massaged me, about six of them give me a massage, and then that finished and they all painted it with black tar. I went home to my mother and I said to her, 'I don't like that factory'. And she said 'Why?' So I said, I couldn't tell what had happened, I said, 'The women swear'. So she said, 'Take no notice of them'. Really I was shocked because it was something that never happened to me before. And of course from then onwards I decided I would have my own back on women, which I did. (Bill Phillips talking about beginning work in an East End factory in the early 1920s: from Humphries, 1988, 61–2)

There are, of course, other discoveries of the 'hidden history' of work-place sexuality, notably Burrell's (1992) rightly celebrated article. It is indeed interesting to be informed that in the Middle Ages bishops received a punishment of eight years' fasting for fornicating with cattle; or about the inability of the authorities to eradicate sodomy in the navy and lesbianism in prisons. Burrell's preference for stories from and about total institutions is influenced by the unfortunate Foucauldian notion that all organizations resemble prisons; hence resistance can be found most where there is control and constraint. But there is a more widespread tendency for what little evidence there is to be skewed towards the old, the extreme and the exotic or marginal.

The sexual division of labour does, of course, still produce a substantial number of sex-segregated workplaces. But in the post-war period this has undergone long-term decline, with the major factor being the rise of the female employee. It is that trend and the associated increase in the social status of women which is identified as the trigger factor by the managerial literature that requires organizations to devote more attention to 'coping with Cupid' (Quinn, 1977, 30; Collins, 1983, 143; *Business Week*, 1984). Roy (1974, 48) observed in his case study that the tendency of the company to employ divorced or separated women and their shared membership of small workgroups with men was a major factor facilitating the formation of sexual alliances in the factory. This points to the simple role of opportunity in providing for a variety of forms of sexual misbehaviour in more occupations and organizational contexts. Large organizations in themselves provide a structural and spatial framework for increased proximity and contact which management cannot monitor and control as directly as in smaller firms. Proximity is mainly geographic and work related; though work includes business trips and social events as well as integration in the labour process itself. One large-scale study showed that, 'Affection for a co-worker of the opposite sex shows a systematic increase with the amount of work done jointly by the two sexes' (Haavio-Mannila, 1988, 33); with dentists, waiters, nurses, journalists, architects and police officers amongst the prominent occupations.

Such an interpretation is consistent with the evidence on patterns of sexual harassment. Gutek's authoritative survey indicates that whereas segregation leads to role spillover, men and women working together in equal numbers produces 'virtually no socio-sexual problems' (1985, xiii). The 'spillover' thesis has been criticized, in part for over-emphasizing the extent to which the sex ratio of an occupation is the key factor (Connell, 1987). Certainly harassment can become a problem in any circumstances where management encourages or legitimizes a hostile culture, as the mass lawsuit by female employees at the Mitsubishi car plant in Illinois indicates. But it does highlight the general issue that the intensity of harassment where women are breaking into non-traditional areas suggests that sexuality is a medium through which some men express perceived threats to their interests and identity (Cockburn, 1983; Livingstone and Luxton, 1989, Di

Tomaso, 1989), an issue to which we return in the next section. The demonstration of British 'navy wives' against the desegregation of shipboard command and facilities signifies that such threats may not be confined to men.

But integration is not the only factor, nor the only new tendency 'entering' the workplace from what was previously the private sphere. The phenomenon labelled 'organization man' necessitated the subsumption of personal identity into the corporate collectivity. As men became associated with the public sphere of work, their wives were vetted as guardians of the private (Roper, 1994). But as time passed, social and cultural changes led to greater employee investment in the personal sphere and a variety of 'private' identities. What is more important, many employees were determined to bring them into the organization, creating an exchange and overlap between organizational and social selves.

> Employees too, have personal needs they introduce into the workplace, despite the management. For many people, women and men, work is the main arena in which they are most 'in the public sphere', most feel themselves to be social, expect to meet new friends. (Cockburn, 1991, 151)

The decline (though certainly not elimination) of formal cultures, work role norms and even dress codes provide opportunities for sexually oriented interaction and display. Compare many modern workplaces with Snizek's endearing description of an older era: 'Should a worker attempt to work while smartly dressed, or in what are referred to as "street clothes", he is likely to be chided by fellow workers as perhaps having a heavy date after work, aspiring to enter management, or just being queer' (1974, 69). Recent reports show that managerial decisions to allow casual dress have led to everything from jeans to leggings and skimpy tops. As a result, 'Managers are sometimes forced to act as clothing police, a role that many do not enjoy' (*Financial Times*, 22 January 1997).

In some senses such changes are only organizational reflections of much broader social and cultural transformations. Giddens has argued that sexuality has become more 'plastic' and decentred, freed from reproduction. In turn this helps to diminish the connection of sexuality with male needs and definitions: 'The claiming of female sexual pleasure came to form a basic part of the reconstitution of intimacy, an emancipation as important as any sought after in the public domain' (1992, 178).

Intimacy is not just a question of a narrow physical sexuality. It also speaks to the partial release of romantic love and friendship from the bonds of marriage and motherhood. While Giddens does not seek to extend his analysis to the organizational sphere, we would argue that such developments have helped to open up the workplace as a 'playground' and to encourage greater conviviality. Nevertheless, the playing of sex games, as we indicated earlier, has negative and positive dimensions. This transformation of intimacy is a process managed by women and one in which many men benefit – for example through the construction of close female friendships – but declining male control of sexuality inside and outside of work 'also generates a rising tide of male violence towards women' (Giddens, 1992, 3).

In this section we have staked out a theoretical position that attempts to understand the multi-dimensional and often contradictory character of sexual misbehaviour as it is shaped by changing boundaries between public and private. With this framework in mind, we now want to examine some of the best empirical studies of the workplace. Such studies have seldom been motivated by a desire to uncover sexuality and sexual misbehaviour, but they have found it anyway and revealed in doing so its contradictory character.

Masculinities/femininities

It is said that workplace studies were, until recently, dominated by the 'three Ms' – male, manufacturing and manual workers. In most senses the first of these – maleness – was largely taken for granted. The older tradition of industrial sociology (Roy, 1952; Lupton, 1963), as we saw in Chapter 2, was dominated by the problematic of output restriction; and even where work-shop behaviour of women diverged sharply from that of men, as with Lupton's study, he was determined to use any explanation but gender to account for the difference. While the tensions between male and female workers did occasionally surface in later, radical accounts of the frontier of control (Beynon, 1975; Nichols and Armstrong, 1976), they remained mar-ginal to the main story.

In part, such emphases reflected the legacy of separate spheres, if not work and home, then at least separate workgroups. In such homosocial set-tings, 'working class masculinities can be seen as valuing such practices as group solidarity with other men, physical toughness, resistance to both auth-ority and danger, and facility with machines' (Hearn, 1992, 164). But differ-ent emphases also reflect what writers are looking at and for. It took Willis's (1977) famous study of the transition from school to work to bring out more adequately the role of masculinity and sexual identity in positively affirm-ing the conditions of (manual) labour power and differentiating it from the work of 'effeminate' pen pushers. This is a theme picked up later by David Collinson, who quotes one worker as saying: 'fellas on the shop floor are genuine. They're the salt of the earth, but they're all twats and nancy boys in th'offices' (Collinson, 1992, 135).

Sexuality and specific patterns of misbehaviour are pertinent to men's 'lifelong wrestling match with the experience of wage labour' (O'Connell, 1983, 31). It is present, as we have seen, in perceptions of the nature of work itself. This has been best captured in Cockburn's brilliant study of print-workers beset by new technology, aggressive employers, and not least by potential female competitors. The entry of women onto their territory is held to spoil the job: 'Some of the shine would go right out of the job for me. Prestige might not exactly be the right word, but it carries what is known

Within the all-male environment of the Components Division, masculine sexual prowess is a pervasive topic. Mediated through bravado and joking relations, a stereotypical image of self, which is assertive, independent and powerful and sexually insatiable is constructed, protected and embellished. By contrast women are dismissed as passive, dependent and only interested in men.

Photos of female nudes could be found on most of the shop floor walls in the division. Many of these had been supplied by the 'Porn King' who maintained a large 'sex library' of magazines for shop floor edification. In addition, proud boasts and comments such as the following were part of the daily fabric of shop floor interaction.

'Men come from the womb and spend the rest of their lives trying to get back in. You'll never win with women because they're sitting on a goldmine. They'll always have the power. At school I was very shy. I went red if girls talked to me. If they talk to me now. I'll shag them' . . . . [Boris] maintained a 'sex diary' that listed all his past 'conquests'. Concerned to 'trap' females, Boris graded out of ten the 'performance' of his twenty 'victims' . . . . Boris proudly boasted of his escapades and the 'carpet burns on my knees'. His exaggerated accounts of sexual exploits were received with disbelief and ridicule on the shop floor. A recurrent comment by Ernie was, 'He's a Don Juan is Boris. When he's had Juan he's Don!' (Collinson on life in a lorry-producing factory, 1992, 114)

as a macho bit, composing' (1983, 180). This sense of pollution of the 'purity' of masculine work can be found in other enclaves such as the fire service, where the entry of women is felt to disturb the intimacy of the group precisely because of the 'strangeness' of their sexuality (Salaman, 1986). The continuous stream of sexual harassment cases in different regional police forces in the UK illustrates this point. Research has shown that a recurring theme of policing is its emphasis on physicality and masculinity, which is challenged by the promotion of equal opportunity policies (Keith and Collinson, 1994a, 1994b). Misbehaviour by such homosocial groups is then characterized by rituals and practices which construct the work environment and discipline both sexes in the name of masculinity.

Masculinity is not just expressed through language and in the environment of organizations. Joking rituals, pranks and 'horseplay' are the most pervasive forms of sexual misbehaviour. Case studies report car workers having daily races accompanied by boasting about respective performances (Gottfried and Graham, 1993, 619); or quasi-sexual and explicitly sexual assaults among slaughtermen (Ackroyd and Crowdy, 1990). The latter is typical of horseplay manifested through physical contact between men. While it is possible to see this in terms of a homosexual subtext, it is more likely to reflect the assertion of male sexual prowess in the most easily available form (Hearn, 1985, 125). This demonstrates that we are not talking here of male behaviour or male sexuality 'in general', but most often in specifically homosocial contexts. Though masculinity is put on public display as a counterpoint to femininity, it draws strength from the absence of or separation from women: 'Men are not men in the company of women', as Cockburn quotes one printworker (1983, 189). Where roles overlap there is more room for some men to dissent, as the same author shows in a service or office context (1991, 146).

The social construction of femininity has long been seen as more central to female wage labour, particularly since the deservedly influential studies of women factory workers by Pollert (1981), Cavendish (1982) and West-wood (1984). Given the existing division of labour and power, 'Factory politics is also sexual politics' (Pollert, 1981, 21). One of the consequences is that female workplace behaviour is, in part, conditioned by those public displays of masculinity outlined above. While women managers may feel constrained to blend in through desexualization (Sheppard, 1989), lower down the ladder a recurrent response has been to use femininity to take men on at their own game. Studies of office (Pringle, 1988), service (Filby, 1992; Adkins, 1992) and factory workers (Gottfried and Graham, 1993) demonstrate that women engage in discursive practices – 'sexy chat' – that respond and set limits to banter, and reappropriate derogatory language or sexual innuendo.

Gottfried and Graham distinguish between 'gossip' which uses shared knowledge to solidify informal networks and 'bitching' which is mobilized against a target. A particularly good example of the latter is the 'scolding routines' utilized by betting shop staff in Filby's study. Aggressive joking and ridicule put customers in their place and provided a running commentary and critique of male sexuality: 'Three or four of the older punters were regularly ridiculed for their alleged tendency to surreptitious masturbation. "I'll get Denise to rub it for you Fraser", was how a regular was brought to book on one occasion' (1992, 32).

But it would be wise to avoid seeing misbehaviour as something always defined by or reacting to men. Most studies report on work taking place in homosocial contexts, so the emphasis is inevitably on the distinctive characteristics of collective female cultures. The two most detailed shop floor studies from Pollert and Westwood show a remarkably similar picture. Some of the practices are the conventional responses to rules and control and the 'having a laff' common to factory workers everywhere. But, 'romance breathed life and energy into shop floor culture' (Westwood, 1984, 104). These 'dreams of escape' (Pollert, 1981, 101) may be a reaction to dead end jobs and boring work. The rituals of rings, wedding photos, fashion and flirtations in the canteen also appear to be conformist or just 'cutting-off'. But they can have their own disruptive effects, if for no other reason than that the skiving and celebrations of engagements, weddings, retirements and birthdays enable time to be appropriated and work discipline resisted. That, however, is not the only thing going on. Rituals of romance and female horseplay allow for the assertion of a positive, if contradictory, identity.

Nor is this behaviour necessarily new. Benson's historical account of US department store life describes similar work culture rituals, as well as more disruptive activities by saleswomen: 'Bosses constantly complained of high spirits and boisterous sociability in the departments, and did their

Julie's gymslip paled into respectability when it was confronted with Tessa's costume, described by Avril as 'a pornographic Andy Pandy suit'. Hands covered smiles, heads rolled and everyone stared at Tessa almost in disbelief before they burst into raucous laughter . . . . It was an oversize Babygro, a fairly loose fit on Tessa, with two large pink cloth breasts attached to the front and two hands appliquéd on the seat of the suit across Tessa's bottom . . . .

Dressed in these clothes the twins spent the morning touring the department and organising the collection and distribution of a large number of cakes, sweets, crisps and drinks. After we had been downstairs [to the large factory canteen] for the third time we settled into our canteen and laid out cakes and drinks for all the twins' friends who then came, unit by unit, to eat and chat, laugh and giggle at the way the twins were dressed and to make jokes about sexual adventures . . . .

[Julie and] Tessa were bundled into one of the large 'wheely baskets' normally used for moving work or scraps around the factory. Michelle, Jo, Lisa and others then pushed the basket at increasing speeds around the department between the machines, around the press, up and down the gangways, amid shrieks of delight from the rest of the department who threw scraps and pieces of paper into the basket onto the screaming twins who looked terrified.

Everyone was now exhausted and most sat down heavily with coffee or tea and a fag. Before anyone had time to light up, we were faced with a group of visitors – men in grey suits who looked stunned at the sight of this female debris littered round the coffee machines.

(Pre-marriage rituals at 'Stitcho', from Westwood, 1984, 113–17)

unsuccessful best to stamp out loud laughing, talking, singing, and horse-play' (1992, 176). In this and other studies, collectivity in work is sustained and enhanced by homosociability outside in the form of outings after work and at the weekend, and close neighbourhood ties: 'The stronger their all-female out-of-work ties, the more collective-spirited, self-assured, assertive and "non-conformist" were the girls at work' (Pollert, 1981, 148).

We have put the emphasis on the preponderance of homosociability in underpinning sex games, reflecting the limited integration in traditional sectors. Even here there are differences between the sexes. While both are conditioned by the same power relations, 'femininity games' appear to be more convivial, whereas many of the masculine equivalents are defensive and reflect the fear of traditional dominance and identities being undermined.

Resistance and transgression

The kind of rituals discussed above, like all forms of sexual misbehaviour, are likely to have 'a multiplicity of meanings and qualities' (Hearn and Parkin, 1987, 99). For example, Collinson rightly notes the double-edged nature of shop floor humour: 'specific masculinities often crucially shaped acts of shop floor resistance (against managers) and discipline (over women and other men)' (1992, 34). It is important, therefore, not to over-burden them with romantic, unrealistic or inappropriate expectations. Yet that is what frequently happens in the literature. Sex games are judged against a model of resistance and found wanting. This parallels the course of Chapter 2 and employee recalcitrance more generally, except that the practices are expected less to be the 'class struggle in miniature' than the gender war by any other name.

Westwood and Pollert are consistently disappointed at the limits to the actions of the women they studied and shared experiences with. For Pollert (1981, 21, 143–5), the use of femininity as a weapon is 'pernicious' because it is complicit with the language of control, diverts attention from the need to organize collectively and takes the sting out of conflicts. Westwood (1984, 6, 231) finds that though an oppositional culture, shop floor feminism sub-verts the real potential to challenge the conditions of work and reproduces an oppressive version of womanhood. Pringle (1988, 103, 92) affirms the pleasure derived from imitation and inversion of secretarial stereotypes and rejects the imagery of victims of men and stooges of management, but bemoans the fact that the 'interventions' may be merely letting off steam and that the substitution of parody for political strategy is a regressive move. It can only be designated as 'resistance' (the author's inverted commas) by borrowing some impenetrable waffle from Foucault on a 'plurality of resis-tances'.

The appropriation of identity and time through sex games does, of course, bring women and men up against organizational authority. But we cannot keep on constructing resistance as the only *alter ego* of rules. If games are reconceived as misbehaviour a large burden is lifted and we can see their capacity to transgress and undermine established norms, even when not resisting and fundamentally opposing them. No matter how such behaviour is designated, it can clearly cause management a headache. Our final section examines how the participants in organizations attempt to regulate differ-ent forms of sexual misbehaviour.

Regulating sexuality

Our previous discussions have ranged over a disparate group of practices, from office romances to homosocial rituals, that are not unified merely by attaching sexuality, sexual misbehaviour or any other label to them. Given that complexity, it is similarly impossible to conceive of any cohesive 'rules of regulation'. We can, however, make some preliminary observations.

Contrary to Burrell's view that eradication or containment is a prime managerial concern and that 'sexuality and labour power are not compatible' (1992, 90), sexual misbehaviour often lubricates the wheels of organizational life. The widespread evidence (Collinson and Collinson, 1989, 98) of mana-gerial tolerance or accommodation to some practices may be linked to its own nature. For management is not a socially neutral category and its responses cannot be unaffected by the fact that it is largely male. It is also worth treating the process of management in a complex way. Organizations come under a variety of types of pressure to regulate sexual misbehaviour, in part because of the diversity of practices. Recent years have seen attempts from sections of employees at 'self-management', in the form of demands for disciplinary procedures or codes of behaviour to deal with harassment or indeed consensual contacts. More broadly, the attitude of co-workers will depend on the circumstances. Gutek's (1985) authoritative survey shows that most employees do not regard workplace sexuality as a serious problem, particularly when it is horseplay or joking behaviour. They may also collude in romances by covering up or turning a blind eye to the colleagues' activities. The reaction is likely to depend on whether the misbehaviour disrupts or threatens the 'organizational web' which structures everyday interaction. For example, studies (Collins, 1983, 147; *Business Week*, 1984, 63) show that members of workgroups often fear that 'pillow talk' will distort formal and informal lines of communication. The same point applies to management itself, except that the vulnerability of the 'web' depends more explicitly on the question of power. Such managerial literature also demonstrates an obsession with the breakdown of authority, happily admitting that this is the reason why it was women that 'got the bullet': 'Where sexual liaisons did arise at work, most male executives agreed that these relationships were only for sexual gratification and that, if they threatened the organizational order, the woman should go' (Collins, 1983, 143).

To make any further general observations, we must divide the practices. The subsequent discussion distinguishes between transgressive, coercive and convivial categories.

Transgressive

This returns us to the widespread sex games, largely structured around horseplay and homosocial rituals, described earlier as subverting if not always resisting organizational order. Such practices are the most likely ones that male managers would 'turn a blind eye to' given the existing cultures of masculinity and the limited challenges from other sources in often sex-segregated contexts.

This does not explain why studies also show that management is largely tolerant of female horseplay. In the pre-wedding incident in Stitchco described earlier, the managing director, despite being embarrassed in front of visitors, made a show of 'joining in the fun': the ritual was too important and too deeply entrenched in shop floor culture to be outlawed (Westwood, 1984, 119). In fact, senior management only complained when health and safety issues were raised, particularly when women were tied to traffic lights or in the middle of the dual carriageway. Such attitudes may also be influenced by male managers not knowing how to act on 'female territory', or because the extent of disruption can be contained or localized. Management again may be implicated in the process. After all, if male

Some things have been noted by people that have been in the shop I have been told I have to put a stop to. One is what is called skylarking, messing about, singing, dancing, shouting, whatever you may do. Now I'm not trying to be a kill-joy but you have got to look at yourselves at work . . . and consider your opposite numbers whether they be building societies, banks, insurance offices or places like that . . . Do you go into a bank or building society and see them singing and dancing and chanting, messing about, hugging each other, kissing each other?

At this point the women staff began to protest variously that, 'the customers liked it'; the shop would lose punters if they cut out their performances; it was a happy shop; they were 'all actors'; and the customers expected it. The manager retreated somewhat in suggesting that they were only to moderate their behaviour not change completely:

You must have thought to yourselves sometimes . . . what I have just done may be a little over the top . . . now I have thought it and no doubt other people have thought it, but I can't say that I could sit up there every afternoon saying that everything you do is over the top, just sometimes, so just moderate it, that is all we are asking you to do. (Filby, 1992, 35)

bosses consistently use sexual banter with their administrative staff, restraint can be difficult if the process develops a life of its own. Filby's case study of betting shops provides a good example. Implicitly encouraged by management as part of attracting customers, women had developed a number of 'routines': joking, scolding and 'periodic embraces and kisses with varying degrees of drama' (1992, 35). He argues that this posed problems in terms of control of sexuality, which a change of management brought to a head.

Overstepping informal bounds causes problems, particularly in a service situation. There have been recent reports that managers have found it difficult to deal with the growing use of strippergrams as a more elaborately staged sexual prank. Even in these instances, as with many forms of misbehaviour, management is still likely to seek to redirect and control the phenomena. Straight suppression is likely to be counter-productive.

Coercive

It could be argued that this 'counter-productiveness' was the motivating force behind the traditional managerial attitudes to the coercive practices typified by sexual harassment. But that assumes that management saw a problem. As we stated earlier, a whole body of survey evidence demonstrates that harassment is a long-term submerged phenomenon, yet it has largely been ignored. What then has changed? Evidence from North America and Britain (Gutek, 1985; IRS, 1992; Wright and Bean, 1993; Stockdale, 1996) pinpoints the fear of being sued and the influence of wider legislation; the growth of equal opportunities policies and the need to recruit and retain women. The former reasons are particularly important in the US where victims can sue under headings such as 'psychotraumatic disability'. An extra push has sometimes been given by unions, who have triggered a significant minority of employers to adopt equal opportunities policies in Britain, notably in the public sector (IRS, 1992).

Employers are increasingly aware of the wider social climate and there-fore the need to redefine organizational cultures when, as an American Society of Personnel Administrators survey put it, 'boys can no longer be boys' (Ford and McLaughlin, 1987, 100). It can also be connected to the internal evolution of managerial thinking about 'the human resource' and 'managing diversity'. Personnel and related functions can mobilize the lan-guage of organizational and employee effectiveness, with respect not just to the victim, but even to the perpetrator: 'an individual who devotes time and energy during the working day to his/her own personal needs for sexual gratification and power is divesting the company of those same energies . . . as long as the maximisation of profit remains pivotal for business, the con-nection must be reinforced that dealing with the issue of sexual harassment remains in the best financial interest of management' (Wright and Bean, 1993, 31, 36).

Alternatively the need for policies can be couched in the framework of professionalism and 'unprofessional conduct' (Gutek, 1985). The outcome has been a rapid growth in the last few years of formal harassment policies, or the inclusion of the issue under formal grievance procedures; though this is more widespread in the US than the UK (Davidson and Earnshaw, 1990). Even the then Department of Employment in Britain issued a guide for employers in 1990, with the Tory minister, Robert Jackson, pronouncing that harassment is 'bad for morale, bad for business efficiency and can cost employers money' (IRS, 1992, 6). As Pringle (1988, 97) notes, these develop-ments can be seen as a belated addition to the modernization of organiz-ations in which a single, rational and objective standard is applied across the board. Detailed procedures are increasingly regarded as a necessary means of regulating organizational life by employees as well as managers.

Understandably, given the time frame, we do not have a lot of evidence on the effectiveness of such policies. In her case studies, Cockburn (1991) notes that, in two private service organizations she studied, there was a preference for informality, quiet words on the side and shifting harassers to new territory. The limitations of formal policy in relation to underlying power structure isn't really news. Not surprisingly, writers in this area (Robertson et al., 1988) advocate that disciplinary procedures be supple-mented by education, information, incorporation of harassment criteria in performance appraisal and general cultural changes to redefine the 'ambi-ence' of organizations. As Gutek admits, this may take us into 'nebulous' and more difficult areas, particularly when the goal of policy is not only to eliminate sexual harassment, but to 'separate work and sex' (1985, 177).

While this conflation of sexuality and harassment is peripheral to Gutek's main policy prescriptions, it is central for others. Wise and Stanley (1990) argue for a move away from a ' trade-union-influenced' model which, they believe, misleadingly gives the impression that harassment is a distinct category of extreme and inappropriate behaviour. Similarly, Carter and Jeffs (1992) pour scorn on the naive belief of professional social work bodies in rational decision-making and formal regulations. If harassment is not aberrant behaviour but normal, and sexuality at work is on a simple continuum with 'flirtations, sexual joking and "getting off" at work' (Wise and Stanley, 1990, 26) then, logically, it cannot be dealt with by existing codes based implicitly on an 'individual deficit' model which assumes that specific perpetrators can be identified and disciplined. Such writers find it extremely difficult to be specific about further policy measures, but the argument drifts inevitably towards extending the range of regulation.

Convivial

Convivial relations have always posed problems for management of how or even whether to intervene. In recent times we have seen the emergence of well-publicized calls for policies of tighter regulation, notably for codes of conduct that would, 'prevent consensual relationships between members and students'. The latter is a quote from a motion put to the Association of University Teachers' (AUT) conference, illustrating the point that pressures for regulation on this territory may come from 'below', though they are subsequently appropriated by management.

Intellectually the underpinning of such moves is provided by the kind of arguments examined in the previous section. Arguments by academics and AUT activists make quite clear that any 'unequal' relationship is by definition coercive and that where power is present, consent is automatically 'suspect' (Carter and Jeffs, 1992, 241). Reluctant, but admitted 'authoritarians', they and other writers regard US-style rules and guidelines which forbid such relations, or exclude consent as a defence, as providing known boundaries and an impetus for cultural change. While it is not appropriate here to go into the detail of policy development, such solutions tend to be justified by a catalogue of incidents which stress only 'the power of the male sexual narrative' (Harlow et al., 1992, 134), and where even examples of consent are reinterpreted as the consequences of harassment (Wise and Stanley, 1990, 20). We have here an impoverished and one-dimensional view of the immensely varied emotional and sexual character of relationships, as well as being back with a vengeance to women constructed solely as victims. Indeed victim is presented 'sadly' as the appropriate term for describing many women's experiences in education by Carter and Jeffs (1992, 243). Holloway and Jefferson (1995) also observe that such perspectives remove the ambivalence that shapes the motives and actions of both sexes: any theory of subjectivity must embrace a notion of multiplicity and contradiction. One of the problems is that much of this literature, though relying on analytical categories of a universal nature, draws from organizational experiences of a highly specific nature; not just higher education, but professional training, social work and care settings which undoubtedly provide opportunities for and evidence of coercive misbehaviour.

The spread of intervention and regulation would certainly go against the trend towards toleration of consensual relations. Roy's case study is fairly typical in reporting the personnel director's view that 'what the employees did after work hours was none of the company's business, unless entanglements affected the work situation' (1974, 56). Such pragmatism has also been shaped by reluctance to enter onto difficult territory, one manager being quoted as preferring the 'blind eye', given that, 'I wouldn't know what to do if I saw something' (*Business Week*, 1984, 22). Another piece described flirting and affairs as 'sticky issues' for managers to handle. Perhaps that was an unfortunate phrase, but it helps to explain the preference for handling events informally. If such practices are perceived as a potential problem, they are more likely to be 'nipped in the bud' with a quiet chat, or at its most formal, be subject to a bit of counselling.

Managerial attitudes are not always benign; it depends largely on the dynamics of workgroup relations. For one thing is clear – relationships are never private, particularly when fellow employees report observing embracing in closets, kissing in supply rooms and fondling in the parking lot. Though love is blind, other people are not. This collection comes from the most detailed study of romantic relationships at work, by Quinn (1977). He reports a large variety of potential changes in actual and perceived power and competence. Impacts on others can be positive, negative or non-existent, but a significant minority do cause problems among colleagues, though this may depend on the stage of the relationship.

Pragmatism is, however, on the wane. An increasing number of management journals are openly discussing the creation of rules for romance. Collins is typical in arguing that, 'The "gentlemanly" hands-off way of approaching personal matters disrupts the goals of the corporation' (1983, 152). What they do about it is still problematic, but a US report (Ford and McLaughlin, 1987) shows that increasing numbers of organizations have formal policies on consensual as well as coercive sexuality. Some of them may be contained within more general frameworks such as the Ethics Compliance Programme of computer giant Unisys. This may be seen as part of a more general shift towards expanding the scope of managerial activism in the cultural sphere, as we shall argue later. In this, they are frequently prodded by academics. This is not new. The attitudes of management in Roy's factory changed when a psychologist colleague argued that extramarital relations were having an adverse effect on production; leading the personnel director to exclaim that: 'We should have told them that if we heard any more of this monkey business going on, they would be fired' (1974, 57).

Her solutions to the 'sex problem' included not hiring divorcees or women who had separated from their husbands. That would neither be legal nor very politically correct nowadays. Codes of conduct are a growth area. But managerial intervention can be governed by a new set of informal guidelines. Central to much of what is being advocated is treating relationships in terms of conflicts of interest which managers must resolve as they would any other business problem. For Collins, 'bosses must not be swayed by emotion' (1983, 151), but should persuade the lower-ranked person to leave (though he is careful to say that if both are equal the women should stay).

Conclusion

It is important to keep organizational sexuality in perspective. There are those who believe that the recent explosion of interest gives the issue a centrality that it does not deserve. We are sympathetic to Witz and Savage's (1992, 54) qualms about 'the over-hasty displacement of the "gender paradigm" and the over-eager substitution of the "sexuality paradigm"'. They are also right to be sceptical of the influence of Foucauldian and postmodern perspectives in this process. In our view the treatment of sexuality is literally *over*-powered, leading to an obscuring of theoretical and practical boundaries. Nevertheless sexuality and the regulation of misbehaviour is an important aspect of the reordering of public–private relations. While we explore the wider trends in detail in the next chapter, some preliminary remarks are useful.

Sexual misbehaviour is clearly a very mixed bag and some forms of control are entirely appropriate. But the blurred lines are problematic. The growth of formal and informal codes to regulate conviviality marks a reversal of existing trends in a number of ways. Such initiatives reintroduce a calculative or instrumental rationality in an area which was becoming regarded as a private domain. In this, there is a clash, with pressure on organizations to recognize the rights of employees to have specific identities, such as being gay. A series of consultants in the *Harvard Business Review* have advised companies to let their employees come out of the closet and to treat their sexuality as a *private* matter (Williamson, 1993). It is therefore doubly ironic that as sexual orientation is becoming less the public property of the organization, wider measures seek to return us full circle to the desexualized workplace. Attempts to regulate sexuality have profoundly ambiguous consequences for management and employees. As Burrell (1992, 91) recognized some time ago, managerial action may exacerbate rather than solve the issues. It could also be argued that the extension beyond harassment is unnecessary as well as problematic. Gutek (1985, 161) observes that: 'As this study showed, work environments characterised by sexual comments and overtures are the same ones that frown on dating among employees, whereas sex integrated environments that have no regulations about employed dating also have relatively little overt expression of sexuality'.

7 The End of Organizational Misbehaviour?

We began this book with the aim of pulling together the often disconnected threads from different studies and traditions dealing with employee recalcitrance, resistance and self-organization. In the course of our journey we have shown that in the present century, and particularly in the decades following the Second World War, social scientists have discussed a rich variety of such forms of behaviour, ranging from analyses of work limitation, absenteeism and time-wasting to sabotage, destructiveness and theft. Theorists have seldom realized the complete range of variations which forms of misbehaviour can adopt, and have often misunderstood their nature and the forces that give rise to such behaviour. With this in mind we have attempted to expand that agenda, in particular by focusing on struggles around identity as they are emerging today, including those of sexuality and humour. Our other main concern has been to locate employee action in a different explanatory framework – hence the term misbehaviour and the emphasis on the specifically organizational dimensions to it.

But in the course of producing the book, it became obvious that our investigations were at odds with the dominant trends in academic study of the workplace, where there has been a sudden loss of concern about misbehaviour and dissent. This chapter therefore identifies and discusses an apparent paradox: that although there is a rich history of misbehaviour in organizations, there is now a large amount of authoritative opinion which suggests that the employee has been effectively tamed and subdued; that the battle that managements have waged to secure a degree of conformity from employees, has been decisively resolved in their favour. Although writers vary in the reasons they give, commentators of very different theoretical positions and political views share many of the same assumptions and views about the nature and effects of new social and technical means of regulation and surveillance. Yet the accounts of new developments in management, which have supposedly brought about fundamental changes in the dispositions of employees, are inaccurate and misconceived. Many readers will have read or become aware of our *Sociology* article 'All Quiet on the Workplace Front? A Critique of Recent Trends in British Industrial Sociology' (Thompson and Ackroyd, 1995), where we critiqued the virtual removal of labour as an active agency of resistance in a considerable portion of theory and research. We make no apology for substantially drawing on that piece for this concluding chapter, for it was always part of the book project. What we have done, however, is to broaden the range of writers and issues examined, and to respond to the issues raised in the subsequent debate, in order, finally, to reflect on the potential for 'reconceptualizing resistance'.

Of course, it is perfectly possible to argue that the apparent marginality of resistance and dissent is the outcome, not of changes in theory, but of transformations in the broader conditions of labour. So it is here that we turn first.

The institutional and structural context

It became commonplace in the 1980s to proclaim that the 'forward march of labour' had been halted. While most accounts were not constructed as broadly as Hobsbawm's (1981) famous article, the clear implication of much of the discussion was that labour as a subject of industrial and political action had been broken or at least severely damaged. Much of the explanation of that supposed decline was sought in factors outside the organization. Such arguments are not supported by an accurate appreciation of the informal organization of employees such has been developed in this book.

The restructuring of labour markets, traceable directly and indirectly to greater competition in domestic product markets, has been instrumental in changing perceptions of the place of labour (Fogarty and Brooks, 1986; Lovering, 1990). These changes seem even more significant against the background of growth in 'peripheral' and 'non-standard' forms of employment, not to mention the increasingly hostile environment for trade unionism, which will be discussed more directly below. Several factors have, in fact, combined to weaken the formal aspects of labour organization and perceptions of its likely continued importance. These changes are appropriately linked to longer-term processes of structural change in the nature and location of capital – decline of plant size, growth of new plants, movement of firms away from the older urban areas (Ackroyd and Whitaker, 1990), and the shift from manufacturing to services and from manual to white collar employment. As one commentator put it early in the debates, 'Certain conditions external to the workplace . . . have changed so dramatically as to affect future activity within the workplace' (Lane, 1982, 13). Taken together with changes inside organizations to individualize the employment relationship, discussed later, they are seen to lead to a fracturing of collectivism (Bacon and Storey, 1994), or the 'end of institutional industrial relations' (Purcell, 1993). It is argued by some that unions would, in these circumstances, be best advised to pack up their collectivist kit-bags and embrace the new agenda of individualism. Bassett and Cave (1993) argue that unions can mirror the individualism at the heart of the employment relationship by improving and expanding the range of services offered to their membership.

Further external obstacles to traditional union functions of interest aggregation and solidaristic action have been provided through changes in the mode of state regulation. Under successive Conservative administrations in Britain three significant dimensions of policy can be identified: a strategy of deregulation of labour markets and promotion of a low wage, low skill economy as a means of attracting inward investment; injection of a market rationality in public services through competitive tendering; and the sustained legislative assault on union organization, employment rights and collective bargaining. The last, in particular, aims to deny workers access to traditional sources of collective power (Smith and Morton, 1993), but all three potentially undermine the means of regulating external and internal labour markets, on which that power has rested. Though these comments and policy dimensions refer to Britain, a combination of economic restructuring, labour market deregulation and declining union densities is identifiable across many advanced industrial societies; generating similar or parallel debates. British governments have simply gone somewhat further and faster towards opening the domestic economy to external competition than has been the case elsewhere, stimulating the need for more extensive corporate change; that is all.

Some academics, particularly in Britain, have been understandably suspicious of this over-hyped agenda of paradigm shifts and structural transformation. For most of the 1980s, many industrial relations theorists were reluctant to accept that significant changes had taken place in the basic mechanisms of representation and bargaining, or of managerial ideology and action (MacInnes, 1987a, 1987b; Kelly, 1990). Other workplace theorists demonstrated effectively that 'novel' forms of employment and flexibility show considerable continuity with the past or are confined to particular sectors (Pollert, 1991). Later stages of the debate see the forms of flexibility adopted in Britain not only as embodying continuities with the past, but also as constituting adaptations to the particular institutional context (Ackroyd and Procter, 1998a, 1998b).

It is not our purpose here to provide additional evidence and commentary on these areas of debate. But, in explaining contemporary workplace change, it would be foolish to deny the impact of structural changes in labour and capital markets: the development of a hostile political and legal climate, however unevenly designed or implemented. Indeed, much of the previous optimism concerning 'the resilience of older patterns of behaviour and attitudes' (MacInnes, 1987b, 9) has been broken by the publication of the third, 1990 British Workplace Industrial Relations survey (WIRS) (Millward et al., 1992) and its pessimistic reading of the substantial decline in national, multi-employer bargaining, union recognition, industrial action, and membership density.

Whatever the accuracy of claim and counter-claim, the debate also reveals the limitations of the focus of much existing research and frameworks of debate. There is a variety of interrelated problems. First, the decline of trade unions has too often been taken to be synonymous with disappearance of workplace resistance and recalcitrance. Second, the decline of traditional forms of male, full-time manufacturing labour is taken as equivalent to the marginalization of all labour. Third, the challenge to historically dominant forms of collectivism is substituted for the end of collectivism as such.

In the case of industrial relations, this is to be expected, as mainstream writing has long tended towards a preoccupation with order and its underpinning by procedural and institutional forms and practices. For all its valuable data, 'WIRS inherited the Donovan equation of industrial relations with management–trade union relations' (Sisson, 1993, 203). This is not inherent to industrial relations as a discipline. As Brown and Wright (1994) recently reminded us, the best traditions of IR overlapped with those of industrial sociology, focusing on informal effort bargaining and the contested management of the employment relation. But in a period when workplace studies of different kinds are dependent on large data sets and increasingly available quantitative survey materials rather than in-depth or longitudinal fieldwork, that kind of orientation is difficult. Brown and Wright also point out that, 'In the radically changed labour market context of the 1980s, the diminishing number of researchers engaged in workplace studies tended to follow earlier leads to focus on management behaviour as the prime mover in workplace bargaining' (1994, 160). But we are suspicious of any view that external changes have necessary or automatic organizational effects independent of the strategic responses of economic and political actors. Historically, too many commentators have been prone to proclaim the death of solidarity or collective action without fully accounting for the contingent economic, cultural and political conditions, or the processes of learning, adaptation and reorganization by labour. What is true of IR is also relevant for other developments in the workplace. It is to this wider terrain that we now turn.

New management practices and the disappearance of misbehaviour

Managerial accounts: things can only get better

Managerial writing has had to perform a delicate balancing act in the last two decades. On the one hand it has had to acknowledge that employees have to operate in a harsher economic and legal climate, with rising job insecurity. The end of the career is, however, offset by the opportunities to develop entrepreneurial skills and a wider range of competencies so that we can all become, in Charles Handy's (1995) words, 'portfolio people'. If there are signs of contradiction in the organizational environment, inside the workplace, largely benign intent and effects are attributed to managerial action. Contemporary managerial practices are framed in a variety of ways for public consumption, with varieties of 'hard' and 'soft' Human Resource Management (HRM) and Total Quality Management (TQM) at the centre. But the core argument remains broadly the same: that management is mobilizing human resources, commitment and soft skills in an unprecedented way to meet new requirements for flexibility and quality, and shifting from command and control to empowerment, trust, involvement and collegiality to facilitate real organizational change.

Many of these arguments are linked to 'paradigm break' theories that suggest new kinds of organization for a new post-something era. At a more general level, however, managerial accounts have long favoured evolutionary frameworks which specify a historical sequence of events, in which the accommodation of workers is progress towards higher trust and involvement of employees in cooperation and partnership between employers and employees. For these writers the idea that we have moved decisively away from the direct control and direction associated with Taylorism and Fordism is to be understood in terms of a developmental sequence in the character of managerial regimes. The disappearance of overt conflict and forms of misbehaviour is thus to be sought through the disappearance of confrontational politics within the firm.

One such argument by George Thomason (1991), doyen of British personnel writers, suggests a sequence from what he calls pre-personnel management (PPM), with effectively no specialist policy towards labour other than harsh direct discipline, to progressively less harsh and more cooperative policies. Thus from roughly the end of the last century we have the emergence of traditional personnel management (TPM) in which there is a heavy concentration on contracts of employment, rules of conduct at work and procedures for the conduct of employee relations, together with corrective regulation of work conduct by close supervision. Such regimes are specifically linked to Taylorism and Tayloristic modes of thought. However, such regimes allegedly give way to new forms of regulation; first there is what Thomason calls human resource development (HRD) which is followed by human resource management (HRM). Both of these are apparently quite marked changes of direction for management in which there is a much greater attempt to win over the allegiance of employees. In this thesis, policy has moved away from exerting control towards fostering competence and responsibility, towards 'creating competence and winning hearts and minds' (Thomason, 1991, 6). In this account the disappearance of dissent and misbehaviour is the consequence of effective changes in the emphasis of management policy.

A similar analysis, which is perhaps of more interest because it is specifically concerned with the role of management in relation to deviancy and dissent, is given by Stuart Henry (1987b). Henry identifies four types of what he calls 'private justice', meaning justice as administered by corporations. Henry is calling attention to the way in which management regimes function in a disciplinary way. Indeed it is obvious that management can be seen, along with the courts and the police, as an element in a societal control system. Very much like Thomason, Henry is arguing for an evolutionary sequence in which the 'punitive-authoritarian discipline' of early capitalism gives way in the later part of the nineteenth century to what he calls 'corrective-representative discipline'. This label Henry uses to sum up the attributes of the regime which is concerned with direct supervision, but while it has strict rules of conduct, these are held to be less punitive than the rules maintained by earlier regimes. In the case of corrective-representative discipline, the rules are held to be comprehensive and to provide very detailed procedures for cases of infringement; in particular, there is scope for some kind of defence by the accused in terms of the rules in force, so that private justice at this stage partially mirrors the criminal justice system.

For Henry there are two more stages in the development of managerial regimes as systems of private justice, each marked by the increasing extent to which employees are consulted about the regulation of their own conduct, and the extent to which the regulation of conduct involves collective agreement. Thus, Henry envisages corrective-representative discipline giving way to what he calls accommodative-participative discipline. Under the latter regime, rules for the regulation of conduct remain, but they reflect the recognition of a greater plurality of interests in organizations. The purpose of rules, according to Henry, is to ensure that 'justice' can still be served when conflicting interest groups compete and try to preserve their bargaining positions. Management as the control of dissent and misbehaviour, by this argument, becomes increasingly a matter of the outcome of negotiation between parties, and therefore what counts as unacceptable conduct becomes more and more a matter of agreed definition. Under such a system, formal written rules are supplemented by the recognition of what has become customary, and are much more subject to discussion and renegotiation than was the case in the past. The jurisdiction of rules, however, grows more inclusive, and, according to Henry, rules will cover all categories of employees with the exception of very senior managers and owners.

Finally, accommodative-participative discipline gives way to what is grandly labelled 'celebrative-collective discipline', in which rules become very informal and unwritten and control is exerted in the name of the collectivity rather than some authoritative part of it. Moreover, rules are allegedly decided entirely by all the membership, who voluntarily participate in recognizing them and in disciplining themselves and other members. Discipline is finally turned inside out: from being entirely external it becomes entirely internal by a series of developments towards self-control.

Henry lists the types of deviance that are supposed to differentiate types of disciplinary system. But when these are examined it is found that he lists disobedience to instructions and rules, theft and damage as central to the first three of them. In short, he has difficulty in clearly differentiating regimes in terms of their associated misbehaviour, a point that might lead one to think that these regimes are, actually, not so different as Henry wishes to suggest. But more importantly, the actual evidence in such writings for radical departures from old ways of management through authority and punitive control can be greatly exaggerated. Lip-service is often paid to the need to develop new ways of incorporating labour, the necessity of developing high trust relations, the need to develop self-regulation amongst employees and so on, but in practice attempts to do this are rather rare and, where they exist, they only partially conform to the models set out by Thomason and Henry. These writers studiously avoid simply recognizing the capacity for self-organization which employees evidently have, and which we have extensively analysed in this book beginning with Chapter 3. A need for new managerial regimes and the appropriateness of the way that they might act is clear in theory, but it is very hard to find examples of their realization in practice. This problem of the gap between intent and outcome is, however, not peculiar to managerial theorists.

Radical perspectives

Radical perspectives inject a welcome note of caution into the assessment of the likely effects of the achievement of high trust relations or other features of the 'new organization'. However, although the mechanisms of incorporation of worker attitudes and behaviour are seen to be rather different, their general effect is very much the same. Unfortunately radical scepticism is often confined to questioning the nature rather than effectiveness of new management practices. There are, of course, exceptions among radical industrial sociologists and organization theorists, such as studies by Beaumont (1991), Martinez-Lucio and Weston (1992) and Pollert's (1996) study of union responses to HRM, teamworking and other new initiatives.

   The overall theme of most studies is that the removal of misbehaviour is evidence of the success of a totalizing project of regulation which is at work in corporations and society. We can distinguish two kinds of mechanisms – cultural and socio-technical – through which these controlling intentions are said to be effectively realized. These must be seen as only analytically distinct and it is, for many writers, the conjoining of social scientific and technical capacity that has led to the effective totalization of control.

   Before we look at these two sets of arguments, we need to recognize that a central reason why the main trend has been towards the marginalization of misbehaviour is the shift in radical theory to Foucauldian and post-structuralist perspectives. Descriptions of new management practices rely heavily on Foucauldian conceptual props, admittedly often without much attempt to reproduce the deeper theoretical framework. The panopticon is the favourite in this armoury – Bentham's design principle based on a circular building with central observation tower, which, from prisons to the new model housing estates, facilitated a unidirectional disciplinary gaze. In other words the observed can be seen but cannot see, while the observers see everything but cannot be seen. So effective are such practices that individuals began to discipline themselves to be, in Foucault's words, docile and useful bodies.

   Though it does not always surface explicitly in contemporary writing, Foucault's (1977) account of the rise of a distinctively modern form of disciplinary power acts as an implicit framework. From this perspective, premodern, sovereign power had depended on personalized bonds of obligation.

In contrast, the techniques of disciplinary power were developed and refined in religious institutions, prisons, asylums, hospitals and workhouses at a local level, rather than overseen by the state. Such micro-techniques were concerned with evaluating, recording and observing individuals in an exhaustive and detailed way and they spread to the factory and other institutions. However, the prison remained the purest exemplar and microcosm of disciplinary techniques and knowledge: power is fundamentally carceral in character.

As well as invoking the imagery of disciplinary power, Foucault's work also provides a further theme by its emphasis on the primacy of discourse. This takes its force from the cultural mechanisms for smothering dissent and colonizing the employee. The key social means in the development of control are new techniques of incorporation of personnel. Here there is a good deal of agreement about the overall function of new policies in human resource management and the emphasis on developing strong cultures. In the radical account of these developments however, the policies towards labour are linked with much wider policies of cultural manipulation, of which new policies and attitudes towards the treatment of employees are just a small part. Though initially dismissive of the managerial literature on corporate culture for its inadequate conceptualizations and overestimation of the likely effects on employees (e.g. Smircich, 1983), critical social science soon began to turn to a rehabilitation of the concept as a powerful tool of ideological incorporation. One of the first studies to take a positive view of organizational culture, by Carol Ray (1986) postulates a transition from 'bureaucratic control' within corporations, based on the extreme division of labour and close regulation of conduct according to rules, to 'humanistic control', where attention is given to the intrinsic interest of tasks and supportive supervision. Finally, control crosses the last frontier to 'cultural control', in which the manipulation of the symbols of culture is the basis of moral discipline.

The thrust of this argument is that new practices such as HRM and TQM are the techniques by which management seeks to involve staff and to develop and manipulate an inclusive culture. Despite earlier radical scepticism, the view that control through culture is not only feasible, but actually practised, has gathered momentum (Willmott, 1993; Townley, 1993; Marsden, 1993). Thus, Willmott (1993, 520) suggests that, 'Within organizations, programmes of corporate culturism, HRM and TQM have sought to promote or strengthen a corporate ethos that demands loyalty from employees as it excludes, silences and punishes those who question.' Disciplinary power constrains individuals through their self-knowledge, their belief in their own sovereignty as consumer or employee: 'the modern subject willingly reproduces prevalent relations of domination and exploitation' (Willmott, 1993, 520). The current most likely vehicle for this is the corporate culture programmes discussed earlier: 'individual insecurity, corporate culture and organizational order are mutually constitutive' (Grey, 1994, 4). Willmott supports Deetz's (1992) earlier critique of the colonizing tendencies of the modern corporation, where he argues that, 'The disciplined member of the corporation wants on his or her own what the corporation wants' (1992, 42).

A growing number of case studies have been written which purport to illustrate at length the effectiveness of such incorporating value systems. Amongst the most influential is Kunda's (1995) study of an American information technology firm ('Tech'). The openness of the company allowed the expression of ironic evaluations and cynical interpretations of the company's policies. According to Kunda, this promoted an almost universally cynical attitude in which employees were disarmed of a critical value standpoint from which to evaluate their situation. As a consequence, employees lacked the basis on which morally to evaluate, and so reject, any role that the corporation asked them to adopt.

It is interesting to note that US high-tech, normally computer firms offer fertile ground for gloomy accounts of cultural manipulation. Hayes takes a critical look 'behind the Silicon curtain' to find employees – notably salaried professionals and their managers – seduced by a combination of career opportunities and a work process re-enchanted by the allure of intriguing technical problems. This seduction both compensates for the lonely world outside and creates 'an independent, narcissistic attraction to work' (1989, 31). Similar themes emerge in Casey's (1995) account of life at the Hephaestus Corporation, this time with a more avowed though somewhat superficial Foucauldian gloss. This particular culture is geared towards the production of 'designer employees' through a totalizing process of discursive colonization of all areas of employees' lives. Though the book says that 'corporate colonisation of the self takes place with varying degrees of resistance and struggle' (1995, 161), such terms are emptied of meaning by the use of an individualistic, psychoanalytic conceptual framework in which employees are allowed only three 'psychic strategies' or 'self-styles' – defence, collusion and capitulation. Ironic cynicism is the only thing that occasionally surfaces to disturb the displays of reverence, total dedication and identification. Many of Casey's professional employees are also apparently smitten by 'latent narcissism' (1995, 178). However, this kind of analysis is not wholly confined to the high-tech firm. Smith and Wilkinson give us another Foucault inspired account of the totalizing impact of sophisticated corporate culture and symbolism at Sherwoods in the UK. Policies of total openness, visibility, involvement and shared ideology provide no conditions for subversive conflict. 'There are no fundamental differences of opinion between levels and divisional functions, no plotting, no organizational coups, no muddles, no strife . . . . The company promises, and substantially, it delivers, capitalism without conflict' (1995, 3). This remarkable outcome consigns not only Marx and Weber to the dustbin of history, but even the routine and inoffensive findings of organization studies on the micro-politics of conflict.

Corporate culture as such is not the only focus. In Foucault's work, penology, medicine and psychiatry become the focal points for the development of new power – knowledge discourses which punish deviation from normative standards. This way of thinking has been enthusiastically adopted and updated. The disciplinary gaze doesn't necessarily require an electronic eye, but can operate through discourses controlled by management (Sakolsky, 1992, 235). The work of Townley (1993) and Marsden (1993) focuses on identifying the social technologies of contemporary specialists in human and organizational behaviour as 'power–knowledge' discourses. These latter day 'soft cops' in HRM, accounting and consultancy are concerned to 'observe, examine and normalise performance and behaviour' (Marsden, 1993, 118–19), carrying on a tradition established by human relations and its efforts to habituate the employee to the changing conditions of work in the large corporation. A familiar theme emerges from Townley (1993, 13), for whom, 'The seemingly mundane and innocuous techniques of HRM form a panopticon', through their categorization and measurement of the individual's tasks and behaviour. Labour disappears from the process partly because of the tendency to believe that there is a monopoly of knowledge by management and its agents, a form of discursive closure that marginalizes other representations and identities (Deetz, 1992). The bars of the new iron cage are so invisible, control techniques so subtle, that employee ignorance or incomprehension is counterposed to 'the increasing knowledge-ability of organizations' (Dandeker, 1990, 197).

The growth of teamworking on the shop floor is also a means of incorporation and self-discipline through which workers internalize the various forms of 'the gaze'. In Barker's study of self-managing teams, the disembodied eye of the panopticon becomes the 'omnipresent tutelary eye of the norm ' (1993, 432). Self-management becomes self-discipline, but, nonetheless harsh discipline in these studies; management harnessing peer pressure within teams to identify and punish deviations from the norm. Thus what is produced technically by the electronic panopticon can also be produced socially from within the team in a process which 'operates directly on the subjectivity of individual members' (Sewell and Wilkinson, 1992b, 108). McKinley and Taylor's (1996) fascinating account of Phoneco in Scotland links together the themes of an ambitious corporate culture programme with an elaborate attention to recruitment, selection and training of a 'socially individuated' pro-company workforce; to a Barker-like use of teamwork as a form of mutual control, self-surveillance, peer pressure and review. Some of the Foucauldian language of mobilization of discourse, colonization of consciousness and calculable subjects is present, but without, as we shall see later, the pessimistic conclusions about the possibilities of resistance.

Finally in the cultural sphere, the construction of identity is a major theme of contemporary post-structuralist research (Kerfoot and Knights, 1993; Grey, 1994; O'Doherty, 1994; Casey, 1995). It is part of attempts to theorize subjectivity, though the influences, such as Giddens, are wider than Foucault (Knights and Willmott, 1989; Knights, 1990; Willmott, 1994). Nevertheless, identity is seen as a site of resistance allowed for in the Foucauldian framework. For despite these self-disciplining tendencies, there is a permanent tension between the search for secure identity and the capacity and nature of corporate attempts to deliver. Self-identity can therefore 'be realised only as a constant struggle against the experience of tension, fragmentation and discord' (Knights and Vurdubakis, 1994, 184). In addition, identity and the processes that shape it are not static or one-dimensional. This helps to focus on the capacity for human action given that in a world of competing discourses and multiple identities, individuals can position themselves and find their own location, rather than be simply positioned by them (Brewis and Kerfoot, 1994).

By contrast with this emphasis on the cultural aspects of new management, other writers have sought to give priority to the socio-technical aspect of management systems, though it receives less prominence in the literature overall. In this line of argument centre stage is given to information technology and somewhat different elements of technique, particularly just in time (JIT) and total quality control (TQC). Sewell and Wilkinson (1992a), for example, argue that JIT/TQC regimes both create and demand systems of surveillance which improve on those of previous factory regimes by instilling new kinds of social discipline and thereby contribute to enhanced central control. Both JIT and TQC produce data that can be available to management. On the one hand, with TQC there is the extension of (apparent) autonomy to groups of workers who monitor their own activity – and those of adjacent individuals and groups. With this there is an active reporting system feeding information on performance into the information system. As a new arrangement of production, TQC both secures and monitors quality production. By contrast, JIT monitors and controls materials flows. From this emerges another data flow, which is particularly transparent. These two sources of data allegedly yield the information necessary for high levels of control in the absence of a developed bureaucracy and a numerous supervisory cadre.

For some commentators the development of superior flows of data is the key to understanding the basic dynamics of managerial innovation in the contemporary world (Zuboff, 1989). However, there are some real differences of opinion about the likely effectiveness of the availablility of information. Recognizing that information, which new technology produces and transmits in abundance, is not necessarily sound knowledge on which sound organizational decision-making may be founded, is among the reasons why Zuboff equivocates about the real effects of new technology on managerial ability to oversee organizations. Others have less compunction. Webster and Robbins (1989, 1993) for example, connect the kinds of plant level development envisaged by Sewell and Wilkinson, in which information is assumed to be directly available to managers with disciplinary intentions, with very much more general processes of structural reorganization in corporations. In their view, the desegregation of complex productive processes and the extensive reorganization of large-scale industrial organization nonetheless does not preclude the effective disciplinary observation and control of plants and offices. Electronic technologies, they argue, allow managers both to individuate the organization of production into teams and cells, thereby increasing control, whilst, apparently, delegating responsibilities. Indeed, this must be seen as 'part of a more general neo-Fordist strategy which increases the flexibility of corporations in a wide range of their activities: production, design, marketing and distribution' (1993, 246). With a breathtaking intellectual economy, new forms of organization serve the logic of global capital accumulation and that of local workplace discipline equally effectively.

The Foucauldian influence surfaces again with arguments along the lines that panopticons are now electronic or informational, focused on technical and social supports to JIT and TQM systems (Wilkinson, 1983; Sewell and Wilkinson, 1992a, 1992b; Delbridge et al., 1992; Webster and Robbins, 1993). Most of the emphasis is on the increased and successful use of monitoring and surveillance of workers' activities, though the latter present an alternative history of the information revolution which traces a line of descent from Bentham's original conception, through Taylorism as a means of monopolizing knowledge in management, to the contemporary flexible firm which uses the capacity of IT to centralize information from an increased range of geographically dispersed units.

Whether through cultural or socio-technical means, the empirical claims are much the same: that resistance and informal self-organization have been squeezed out by the success of new management practices. For example, Delbridge et al. (1992, 105) say that 'worker counter-control (in the sense described by Roy and many others) is effectively eliminated', while Barker's concept of concertive control means that workers 'have harnessed themselves into a rational apparatus out of which they truly cannot squirm' (1993, 435–6). Casting her net even wider, Casey asserts that 'the conditions for such alternative [cultural] production are increasingly less conducive to employee initiative. The possibilities of action are reduced as employees' previously semi-autonomous loci of solidarity and protection are taken over by the totalising corporate culture' (1995, 192). The gaze has been truly internalized.

Criticisms

There is a variety of empirical, theoretical and methodological problems with these arguments. The empirical problems are numerous. For the vast majority of employees the organizations that they experience day by day are still authoritarian, rule bound and punitive. The majority of organizations have many continuities with the historically extant forms of management that are based on low trust regimes of one sort or another. Even white collar and service organizations are, quite often, managed by directive and low trust regimes of management. Evidence that commitment to the substance of HRM-style regimes is frequently absent or skin-deep is widespread. It ranges from large-scale surveys by academics and consultants (Edwards et al., 1996; Ingersoll Engineers, 1994); through detailed case studies such as that by Clark on Pirelli (1995) or Scott (1994) on unionized and non-unionized chocolate factories; and comprehensive surveys of the secondary literature (Milkman, 1998). Scott shows how quickly British management reverts to traditional authoritarian methods when faced with pressures, problems and non-compliance. The fact that Milkman's study is a demonstration of how few American companies are following a high trust, high skill road to competitiveness, indicates that the disease is not peculiarly British.

The evidence concerning the installation of new corporate cultures is also patchy to say the least. Where corporate culture change is undertaken, the evidence seems to be that trickle down techniques are used. The message becomes attenuated as it moves down the hierarchy, and there is little to support the idea that the communication of complex messages and cultural symbols will be achieved by such means. While we do not have many accounts of where exactly the trickle peters out, we do have plenty of evidence that employees are not necessarily 'buying into the message'. Again this ranges from analysis of survey data on employee attitudes, sometimes from companies themselves (Coopey, 1995; Hope and Hendry, 1995; Marks et al., 1997); to case studies of change programmes (Scott, 1994; Jones, 1997; Wilkinson et al., 1997). Even studies that find that employees are positive about the objectives of culture change programmes, such as Rosenthal et al.'s examination of the impacts of a customer service initiative in a large supermarket, are careful to note variations and limits: 'It lends little support though, to arguments about the hegemonic qualities of managerial discourse and their homogenising effects' (1997, 496). In contrast to some of the Foucauldian arguments, other studies of teamworking, while noting a variety of managerial attempts to promote normative integration, find little evidence for its success (Sharpe, 1996; Marks et al., 1997). Even where the classic features of imposed self-surveillance are present, success is not guaranteed, as McKinley and Taylor's (1996) study of team resistance to peer review demonstrates. According to these authors, despite a non-union environment, and the extraordinary lengths gone to by the company to disbar any alternative sources of cultural influence with the aim of making teams discipline themselves, there was considerable evidence of resistance and counter-planning. For example, workers tacitly traded monthly scores in the peer review process, engaged in silent strikes and a three-week go-slow.

As we indicated earlier, such evidence for colonized consciousness as there is at the moment, is from small and usually quite specialized companies, notably those in the information technology sector. Let us be generous and agree that some of those who run organizations, as in Smith and Wilkinson's (1995) case study discussed earlier, have engineered conditions in which conflict is minimal or absent on the surface. But generally, where organizations have less uniformly middle class and professional employees, the effectiveness of enculturation is less assured (Grenier, 1988).

As to the effectiveness of socio-technical methods, similar scepticism would seem to be in order. With respect to surveillance based on the integration of personnel information from TQC and new HRM policies, even the conventional organization behaviour and HRM literature creates doubts about whether adequate integration of information can be easily achieved. Indeed, the organizational changes currently taking place are often stripping out the very personnel whose main responsibility such monitoring would be. Of course, new information technologies are promoted as having integrative properties independent of old-style personnel. But we have to be careful not to confuse the technological potential of such devices with the extent of their use (cf. Lyon, 1988, 1994). Companies, such as those running centralized call centres, do use enhanced methods of surveillance, but it does not stop employee resentment and resistance towards monitoring and enforcement of scripted behaviour, as Taylor (1998) shows in his study of travel industry sales workers.

Given this evidence from a variety of perspectives and methodologies, we are inexorably led to the conclusion that some theorists are seeing what they want to see. In principle, many of those promoting accounts of radical cultural and socio-technical change should not have a problem in relation to resistance, for in the Foucauldian framework power and resistance are inseparable. If, as Foucault says, resistance is in the same place as power, where then does it come from? Asking this question, according to Knights and Vurdubakis (1994) commits the sin of 'dualism', where resistance is seen as dichotomous to and outside of power (as in 'control and resistance'). Power, instead, is productive of and generates resistance. It is 'capillary', circulating through and down to the lowest rungs, reaches and localities. Because power can never be total, resistance may break out at different points in the chain and while that resistance recreates power, it promotes a ceaseless process of shifting alliances and tensions. It seems that power needs something else to be productive: 'power has to work on recalcitrant material – otherwise as Foucault has pointed out, it would have no existence' (Knights and Vurdubakis, 1994, 185).

But it is problematic, at least in the sense that no actual accounts of resistance can normally be found in such studies. The idea of the panopticon in which power becomes automatic is particularly dangerous in closing the space to 'see' resistance. McKinley and Taylor (1994, 2–3) accurately identify the consequences of such arguments: 'So seductive is Foucault's metaphor, however, that if simply transposed onto the labour process perspective it can seriously overestimate the scope and depth of management control . . . . The image in these accounts is a form of self-subordination so complete, so seamless that it stifles any dissent, however innocuous.'

Most importantly, there is the problem that because power is everywhere and nowhere, the impression can be given that it is a force from which there can never be any escape. Resistance is part of the formal picture, but is under-theorized and the dice loaded against it because 'only power is positive and productive, while resistance is simply a reaction to its production'

(Dews, 1986, 99). In addition, resistance does not threaten power, because 'It means that discipline can grow stronger knowing where its next efforts must be directed' (Burrell, 1988, 228). Clegg is similarly pessimistic in noting the organizational outflanking of resistance, due to subordinated agencies 'Lacking the organizational resources to outmanoeuvre existing networks and alliances' (1989, 19). As Collinson (1994) observes, this analysis draws on Foucault in arguing that knowledge and information structure access to power. Subordinates either have too little of both, or their knowledge of the likely outcome of action is so predictable that it is similarly inhibitive. A further problem in the neglect of resistance is that it reflects the limitation of Foucault's analysis where, in the desire to avoid explanations at the level of the subject, human agency gets lost in the constitution of the subject solely through discourse (Newton, 1994). If we take all these factors into account, it is hardly surprising that, fragmented, insubstantial and counter-productive, resistance simply disappears from view.

Post-structuralists make it doubly hard for themselves and everybody else by raising a cry of 'dualism' whenever they engage with an opposing argument. As a stick with which to beat their opponents, it is, we would suggest, a blunt instrument which adds nothing to the capacity of researchers to identify and explain actors and actions in the workplace. Of course, in practice, power or control and resistance interpenetrate rather than mechanically produce one another. But separating them, as in labour process theory, has been a necessary heuristic device that enables us to 'see' the reciprocal actions. Without such a separation one merely collapses into another and we are left with the confusing and opaque results observed in the work of Foucault and followers. We have tried, in this book, to develop a framework which identifies a dialectic of innovatory behaviour in the workplace, where particular actors are not endowed with cause (control) and the effect (resistance). But no doubt this will also be found guilty of some form of dualism.

Not only is the Foucauldian framework inherently flawed, it is not, as claimed, a better alternative to accounts of workplace social relations. First of all, it is not actually a specific account of the workplace at all. By treating the workplace as an extension of disciplinary practices and the factory, hospital and other organizations as paler versions of carceral institutions (Burrell, 1988), the specific character of employment relations in a capitalist society is lost. Sakolsky (1992, 237) is clear that the labour process is not analysed in relation to the mode of production, but as a site of disciplinary power. His target may be what he thinks is 'orthodox Marxism', but the dismissal would equally apply to the broad mass of industrial sociology which sees something distinctive in the social relations of the wage–effort bargain. Control is treated merely as another version of discipline, and functionally oriented towards the creation of obedient bodies rather than sustaining exploitation (Clegg, 1989, 176). The contested rationality between capital and labour is reduced to a 'local site of struggle' and labour is not regarded as a distinctive or significant agency. Though the case studies are a useful corrective to the managerialist treatment of developments such as HRM, and some studies have mixed and matched Foucauldian and labour process concepts with some success (McKinley and Taylor, 1998), disciplinary power and surveillance are less effective as alternatives to concepts of control and resistance. When the terms are applied a narrower conceptual basis for understanding tends to result. For example, when work reorganization and teamwork are defined and described through the idea of surveillance (e.g. Sewell and Wilkinson, 1992b, 109) the complexity of various types and dimensions of control gives way to measurement, information gathering, supervision, and electronic tagging. Even if one were to make the highly dubious assumption that surveillance mechanisms are effective in suppressing or incorporating dissent and informal practices, the problem is that everything is subsumed under Foucault's notion of discipline as a type of power with instruments, techniques, procedures and targets. In contrast, in Richard Edwards's (1979, 18) influential labour process framework, the apparatus of discipline is only one of the three components of a system of control.

There are other conceptual and practical limitations. First, it is not a struggle as labour inside the employment relationship, but as subjects of modernity fighting on a universal terrain deriving from the indeterminacy and finitude of human existence (Willmott, 1994). The existential nature of this process of managing threatened identities is spelled out by O'Doherty: 'Increasing ontological insecurity arises as individuals fail to sustain a continuous narrative of self-identity, as they become preoccupied with possible dangers and risks, and as they struggle to maintain trust in their relations with others and in their own self integrity' (1994, 18). This interpretation of the life and trying times of bank workers is, admittedly, wholly at odds with the case study descriptions of work intensification, redundancies, staff shortages, job monotony and other responses which sound conventionally materialist and non-discursive! In these studies workers are not disciplined by the market, or sanctions actually or potentially invoked by capital, but by their own identity and subjectivity (Smith and Thompson, 1992, 15). The approach adopted emphasizes the point that the labour process is just part of the scenery, a backdrop against which a universal struggle takes place, one involving the indeterminacy of identity rather than the indeterminacy of labour. At best, the workplace is a source of illustrative examples of the processes whereby individuals are subjected to increased anxiety and seduced by the security offered by powerful corporate authority (Willmott, 1994, 36).

Second, for many theorists, particularly those concerned with culture and identity, it is a struggle of individuals not collectivities. The constant emphasis on 'the formation and reformation of self' (Jermier et al., 1994, 8) is sharply at odds with our theme of self-organization, which is necessarily collective. In referring to 'the new sociality, provided in the culture of the team-family, the use of the shared new language and the espousal of the new company philosophy of Total Quality Management and globalisation' (1995, 188), Casey takes the argument to its logical conclusion in asserting that as the totalizing culture of business eclipses the older forms of class, occupational and professional solidarity, the only form of solidarity is provided within and by the organization.

Finally, it is also ultimately a futile struggle. Even when employees are not entirely subjugated, seduced or self-disciplined, they are prisoners of their own identity projects. For not only is the search for particular secure identities constantly undermined, the search for security *per se* is a self-defeating trap. Knights argues that for collective solidarity to have anything more than a remote chance of effectiveness, 'It would require that the target of resistance become the very preoccupation with stable meaning' (1990, 329). The futility also arises from the nature of the process. It is difficult to see how anything more than individual consciousness raising, rather than collective action, could be on the agenda. Even if it was, there is a final drawback. Opposition is largely self-defeating since those who play the game become addicts to the rules and the pursuit of sovereign rights through bodies such as trade unions hides the disciplinary processes which produce the struggle in the first place (Deetz, 1992, 42). None of our arguments are intended to deny that issues of subjectivity are not entirely legitimate and a central issue for anyone interested in how social relations in the contemporary workplace are constituted and reproduced. Indeed anyone reading this book, with its recurrent emphasis on the significance of identity as a focal point for managerial and employee action, would be hard put to erect such a straw man. The processes of 'identity work' are of central importance (Thompson and McHugh, 1995) and studies of subjectivity as a control device, such as Hochschild's (1983) account of emotional labour among flight attendants, among the most valuable. Our objections are to the type of analysis, notably to the denial of the specificities of the employment relationship, the subjectivizing of social relations and the erosion of the space for resistance and misbehaviour.

It is ironic that we have now come full circle to the post-Braverman cry of whatever happened to worker resistance? Must we be condemned to repeat the same cycle of denial and rediscovery? Foucauldian theory and research, as we have shown in this chapter, is not the only mechanism for taking labour out of the process. Nor is it a homogeneous body of work. Some of the writing on sexuality reviewed in Chapter 6 shows more complexity in the range of employee responses than was previously imagined, and some case studies using elements of a Foucauldian framework do succeed in identifying resistance. For example, Collinson (1994) demonstrates that specific forms of knowledge, based on restricting information from management, are a key resource through which oppositional practices are maintained, and that such action was linked to shop floor workers' concern to keep their identity and to maintain distance from management.

But locating resistance and misbehaviour is against the grain of the conceptual structure of much recent work and also, to some extent, against the associated epistemology. What is problematic about many current accounts of corporate culture, teamworking or TQM is not the argument concerning what those who design the systems want, but the bizarre belief that they have almost no difficulty getting it. As Anthony observes, 'The so-called sub cultures . . . found within some organizations are stronger and more enduring than the transitory managerial cultural espousals that would overcome them' (1989, 7). However, the shift towards the primacy of discourse and the text encourages the removal of workers from the academic gaze and the distinction between the intent and outcome of managerial strategies and practices. In this respect, current discussion often repeats the errors in understanding of the earlier development of management, labour discipline and 'scientific' systems. Whether it be the establishment of Taylorism, bureaucracy, human relations or new technology, extravagant claims of rationality and effectiveness were made by managerial advocates and too often believed by academics. We now know that workers learned to bend the bars in these particular iron cages. Why should the current crop of new management practices be any different?

Actually, we are beginning to know the answer to that question – they are not. Contrary to claims that the controlling functions of management have 'simply been incorporated into the consciousness of the members themselves' (Sewell and Wilkinson, 1992b, 284), one of the clearest things to come out of good case study work is the realization of how aware employees are of the characteristics of culture and change programmes, whether they endorse the objectives or not. Theorists may confuse and elide intent and outcome, but workers are normally tried and tested experts at spotting the 'reality gap'. Wilkinson et al.'s summary is blunt and fairly typical: 'The employees we have interviewed are under no illusions as to senior management's objectives behind the introduction of TQM . . . . No employee felt that the initiatives had anything to do with improving their working life' (1997, 817). Awareness or even hostility may not lead to resistance given particular market conditions or balance of power resources, but it is likely to encourage workers to maintain informal norms and self-organization. Strong workplace organization and traditional forms of misbehaviour such as work limitation can and do continue to frustrate managerial initiatives and restructuring plans in both traditional and HRM and JIT settings (Scott, 1994; Delbridge, 1995).

One of the remarkable features of current arguments is how much has been claimed on the basis of so little. Rosenthal et al. (1997, 121) rightly observe that, 'The various accounts of the manipulation of meaning are long on the content of ideological or discursive messages and on theories of identity. They are short, however, on the substantiation that managerial ideologies or discourses do indeed work in the ways that they allege'. The gap between strong claims and weak evidence has been described elsewhere by Thompson and Findlay (1998). They show that some of the strongest claims for the 'governance of the soul' are simply read off from the stated goals of senior management and corporate discourses, or that employee concerns with maintenance of identity are attributed on the basis of a small number of often highly selective and unsystematic quotes.

We are not saying that resistance and misbehaviour is always present in the same force or form. But it is there if workplace researchers have the time or inclination to look. Examining WIRS 3, Sisson (1993, 206) observes that forms of 'unorganized conflict' were much in evidence even in union-free firms. The best chance of picking up on what is happening on the ground continues to be the kind of longitudinal, observational study under-taken by McKinley and Taylor (of Phoneco: see 1994). But even less inten-sive qualitative and survey work can be sensitive to the epistemological problems of evaluating 'subjectivity' and seek to develop methodological instruments capable of asking more complex questions about relationships between behaviour and attitudes (see Rosenthal et al., 1997, and Marks et al., 1997). It is often not possible to have that kind of access, time or resources. Sometimes, interviewing managers, a tour round the factory and a chat with the union convenor is all that is possible. But neither the blink-ers of specific theories nor the limitations of particular methodologies should be used to close down the potential for digging deeper or seeing differently. Rather, as social scientists, we have to put labour back in, by doing theory and research in such a way that it is possible to 'see' resistance and misbehaviour, and recognize that innovatory employee practices and informal organization will continue to subvert managerial regimes.

Reconceptualizing resistance

This analysis, which has built on Thompson and Ackroyd (1995 – hereafter referred to as 'All Quiet?'), has, if the citations are anything to go by, already touched a nerve among many researchers who have welcomed the empha-sis on bending the methodological and theoretical stick away from all-seeing, all-knowing management, back towards self-aware, self-active labour. For some commentators, notably Martinez-Lucio and Stewart (1997), however, we have taken a few steps too far. As the debate raises some important general issues, it is worth discussing in some detail.

Martinez-Lucio and Stewart broadly welcome our critique, but claim that 'All Quiet?' questioned both the existence of collectivism, and indeed the need for it. They go on to argue that conflict is treated 'as a cipher for indi-vidual autonomy', and that we use 'employees' as a category rather than 'labour'. For example they say that we 'share an assumption that tradition-alism has declined or will disappear' (1997, 62–3).

A lot of this is based on misunderstandings of content and purpose. There is, in fact, considerable common ground, for example in the research agenda they outline at the end of their article. Martinez-Lucio and Stewart are reading a lot into what was basically a critique without an extended alterna-tive. We do not question the existence, need for or conditions that can facili-tate the growth of collectivism. Our point was slightly different: that too many commentators had written off collective resistance because particular types of labour and forms of trade union organization had become weaker.

We hope that the emphasis in Chapter 3 on the resilience of informal self-organization will put some of that misunderstanding right. But in emphasizing a different kind of collective action and organization, we do not dismiss other kinds. As we made clear, the essential conditions for even relatively traditional forms of resistance and misbehaviour are still present. Chill winds of competition in an increasingly globalized production system are compelling capital to focus on more extensive ways of 'taking labour out', and the squeeze on labour is becoming a defining feature of the public sector. While many contemporary theorists attribute the relative quiescence of formal labour organization and action to the power, knowledgeability and ingenuity of management, we see the much less prosaic balance of power arising from a difficult and often hostile economic and political terrain.

No matter what the situation may look like on the surface, there are real tensions in the 'new workplace', for example between the collective regulation of labour process through initiatives such as teamworking and the parallel trend towards the individualization of the employment relationship. The potential for a new politics of production and pro-active agenda for labour to emerge is considerable, as Martinez-Lucio and Stewart (1997) demonstrate in recent work on teamwork and trade unionism in General Motors. Politics cannot repeat and reproduce past patterns of relationships between informal and formal organization. In key periods historically, for example during the rise of the first shop stewards' movement in Britain before and after the First World War and the height of power of the later shop stewards' movement that the Donovan Commission tried to incorporate, there was a direct if uneven line between the two. A combination of organizational restructuring and management action has now 'penetrated' informal self-organization and modified older forms of shop floor autonomy. Old-style work limitation or other things that employers like to call 'Spanish practices' may not be appropriate or feasible in new conditions. But as we have demonstrated, modified forms of self-organization remain the bedrock of employee action and the resource on which more formal and solidaristic behaviour rests, however indirectly.

Returning to the critique made by Martinez-Lucio and Stewart (1997), we also dispute the claim that conflict is treated 'as a cipher for individual autonomy', and the related argument that we use 'employees' as a category rather than 'labour'. Commentators may or may not like our various categories of autonomy that were the main focus of Chapter 3, but they are all collective in character. On the other issue, despite Martinez-Lucio and Stewart's reference to our 'Return to the employee' there are no quotes or references from 'All Quiet?' to back that up. They are not the only authors to invest great significance in the use of the term employee rather than labour (see Jacques, 1996). In this book the terms employees and labour are used interchangeably. What Martinez-Lucio and Stewart appear to have missed in 'All Quiet?' is that our objection is, precisely, that when Foucauldian theory is applied to the workplace, it treats it as just another terrain of the individual's struggle for identity in postmodernity. Whether we talk of labour or employees the same point is intended – that there are conditions and struggles specific to the labour process and the employment relationship.

So, for us it is neither a question of 'waiting for the fightback' or disregarding the capacity of unions to renew their own organization and strategy. Hopefully this book will put some of the misunderstandings right. But we do not want to make a narrow textual defence. There are actual or potential differences which arise from some of our most basic themes. Most notably, we would challenge the idea that traditional collectivism is the sole or even main criterion against which workplace researchers should evaluate the actions of labour. For example, when Martinez-Lucio and Stewart argue that 'organizational misbehaviour doesn't lead to resistance', it parallels the weakness of Edwards and Scullion (1982) that we identified earlier. Misbehaviour, as represented in various forms of informal action and self-organization, should not be treated as a junior form of trade unionism or class struggle which should or will one day grow up. Misbehaviour is not an alternative to or better than these grown-up pursuits, it is just different. It is what it is and no more. We investigate it because it is there, because researchers should be realists above all else. There are enough managerialists with one or both eyes shut without joining them.

We accept that one of the problems is that an alternative account of workplace misbehaviour is at best implicit in 'All Quiet?' The idea of organizational misbehaviour is of course provocative as well as controversial. We began to use the term because it stands the basic assumptions of mainstream OB on its head. Some people are critical of it because it may give ground to management and implies illegitimacy and 'badness'. In our text we counter this by showing that designating misbehaviour is a matter of perspective and definition, and that the identification and prosecution of misbehaviour is to be understood in terms of continuing structural imbalances of power. In view of this it is interesting that, in these supposedly postmodern times, some readers are seemingly still not subtle enough to notice the heavy use of irony in the deployment of key terms such as 'organizational misbehaviour' and 'irresponsible autonomy'.

It has also been said that misbehaviour is over-extended as a category. Again we recognize the problem and we have tried to avoid using misbehaviour as a new generic term to *replace* resistance, recalcitrance or anything else. Of equal importance, we do not pretend that this is a work of social theory, let alone that it is in opposition to the tenets of Marxian perspectives on capital and labour or Weberian accounts of market conflicts between power and status groupings. To put it on the record, we accept the framework that has arisen out of labour process analysis (see Edwards, 1986b; Thompson, 1990) which recognizes a 'structured antagonism between capital and labour', but regards any connection between workplace conflicts and wider social changes as analytically distinct and politically contingent.

Our essential purpose has been to take this kind of argument and ratchet it down one notch further. In other words, whereas a second generation of labour process writers developed a concept of worker resistance that was to be treated as a phenomenon in its own right rather than a conceptual and practical derivation of class struggle, we are asking readers to accept that there is another realm of workplace behaviour that should not be understood merely as a form of or step towards what has become identified with the term resistance. Therefore, rather than trying to replace existing accounts, we have been trying to fill a gap, adding a dimension and vocabulary to get people to think differently about workplace behaviour. We freely admit that the book has not solved or even attempted to deal with all the boundary and definitional terms concerning action in the workplace. Furthermore we accept that the categories and actions overlap. That is why we have broadened the themes of this last chapter to critique attempts to write off or marginalize all forms of dissenting, oppositional behaviour.

We also take heart from the fact we are not alone. There are welcome signs of a broader reconceptualization of resistance, notably from Edwards et al. (1996). Noting that oppositional behaviour is often covert and difficult to detect, they seek to outline and account for the variety of forms of 'under-life' in organizations. Furthermore they reject the current fashionable pessimism: 'More generally, there is a growing body of evidence . . . suggesting that conflict at workplace level is not so much being removed as re-organized and expressed in new ways' (1996, 284). We agree. Contrary to the current rush to judgement about new forms of management and their effects, it is truly 'early days'. There has always been a dialectic of innovation and adaptation between workplace actors and action. Our account of organizational misbehaviour will, we hope, become a part of a wider and more varied picture of workplace action, while at the same time encouraging researchers to exercise greater caution concerning the nature and impacts of new management practices.

References

Ackers, P., Smith, P. and Smith, C. (eds) (1996) *The New Workplace Trade Unionism: Critical Perspectives on Work and Organisation*. London: Routledge.

Ackroyd, S. (1976) 'Sociological Theory and the Human Relations School', *Sociology of Work and Occupations*, 3, 4: 399–420.

Ackroyd, S. (1984) 'Extended Review, The Social Organisation of Industrial Conflict', *Sociological Review*, 32, 1: 116–26.

Ackroyd, S. and Crowdy, P. (1990) 'Can Culture be Managed? Working with "Raw" Material: The Case of the English Slaughtermen', *Personnel Review*, 19, 5: 3–13.

Ackroyd, S, and Procter, S. (1998a) 'Are the British Bad at Flexible Manufacturing?', in R. Delbridge and J. Lowe (eds) *Manufacturing in Transition*. London: Routledge.

Ackroyd, S. and Procter, S. (1998b) 'British Manufacturing Organisation and Workplace Industrial Relations', *British Journal of Industrial Relations*, 36, 2: 163–83.

Ackroyd, S. and Whitaker, A. (1990) 'Manufacturing Decline and the Organisation of Manufacturing in Britain', in P. Stewart, P. Garrahan and P. Crowther (eds) *Restructuring for Economic Flexibility*. Aldershot: Avebury.

Adams, S. (1984) *Roche vs Adams*. London: Jonathan Cape.

Adams, S. (1996) *The Dilbert Principle*. London: Boxtree.

Adkins, L. (1992) 'Sexual Work and the Employment of Women in the Service Industries', in A. Witz and M. Savage (eds) *Gender and Bureaucracy*. Oxford: Blackwell.

Alvesson, M. (1987) 'Organisations, Culture and Ideology', *International Studies of Management and Organisation*, 17, 3: 4–18.

Alvesson, M. (1991) 'Corporate Culture and Corporatism at the Company Level: A Case Study', *Economic and Industrial Democracy*, 12, 2: 347–67.

Alvesson, M. and Willmott, H. (eds) (1992) *Critical Management Studies*. London: Sage.

Analoui, F. (1992) 'Unconventional Practices at Work', *Journal of Managerial Psychology*, 7, 5: 3–31.

Analoui, F. and Kakabadse, A. (1993) *Sabotage*. London: Spokesman.

Anderton, B. and Keily, J. (1988) 'Employee Theft', *Personnel Review*, 17, 5: 37–43.

Anthony, P.D. (1989) 'The Paradox of Organisational Culture or "He Who Leads is Lost"', *Personnel Review*, 19, 4: 3–8.

Aronowitz, S. and Brecher, J. (1975) 'The Postal Strike', in *Root and Branch: The Rise of Workers' Movements*. Greenwich, CT: Fawcett Publications.

Arvedson, L. and Hedberg, M. (1986) 'Absenteeism: A Concept Whose Time Has Come and Gone', *Economic and Industrial Democracy*, 7, 4: 561–3.

Bacon, N. and Storey, J. (1994) 'Individualism and Collectivism and the Changing Role of Trade Unions'. Paper presented at the 12th Labour Process Conference, Aston.

Baldamus, G. (1957) 'The Relationship between Work and Effort', *Journal of Industrial Economics*, 6, 3: 192–201.

Baldamus, G. (1961) *Efficiency and Effort: An Analysis of Industrial Administration*. London: Tavistock.

Barker, J.R. (1993) 'Tightening the Iron Cage: Concertive Control in Self Managed Teams', *Administrative Science Quarterly*, 38, 3: 408–37.

Barsoux, J.-L. (1993) *Funny Business: Humour, Management and Business Culture*. New York: Cassell.

Bassett, P. and Cave, A. (1993) *All for One: The Future of the Unions*. London: Fabian Pamphet 559.

Bate, P. (1994) *Strategies for Cultural Change*. Oxford: Butterworth Heinemann.

Bean, R. (1975) 'The Relationship between Strikes and "Unorganized" Conflict in Manufacturing Industries', *British Journal of Industrial Relations*, 13, 1: 98–101.

Beaumont, P.B. (1991) 'Trade Unions and Human Resource Management', *Industrial Relations Journal*, 22, 4: 300–8.

Behagg, C. (1990) *Politics and Production in the Early Nineteenth Century*. London: Routledge.

Behrend, H. (1957) 'The Effort Bargain', *Industrial and Labour Relations Review*, 10, 4: 503–15.

Bennis, W. (1966) *Changing Organisations*. New York: McGraw-Hill.

Benson, S.P. (1992) 'The Clerking Sisterhood: Rationalization and the Work Culture of Saleswomen in American Department Stores, 1890–1960', in A.J. Mills and P. Tancred (eds) *Gendering Organisational Analysis*. London: Sage.

Beynon, H. (1975) *Working for Ford*. Harmondsworth: Penguin.

BIM (British Institute of Management) (1961) *Absence from Work: Incidence, Cost and Control*. London: British Institute of Management.

Boland, R.J. and Hoffman, R. (1983) 'Humour in a Machine Shop', in L. Pondy et al. (eds) *Organisational Symbolism*. Greenwich, CT: JAI Press.

Boye, M.W. and Jones, J.W. (1997) 'Organisational Culture and Employee Counterproductivity', in R.A. Giacalone and J. Greenberg (eds) *Anti-social Behaviour in Organisations*. London: Sage.

Bradney, P. (1957) 'The Joking Relationship in Industry', *Human Relations*, 10, 2: 179–87.

Braverman, H. (1974) *Labour and Monopoly Capital*. New York: Monthly Review Press.

Breakwell, G.M. (1986) *Coping with Threatened Identities*. London: Macmillan.

Brecher, J. (1978) 'Uncovering the Hidden History of the American Workplace', *Review of Radical Political Economics*, 10, 4: 1–23.

Brewis, J. and Grey, C. (1994) 'Re-Eroticizing the Workforce: An Exegesis and Critique', *Gender, Work and Organisation*, 1, 2: 67–82.

Brewis, J. and Kerfoot, D. (1994) 'Selling Our "Selves"? Sexual Harassment and Intimate Violations in the Workplace'. Paper presented at the BSA Conference, Sexualities in Their Social Contexts, University of Central Lancashire, March.

Brockway, M. (1975) 'Keep on Trucking', in Root and Branch (eds) *Root and Branch: The Rise of the Workers' Movement*. Greenwich, CT: Fawcett Publications.

Brooks-Gordon, B. (1995) 'Struggling in the City: The Subordination of Women Traders in the City of London Oil-Broking Market and their Coping Strategies'. Paper presented at the Women and Psychology Conference, University of Leeds.

Brown, G. (1977) *Sabotage: A Study in Industrial Conflict*. Nottingham: Spokesman Books.

Brown, R.K. (1992) *Understanding Industrial Organisations*. London: Routledge.

Brown, W. and Wright, M. (1994) 'The Empirical Tradition in Workplace Bargaining Research', *British Journal of Industrial Relations*, 32, 2: 153–64.

Burawoy, M. (1979) *Manufacturing Consent: Changes in the Labour Process under Monopoly Capitalism*. Chicago: Chicago University Press.

Burrell, G. (1988) 'Modernism, Postmodernism and Organizational Analysis: The Contribution of Michel Foucault', *Organisation Studies*, 9, 2: 221–35.

Burrell, G. (1992) 'Sex and Organisations', in A.J. Mills and P. Tancred (eds) *Gendering Organisational Analysis*, London: Sage. (Originally published in 1984.)

Business Week (1984) 'Romance in the Workplace: Corporate Rules for the Game of Love', *Business Week*, 18 June: 20–25.

Carter, P. and Jeffs, P. (1992) 'The Hidden Curriculum: Sexuality in Professional Education', in P. Carter, T. Jeffs and M. Smith (eds) *Changing Social Work and Welfare*. Buckingham: Open University Press.

Casey, C. (1995) *Work, Self and Society: After Industrialism*. London: Routledge.

Cavendish, R. (1982) *Women on the Line*. London: Routledge and Kegan Paul.

CBI (Confederation of British Industry) (1970) *Absenteeism: An Analysis of the Problem*. London: Confederation of British Industry.

Chadwick-Jones, J., Brown, C. and Nicholson, N. (1982) *The Social Psychology of Absenteeism*. New York: Praeger.

Charkham, J. (1994) *Keeping Good Company*. Oxford: Oxford University Press.

Clark, H., Chandler, J. and Barry, J. (1994) *Organisations and Identities*. London: Chapman and Hall.

Clark, J. (1995) *Managing Innovation and Change*. London: Sage.

Clarke, T. (1977) 'The *Raison d'être* of Trade Unionism', in Tom Clarke and Laurie Clements (eds) *Trades Unions under Capitalism*. Glasgow: Fontana.

Clarke, T. and Clements, L. (eds) (1977) *Trades Unions under Capitalism*. Glasgow: Fontana.

Clegg, H. (1976) *Trade Unionism under Collective Bargaining*. Oxford: Blackwell.

Clegg, H. (1979) *The Changing System of Industrial Relations in Britain*. Oxford: Blackwell.

Clegg, S.R. (1975) *Power, Rule and Domination*. London: Routledge and Kegan Paul.

Clegg, S.R. (1989) *Frameworks of Power*. London: Sage.

Clegg, S.R. (1990) *Modern Organisations*. London: Sage.

Clegg, S. and Dunkerley, D. (1980) *Organisations, Class and Control*. London: Routledge and Kegan Paul.

Cliff, T. (1974) *The Employers' Offensive*. London: Pluto.

Cockburn, C. (1983) *Brothers: Male Dominance and Technological Change*. London: Pluto.

Cockburn, C. (1991) *In the Way of Women: Men's Resistance to Sex Equality in Organisations*. London: Macmillan.

Cohen, S. (ed.) (1971) *Images of Deviance*. Harmondsworth: Penguin.

Cohen, S. and Taylor, L. (1976) *Escape Attempts: The Theory and Practice of Resistance to Everyday Life*. Harmondsworth: Penguin.

Coleman, J.S. (1970) 'Social Inventions', *Social Forces*, 48, 4: 163–73.

Collins, E.G.C. (1983) 'Managers and Lovers', *Harvard Business Review*, September–October: 142–53.

Collins, O., Dalton, M. and Roy, D. (1946) 'Restriction of Output and Social Cleavage in Industry', *Applied Anthropology*, 5, Summer: 1–14.

Collinson, D.L. (1988) 'Engineering Humour: Masculinity, Joking and Conflict in Shop Floor Relations', *Organisation Studies*, 9, 2: 181–99.

Collinson, D.L. (1992) *Managing the Shopfloor: Subjectivity, Masculinity and Workplace Culture*. Berlin: William de Gruyter.

Collinson, D.L. (1994) 'Strategies of Resistance: Power, Knowledge and Subjectivity in the Workplace', in J. Jermier, W. Nord and D. Knights (eds) *Resistance and Power in the Workplace*. London: Routledge.

Collinson, D.L. and Collinson, M. (1989) 'Sexuality in the Workplace: The Domination of Men's Sexuality', in J. Hearn et al. (eds) *The Sexuality of Organisations*. London: Sage.

Connell, R.W. (1987) *Gender and Power*. Cambridge: Polity Press.

Coopey, J. (1995) 'Managerial Culture and the Stillbirth of Organisational Commitment', *Human Resource Management Journal*, 5, 3: 56–76.

Coventry Machine Tool Workers' Committee (1979) *Crisis in Engineering: Machine Tool Workers Fight for Jobs*. Nottingham: Institute of Workers' Control.

Cronin, J. (1979) *Industrial Conflict in Modern Britain*. London: Croom Helm.

Crouch, C. (1982) *Trade Unions: The Logic of Collective Action*. London: Fontana-Collins.

Crouch, C. and Pizzorno, A. (eds) (1978) *The Resurgence of Class Conflict in Western Europe Vol. 1*. London: Macmillan.

Crystal, G. (1991) *In Search of Excess: The Overcompensation of American Executives*. New York: Norton.

Cunnison, S. (1964) *Wages and Work Allocation*. London: Tavistock.

Dalton, M. (1948) 'The Industrial Rate Buster', *Applied Anthropology*, 7, 1: 5–23.

Dandeker, C. (1990) *Surveillance, Power and Modernity: Bureaucracy and Discipline from 1700 to the Present Day*. Cambridge: Polity Press.

Davidson, M.J. and Earnshaw, J. (1990) 'Policies, Practices and Attitudes towards Sexual Harassment in UK Organisations', *Personnel Review*, 19, 3: 23–7.

Davies, C. (1982) 'Ethnic Jokes, Moral Values and Social Boundaries', *British Journal of Sociology*, 33, 3: 383–403

Day, R.A. and Day, J. (1997) 'A Review of the Current State of Negotiated Order Theory: An Appreciation and Critique', *Sociological Quarterly*, 18 (Winter): 126–42.

Deetz, S. (1992) 'Disciplinary Power in the Modern Corporation', in M. Alvesson and H. Willmott (eds) *Critical Management Studies*. London: Sage.

Delbridge, R. (1995) 'Surviving JIT: Control and Resistance in a Japanese Transplant', *Journal of Management Studies*, 32, 6: 803–17.

Delbridge, R., Turnbull, P. and Wilkinson, B. (1992) 'Pushing Back the Frontiers: Management Control and Work Intensification Under J.I.T./ T.Q.M. Factory Regimes', *New Technology, Work and Employment*, 7, 2: 97–106.

Dennis, N., Henriques, F. and Slaughter, C. (1956) *Coal Is Our Life*. London: Eyre and Spottiswoode.

Dews, P. (1986) 'The "Nouvelle Philosophie" and Foucault', in M. Gane (ed.) *Towards a Critique of Foucault*. London: Routledge.

Di Tomaso, N. (1989) 'Sexuality in the Workplace: Discrimination and Harassment', in J. Hearn et al. (eds) *The Sexuality of Organisations*. London: Sage.

Ditton, J. (1972) 'Absent at Work: How to Manage Monotony', *New Society*, 21: 697–81.

Ditton, J. (1977a) *Part-time Crime: An Ethnography of Fiddling and Pilferage*. London: Macmillan.

Ditton, J. (1977b) 'Perks, Pilferage and the Fiddle: The Historical Structure of Invisible Wages', *Theory and Society*, 4, 1: 39–71.

Ditton, J. (1978) *Contrology: Beyond Criminology*. London: Macmillan.

Donaldson, L. (1985) *In Defence of Organisation Theory*. Cambridge: Cambridge University Press.

Douglas, M. (1975) *Implicit Meanings*. London: Routledge and Kegan Paul.

Drew, P. (1987) 'Po-Faced Receipts of Teases', *Linguistics*, 25, 2: 219–53.

Dubois, P. (1977) *Sabotage in Industry*. Harmondsworth: Penguin.

DuGay, P. (1996) *Consumption and Identity at Work*. London: Sage.

Duncan, W. and Feisal, J.P. (1989) 'No Laughing Matter: Patterns of Humour in the Workplace', *Organisational Dynamics*, 17, 4: 18–30.

Dunlop, J.T. (1958) *Industrial Relations Systems*. New York: Holt.

Edwards, P. (1986a) *Managing the Factory: A Survey of General Managers*. Oxford: Blackwell.

Edwards, P. (1986b) *Conflict at Work: A Materialist Analysis of Workplace Relations*. Oxford: Blackwell.

Edwards, P. (1988) 'Patterns of Conflict and Accommodation', in D. Gallie (ed.) *Employment in Britain*. Oxford: Blackwell.

Edwards, P. and Scullion, H. (1982) *The Social Organisation of Industrial Conflict*. Oxford: Blackwell.

Edwards, P., Collinson, D. and Della-Rocca, G. (1996) 'Workplace Resistance in Western Europe: A Preliminary Overview and Research Agenda', *European Journal of Industrial Relations*, 1, 3: 283–94.

Edwards, R. (1979) *Contested Terrain: The Transformation of Industry in the Twentieth Century*. London: Heinemann.

Eldridge, J. (1968) *Industrial Disputes*. London: Routledge.

Emerson, J. (1969) 'Negotiating the Serious Import of Humour', *Sociometry*, 32: 169–81.

Filby, M. (1992) 'The Figures, the Personality and the Bums: Service Work and Sexuality', *Work, Employment and Society*, 6, 1: 23–42.

Finchman, M. (1984) 'A Theoretical Approach to Understanding Employee Absence', in P.S. Goodman and R. Atkin, *Absenteeism*. San Francisco: Jossey-Bass.

Fineman, S. (1993) *Emotion in Organisations*. London: Sage.

Fitzpatrick, J. (1980) 'Adapting to Danger: The Participant Observation Study of an Underground Mine', *Sociology of Work and Occupations*, 7, 2: 131–58.

Fogarty, M. and Brooks, D. (1986) *Trade Unions and British Industrial Development*. London: Policy Studies Institute.

Ford, R.C. and McLaughlin, F.S. (1987) 'Should Cupid Come to the Workplace: An APSA Survey', *Personnel Administrator*, October: 100–10.

Foucault, M. (1977) *Discipline and Punish*. London: Allen and Unwin.

Fournie, D. (1988) *Why Employees Don't Do What They're Supposed to Do and What to Do About It*. New York: Liberty Hall Press.

Fox, A. (1974) *Beyond Contract: Work, Power and Trust Relations*. London, Faber and Faber.

Fox, S. (1990) 'The Ethnography of Humour and the Problem of Social Reality', *Sociology*, 24, 3: 431–46.

Franklin, P. (1990) *Profits of Deceit: Dispatches from the Front Lines of Fraud*. London: Heinemann.

Friedman, A. (1977) *Industry and Labour: Class Struggle at Work and Monopoly Capitalism*. London: Macmillan.

Friedman, A. (1987) 'The Means of Management Control and Labour Process Theory', *Sociology*, 21, 2: 287–94.

Gallacher, W. and Campbell, J. (1972) *Direct Action: An Outline of Workshop Social Organisation*. Reprints in Labour History. London: Pluto. (Originally published in 1919.)

Giacalone, R.A. and Greenberg, J. (eds) (1997) *Anti-Social Behaviour in Organisations*. London: Sage.

Giddens, A. (1992) *The Transformation of Intimacy: Sexuality, Love and Eroticism in Modern Societies*. Cambridge: Polity Press.

Glaberman, M. (1976) 'The Working Class', *Radical America*, 10, 1: 23–40.

Goffman, E. (1963) *Asylums*. Harmondsworth: Penguin.

Goffman. E. (1969) *Interaction Ritual*. Harmondsworth: Penguin.

Goodman, P.S., Atkin, R.S. and Associates (1984) *Absenteeism: New Approaches to Understanding, Measuring and Managing Employee Absence*. London: Jossey-Bass.

Goodrich, C. (1975) *The Frontier of Control: A Study of British Workshop Politics*. London: Pluto. (Originally published in 1920.)

Gospel, H. (1995) 'The Decline of Apprenticeship Training in Britain', *Industrial Relations Journal*, 26, 1: 32–44.

Gottfried, H. and Graham, L. (1993) 'Constructing Difference: The Making of Gendered Subcultures in a Japanese Assembly Plant', *Sociology*, 27, 4: 611–28.

Grenier, G.J. (1988) *Inhuman Relations, Quality Circles and Anti-Unionism in American Industry*. Philadelphia: Temple University Press.

Grey, C. (1994) 'Organisational Calvinism: Insecurity and Labour Power in a Professional Labour Process'. Paper presented at the 12th Annual Labour Process Conference, Aston.

Gutek, B. (1985) *Sex and the Workplace*. London: Jossey-Bass.

Gutek, B. (1989) 'Sexuality and the Workplace: Key Issues in Social Research and Organisational Practice', in J. Hearn et al. (eds) *The Sexuality of Organisations*. London: Sage.

Haavio-Mannila, E. (1988) 'Emotional Relations at Work', *Finnish Labour Bulletin*, 2,1: 28–35.

Handy, C. (1995) *The Future of Work*. London: W.H. Smith Contemporary Papers, no. 8.

Harlow, E., Hearn, J. and Parkin, W. (1992) 'Sexuality and Social Work Organisations', in P. Carter, T. Jeffs and M. Smith (eds) *Changing Social Work and Welfare*. Buckingham: Open University Press.

Hayes, D. (1989) *Behind the Silicon Curtain: The Seductions of Work in a Lonely Era*. London: Free Association Books.

Hearn, J. (1985) 'Men's Sexuality at Work', in A. Metcalfe and M. Humphries (eds) *The Sexuality of Men*. London: Pluto.

Hearn, J. (1992) *Men in the Public Eye: The Construction and Deconstruction of Public Men and Public Patriarchies*. London: Routledge.

Hearn, J. and Parkin, W. (1987) *'Sex' at 'Work': The Power and Paradox of Organisational Sexuality*. Brighton: Wheatsheaf.

Hearn, J., Sheppard, D.L., Tancred-Sheriff, P. and Burrell, G. (eds) (1989) *The Sexuality of Organisations*. London: Sage.

Hebdige, D. (1979) *Sub-Culture: The Meaning of Style*. London: Methuen.

Henry, S. (1987a) *The Hidden Economy: The Context and Control of Borderline Crime*. Oxford: Martin Robertson.

Henry, S. (1987b) 'Disciplinary Pluralism: Four Models of Private Justice in the Workplace', *Sociological Review*, 35, 2: 279–319.

Herzberg, F. (1959) *The Motivation to Work*. New York: John Wiley.

Hickson, D. and McCullough, A.F. (1980) 'Power in Organisations', in G. Salaman and K. Thompson (eds) *Control and Ideology in Organisations*. Buckingham: Open University Press.

Hill, S. (1981) *Competition and Control at Work*. London: Heinemann.

Hinton, J. (1973) *The First Shop Stewards' Movement*. London: Allen and Unwin.

Hirschman, A.D. (1970) *Exit, Voice and Loyalty*. Cambridge, MA: Harvard University Press.

Hobbs, D. (1988) *Doing the Business: Entrepreneurship, the Working Class, and Detectives in the East End of London*. Oxford: Clarendon Press.

Hobbs, D. (1995) *Bad Business*. London: Oxford University Press.

Hobsbawm, E.J. (1981) 'The Forward March of Labour Halted?', in M. Jaques and F. Mulhern (eds) *The Forward March of Labour Halted?* London: New Left Books. (Originally published in *Marxism Today*, September 1978.)

Hochschild, A.R. (1983) *The Managed Heart: Commercialization of Human Feeling*. Berkeley: University of California Press.

Holloway, W. and Jefferson, T. (1995) 'PC or not PC: Sexual Harassment and the Question of Ambivalence', *Human Relations*, 9, 3: 373–93.

Homans, G. (1950) *The Human Group*. New York: Harcourt Brace.

Hope, V. and Hendry, J. (1995) 'Corporate Culture: Is It Relevant for the Organisations of the 1990s?' *Human Resource Management Journal*, 5, 4: 61–73.

Humphries, S. (1988) *A Secret World of Sex, Forbidden Fruit: The British Experience 1900–1950*. London: Sidgwick and Jackson.

Hyman, R. (1972) *Strikes*. London: Fontana-Collins.

Hyman, R. (1975) 'Industrial Conflict and Political Economy', in *Socialist Register, 1975*. London: Merlin Press.

Hyman, R. (1987) 'Strategy or Structure? Capital, Labour and Control', *Work, Employment and Society*, 1, 1: 25–55.

Hyman, R. and Brough, I. (1975) *Social Values and Industrial Relations*. Oxford: Blackwell.

Ingersoll Engineers (1994) *The Quiet Revolution Continues*. Rugby: Ingersoll Engineers.

IRS (1992) 'Focus: Sexual Harassment at the Workplace', *IRS Employment Trends*, 513, June: 1102–4.

Jackson, M. (1977) *Industrial Relations*. London: Croom Helm.

Jacques, R. (1996) *Manufacturing the Employee*. London: Sage.

Jaques, E. (1951) *The Changing Culture of a Factory*. London: Tavistock.

Jermier, J. (1988) 'Sabotage at Work: The Rational View', *The Sociology of Organisations*, 6: 101–34.

Jermier, J., Knights, D. and Nord, W. (eds) (1994) *Resistance and Power in Organisations*. London: Sage.

Jones, O. (1997) 'Changing the Balance: Taylorism, TQM and Work Organisation', *New Technology, Work and Employment*, 12, 1: 13–24.

Kanter, R. (1977) *Men and Women of the Corporation*. New York: Basic Books.

Keith, B. and Collinson, D. (1994a) 'Policing Gender: Barriers to Change in the Police'. Paper presented at the International Labour Process Conference, Aston.

Keith, B. and Collinson, D. (1994b) 'Constructing Control', in J. Hartley and G. Stephenson (eds) *Employment Relations*. Oxford: Blackwell.

Kelly, G. (1972) *Make Conflict Work for You*. New York: Bantam Books.

Kelly, J.E. (1990) 'British Trade Unionism, 1979–89: Change, Continuity or Transformation?' *Work, Employment and Society*, Special Issue, May: 29–65.

Kerfoot, D. and Knights, D. (1993) 'Management, Masculinity and Manipulation', *Journal of Management Studies*, 30: 659–79.

Knights, D. (1990) 'Subjectivity, Power and the Labour Process', in D. Knights and H. Willmott (eds) *Labour Process Theory*. London: Macmillan.

Knights, D. and Vurdubakis, T. (1994) 'Foucault, Power, Resistance and All That', in J. Jermier, W. Nord and D. Knights (eds) *Resistance and Power in Organisations*. London: Routledge.

Knights, D. and Willmott, H. (1989) 'Power and Subjectivity at Work: From Degradation to Subjugation in Social Relations', *Sociology*, 23, 4: 535–58.

Knights, D. and Willmott, H. (eds) (1990) *Labour Process Theory*. London: Macmillan.

Knights, D., Willmott, H. and Collinson, D. (eds) (1985) *Job Redesign: Critical Perspectives on the Labour Process*. Aldershot: Gower.

Kornbluh, J.L. (ed.) (1968) *Rebel Voices: An I.W.W. Anthology*. Ann Arbor, MI: Free Press.

Kunda, G. (1995) *Engineering Culture: Control and Commitment in a High-tech Corporation*. Philadelphia: Temple University Press.

Lane, T. (1974) *The Union Makes Us Strong*. London: Arrow.

Lane, T. (1982) 'The Unions: Caught on the Ebb Tide', *Marxism Today*, 26, 9: 6–13.

La Nuez, D. and Jermier, J. (1990) 'Sabotage by Managers and Technocrats: The Quiet Revolution at Work'. Paper presented at the 8th Aston/UMIST Conference on the Organisation and Control of the Labour Process, Aston, March.

Lawrence, P. (1996) 'Through a Glass Darkly: Towards a Characterization of British Management', in I. Glover and M. Hughes (eds) *The Professional Managerial Class*. Aldershot: Avebury.

Leavitt, H. (1973) *Managerial Psychology*. Chicago: University of Chicago Press.

Lee, R. and Lawrence, P. (1985) *Organisational Behaviour: Politics at Work*. London: Heinemann.

Levine, A.L. (1967) *Industrial Retardation in Britain*. New York: Basic Books.

Likert, R. and Likert, J.G. (1976) *New Ways of Managing Conflict*. New York: McGraw-Hill.

Linstead, S. (1985) 'Jokers Wild: The Importance of Humour and the Maintenance of Organisational Culture', *Sociological Review*, 33, 4: 741–67.

Littler, C. (1982) *The Development of the Labour Process in Capitalist Societies: A Comparative Analysis of Workplace Organisation.* London: Heinemann.

Livingstone, D.W. and Luxton, M. (1989) 'Gender Consciousness at Work: Modifications of the Male Breadwinner Norm among Steelworkers and Their Spouses', *Canadian Review of Sociology and Anthropology*, 26, 2: 240–75.

Lovering, J. (1990) 'A Perfunctory Sort of Fordism: Economic Structuring and Labour Market Segmentation in Britain in the 1980s', *Work, Employment and Society.* (Special Issue: A Decade of Change), May: 9–28.

Lupton, T. (1963) *On the Shop Floor: Two Studies of Workplace Organisation and Output.* Oxford: Pergamon Press.

Luthans, F. (1972) *Organization Behaviour.* New York: McGraw-Hill.

Lyon, D. (1988) *The Information Society: Issues and Illusions.* Cambridge: Polity Press.

Lyon, D. (1994) *The Electronic Eye.* Cambridge: Polity Press.

McGregor, D. (1960) *The Human Side of Enterprise.* New York: McGraw-Hill.

MacInnes, J. (1997a) *Thatcherism at Work.* Buckingham: Open University Press.

MacInnes, J. (1997b) 'Why Nothing Much Has Changed: Recession, Economic Restructuring and Industrial Relations since 1979', *Employee Relations*, 9, 1: 3–9.

McKinley, A. and Taylor, P. (1994) 'Power, Surveillance and Resistance: Inside the Factory of the Future'. Paper presented at the 14th Labour Process Conference, Aston.

McKinley, A. and Taylor, P. (1996) 'Power, Surveillance and Resistance: Inside the "Factory of the Future", in P. Ackers, C. Smith and P. Smith (eds) *The New Workplace Trade Unionism: Critical Perspectives on Work and Organisation.* London: Routledge.

McKinley, A. and Taylor, P. (1998) 'Foucault and the Politics of Production', in A. McKinley and K. Starkey (eds) *Foucault, Management and Organisation.* London: Sage.

MacKinnon, C.A. (1979) *The Sexual Harassment of Working Women.* New Haven, CT: Yale University Press.

Malone, P.B. (1980) 'Humor: A Double Edged Tool for Today's Managers?', *Academy of Management Review*, 5, 3: 357–60.

Mann, M. (1973) *Consciousness and Action among the Western Working Class.* London: Macmillan.

Marglin, S. (1974) 'What Do Bosses Do?', in A. Gorz (ed.) *The Division of Labour.* Brighton: Harvester Press.

Marks, A., Findlay, P. and Hine, J. (1997) 'Whisky Galore: Teamworking and Workplace Transformation in the Scottish Spirits Industry'. Paper presented at the 15th International Labour Process Conference, Edinburgh University.

Mars, G. (1973) 'Chance, Punters and the Fiddle: Institutionalized Pilferage in a Hotel Dining Room', in M. Warner (ed.) *The Sociology of the Workplace.* London: Allen and Unwin.

Mars, G. (1982a) 'Dock Pilferage', in P. Rock and M. McIntosh (eds) *Deviance and Social Control.* London: Tavistock.

Mars, G. (1982b) *Cheats at Work: An Anthropology of Workplace Crime.* London: Counterpoint.

Marsden, R. (1993) 'The Politics of Organisational Analysis', *Organisation Studies*, 14, 1: 93–121.

Marsh, P., Rosser, E. and Harré, R. (1983) *The Rules of Disorder.* London: Routledge.

Martinez-Lucio, M. and Stewart, P. (1997) 'The Paradox of Contemporary Labour Process Theory: The Rediscovery of Labour and the Disappearance of Collectivism', *Capital and Class*, 62, Summer: 49–77.

Martinez-Lucio, M. and Weston, S. (1992) 'The Politics and Complexity of Trade Union Responses to New Management Practices', *Human Resource Management Journal*, 2, 1: 77–91.

Maslow, A. (1943) 'A Theory of Human Motivation', *Psychological Review*, 50: 370–96.

Mayo, E. (1933) *The Human Problems of an Industrial Civilization*. New York: Macmillan.

Milkman, R. (ed.) (1995) *Women, Work and Protest: A Century of US Women's Labour History*. London: Routledge and Kegan Paul.

Milkman, R. (1998) 'The New American Workplace: High Road or Low Road?', in P. Thompson and C. Warhurst (eds) *Workplaces of the Future*. London: Macmillan.

Mills, A.J. and Tancred, P. (eds) (1992) *Gendering Organisational Analysis*. London: Sage.

Millward, N., Smart, D., Stevens, M. and Hawes, W.R. (1992) *Workplace Industrial Relations in Transition: The DE/PSI/ESRC Survey*. Aldershot: Dartmouth.

Montgomery, D. (1980) *Workers' Control in America: Studies in the History of Work, Technology and Labour Struggles*. London: Cambridge University Press.

Morgan, D. (1981) 'Men, Masculinity and the Process of Sociological Enquiry', in H. Roberts (ed.) *Doing Feminist Research*. London: Routledge.

Morgan, G. (1990) *Organisations in Society*. London: Macmillan.

Mulkay, M. (1988) *On Humour*. Cambridge: Polity Press.

Murphy, J.T. (1972) *The Workers' Committee: An Outline of its Principles and Structure*. Reprints in Labour History. London: Pluto Press. (First published in 1917.)

Neuman, J.H. and Barron, R.A. (1997) 'Aggression in the Workplace', in R.A. Giacalone and J. Greenberg (eds) *Anti-Social Behaviour in Organisations*. London: Sage.

Newton, T. (1994) 'Resocializing the Subject?', Working Paper Series, Department of Business Studies, University of Edinburgh.

Nichols, T. and Armstrong, P. (1976) *Workers Divided: A Study in Shop Floor Politics*. London: Fontana-Collins.

Nichols, T. and Beynon, H. (1977) *Living with Capitalism*. London: Routledge and Kegan Paul.

Noon, M. and Delbridge, R. (1993) 'News from behind my Hand: Gossip in Organisations', *Organisation Studies*, 14, 1: 23–36.

O'Connell, R.W. (1983) *Which Way Is Up?* London: Allen and Unwin.

O'Doherty, D. (1994) 'Institutional Withdrawal? Anxiety and Conflict in the Emerging Banking Labour Process'. Paper presented at the 12th International Labour Process Conference, Aston.

Ogbonna, E. and Wilkinson, B. (1990) 'Corporate Strategy and Corporate Culture: The View from the Checkout', *Personnel Review*, 19, 4: 9–15.

O'Neill, J. (1986) 'The Disciplinary Society: From Weber to Foucault', *British Journal of Sociology*, 37, 1: 42–60.

Penn, R. (1985) *Skilled Workers in the Class Structure*. Cambridge: Cambridge University Press.

Peters, T. and Waterman, R. (1982) *In Search of Excellence*. New York: Harper and Row.

Pfeffer, R.M. (1981) *Working for Capitalism*. New York: Columbia University Press.

Pollert, A. (1981) *Girls, Wives and Factory Lives*. London: Macmillan.

Pollert, A. (ed.) (1991) *Farewell to Flexibility?* Oxford: Blackwell.

Pollert, A (1996) 'Teamwork on the Assembly Line: Contradictions and the Dynamics of Union Resilience', in P. Ackers, P. Smith and C. Smith (eds) *The New Workplace and Trades Unionism*. London: Routledge.

Pringle, R. (1988) *Secretaries Talk: Sexuality, Power and Work*. London: Verso.

Punch, M. (1996) *Dirty Business*. London: Sage.

Purcell, J. (1993) 'The End of Institutional Industrial Relations', *Political Quarterly*, 64, 1: 6–23.

Quinn, R. (1977) 'Coping with Cupid: The Management of Romantic Relations in Organisations', *Administrative Science Quarterly*, 22, 1: 30–45.

Radcliffe-Brown, A.R. (1952) 'On Joking Relationships', *Structure and Function in Primitive Society*. London: Routledge and Kegan Paul. (Originally published in *Africa*, 19: 133–40, 1940.)

Ramazanoglu, C. (1987) 'Sex and Violence in Academic Life or, You Can't Keep a Good Man Down', in J. Hanmer and M. Maynard (eds) *Women, Violence and Social Control, Explorations in Sociology, 23*. London: Macmillan.

Ramsay, K. and Parker, M. (1992) 'Gender, Bureaucracy and Organisational Culture', in M. Savage and A. Witz (eds) *Gender and Bureaucracy*. Oxford: Blackwell.

Ray, C. (1986) 'Corporate Culture: The Last Frontier of Control', *Journal of Management Studies*, 23, 3: 287–97.

Reed, M. (1985) *Redirections in Organisational Analysis*. London: Tavistock.

Reed, M. (1992) *The Sociology of Organisations*. Brighton: Harvester Wheatsheaf.

Renold, C.G. (1914) *Sociological Review* (Old Series) 7, 2.

Robertson, C., Dyer, C. and Campbell, D. (1988) 'Campus Harassment: Sexual Harassment Policies and Procedures at Institutions of Higher Learning', *Signs*, 13, 4: 792–812.

Robinson, S.L. and Bennett, R. (1995) 'A Typology of Deviant Workplace Behaviours', *Academy of Management Journal*, 38, 4: 555–72.

Roethlisberger, F.J. and Dickson, W.L. (1964) *Management and the Worker*. Cambridge, MA: Harvard University Press. (First published in 1939.)

Rogers, J.K. and Henson, K.D. (1997) ' "Hey, Why Don't You Wear a Shorter Skirt?": Structural Vulnerability and the Organisation of Sexual Harassment in Temporary Clerical Employment', *Gender and Society*, 11, 2: 215–37.

Roper, M. (1994) *Masculinity and the British Organisation Man since 1945*. Oxford: Oxford University Press.

Rose, M. (1988) *Industrial Behaviour*. Harmondsworth: Penguin.

Rosenthal, P., Hill, S. and Peccei, R. (1997) 'Checking Out Service: Evaluating Excellence: HRM in Retailing', *Work, Employment and Society*, 11, 3: 481–503.

Roy, D. (1952) 'Quota Restriction and Goldbricking in a Machine Shop', *American Journal of Sociology*, 57, 5: 427–42.

Roy, D. (1953) 'Work Satisfaction and Social Reward in Quota Achievement: An Analysis of Piecework Incentives', *American Sociological Review*, 18, 5: 507–14.

Roy, D. (1954) 'Efficiency and the "Fix": Informal Inter-Group Relations in Piecework Machine Shops', *American Journal of Sociology*, 60, 3: 255–66.

Roy, D. (1958) 'Banana Time: Job Satisfaction and Informal Interaction', *Human Organisation*, 18, 1: 158–61.

Roy, D. (1974) 'Sex in the Factory: Informal Heterosexual Relations between Supervisors and Workgroups', in C.D. Bryant (ed.) *Deviant Behaviour*. Chicago: Rand McNally.

Rubery, J. (1980) 'Structured Labour Markets, Worker Organisation and Low Pay', in A. Ainsday (ed.) *The Economics of Women and Work*. Harmondsworth: Penguin.

Sakolsky, R. (1992) 'Disciplinary Power and the Labour Process', in A. Sturdy, D. Knights and H. Willmott (eds) *Skill and Consent: Contemporary Studies in the Labour Process*. London: Routledge.

Salaman, G. (1979) *Work Organisation: Resistance and Control*. London: Longman.

Salaman, G. (1986) *Working*. London: Tavistock.

Sargent, A.G. (1983) *The Androgynous Manager*. New York: American Management Association.

Savage, M. and Witz, A. (eds) (1992) *Gender and Bureaucracy*. Oxford: Blackwell.

Scott, A. (1994) *Willing Slaves: British Workers under Human Resource Management*. Cambridge: Cambridge University Press.

Segal, L. (1987) *Is the Future Female? Troubled Thoughts from Contemporary Feminism*. London: Virago.

Sewell, G. and Wilkinson, B. (1992a) 'Someone To Watch Over Me: Surveillance, Discipline and the Just in Time Labour Process', *Sociology*, 26, 2: 271–89.

Sewell, G. and Wilkinson, B. (1992b) 'Empowerment or Emasculation? Shop Floor Surveillance in the Total Quality Organisation', in P. Blyton and B. Turnbull (eds) *Reassessing Human Resource Management*. London: Sage.

Sharpe, D. (1996) 'Changing Managerial Control Strategies and Subcultural Processes: An Ethnographic Study on the Hano Assembly Line'. Paper presented at the 14th Labour Process Conference, Aston.

Sheppard, D. (1989) 'Organisations, Power and Sexuality: The Image and Self Image of Women Managers', in Hearn et al. (eds) *The Sexuality of Organisations*. London: Sage.

Silverman, D. (1970) *The Theory of Organisations*. London: Heinemann.

Sisson, K. (1993) 'In Search of HRM', *British Journal of Industrial Relations*, 31, 2: 201–10.

Skinner, B. (1953) *Science and Human Behaviour*. London: Macmillan.

Smircich, L. (1983) 'Concepts of Culture and Organisational Analysis', *Administrative Science Quarterly*, 28, 3: 339–58.

Smith, C. and Thompson, P. (1992) 'When Harry Met Sally . . . and Hugh and David and Andy'. Paper presented at the 10th International Labour Process Conference, Aston.

Smith, P. and Morton, G. (1993) 'Union Exclusion and the De-Collectivization of Industrial Relations in Contemporary Britain', *British Journal of Industrial Relations*, 31, 1: 24–38.

Smith, S. and Wilkinson, B. (1995) 'No Doors, No Offices, No Secrets. We Are Our Own Policemen! Capitalism without Conflict', in S. Linstead, R. Grafton-Small and P. Jeffcutt (eds) *Understanding Management*. London: Sage.

Snizek, W.E. (1974) 'Deviant Behaviour among Blue Collar Workers: Work-Norm Violations in the Factory', in C.D. Bryant (ed.) *Deviant Behaviour*. Chicago: Rand-McNally.

Sprouse, M. (ed.) (1992) *Sabotage in the American Workplace*. San Francisco: Pressure Drop Press.

Stanko, E. (1988) 'Keeping Women In and Out of Line: Sexual Harassment and Occupational Segregation', in S. Walby (ed.) *Gender Segregation at Work*. Buckingham: Open University Press.

Steers, R.M. and Rhodes, S. (1984) 'Knowledge and Speculation about Absenteeism', in P.S. Goodman and R. Atkin (eds) *Absenteeism*. San Francisco: Jossey-Bass.

Stockdale, M.S. (1996) *Sexual Harassment in the Workplace: Perspectives, Frontiers and Response Strategies*. London: Sage.

Storey, J. (1983) *Management Prerogative and the Question of Control*. London: Routledge and Kegan Paul.

Storey, J. (1989) 'The Means of Management Control', *Sociology*, 23, 1: 119–24.

Sykes, A.J. (1966) 'Joking Relationships in an Industrial Setting', *American Anthropologist*, 68, 1: 188–93.

Taylor, F.W. (1947) *Scientific Management*. New York: Harper and Row. (First published 1911.)

Taylor, L. and Walton, P. (1971) 'Industrial Sabotage: Motives and Meanings', in S. Cohen (ed.) *Images of Deviance*. Harmondsworth: Penguin.

Taylor, S. (1998) 'Emotional Labour and the New Workplace', in P. Thompson and C. Warhurst (eds) *Workplaces of the Future*. London: Macmillan.

Terry, M. (1977) 'The Inevitable Growth of Informality', *British Journal of Industrial Relations*, 15, 1: 76–90.

Thomas, A.M. and Kitzinger, C. (1994) 'It's Just Something That Happens: The Invisibility of Sexual Harassment in the Workplace', *Gender, Work and Organisation*, 1, 3: 151–61.

Thomason, G. (1991) 'The Management of Personnel', *Personnel Review*, 20, 2: 3–10.

Thompson, E.P. (1968) 'Time, Work Discipline and Industrial Capitalism', *Past and Present*, 38, 1: 5–97.

Thompson, P. (1983) *The Nature of Work: An Introduction to the Debates on the Labour Process*. London: Macmillan.

Thompson, P. (1989) *The Nature of Work*, 2nd edn. London: Macmillan.

Thompson, P. (1990) 'Crawling from the Wreckage: The Labour Process and the Politics of Production', in D. Knights and H. Willmott (eds) *Labour Process Theory*. London: Macmillan.

Thompson, P. and Ackroyd, S. (1995) 'All Quiet on the Workplace Front? A Critique of Recent Trends in British Industrial Sociology', *Sociology*, 29, 4: 610–33.

Thompson, P. and Bannon, E. (1985) *Working the System*. London: Pluto.

Thompson, P. and Findlay, P. (1998) 'Changing the People: Social Engineering in the Contemporary Workplace', in A. Sayer and L. Ray (eds) *Culture and Economy after the Cultural Turn*. London: Sage.

Thompson, P. and McHugh, D. (1995) *Work Organisations*, 2nd edn. London: Macmillan.

Townley, B. (1993) *Reframing Human Resource Management*. London: Sage.

TUCRIC (1983) *Sexual Harassment of Women at Work, a Study from West Yorkshire*. Trade Union Centre, Leeds: TUCRIC.

Turner, B. (1971) *Exploring the Industrial Subculture*. London: Macmillan.

Vaught, C. and Smith, D. (1980) 'Incorporation and Mechanical Solidarity in an Underground Coal Mine', *Sociology of Work and Occupations*, 7, 2: 159–87.

Von Haller, G.B. (1971) *Industrial Psychology*. New York: Prentice-Hall.

Vroom, V. (1960) *Work and Motivation*. New York: John Wiley.

Walby, S. (1986) *Patriarchy at Work*. Cambridge: Polity Press.

Warhurst, C. and Thompson, P. (1998) 'Hands, Hearts and Minds', in C. Warhurst and P. Thompson (eds) *Workplaces of the Future*. London: Macmillan.

Watson, S. (1972) 'Counter-Planning on the Shop Floor', *Radical America*, 5, 3: 22–45.

Webster, F. and Robbins, K. (1989) 'Plan and Control: Towards a Cultural History of the Information Society', *Theory and Society*, 18, 2: 323–51.

Webster, F. and Robbins, K. (1993) 'I'll be Watching You: Comment on Sewell and Wilkinson', *Sociology*, 27, 2: 243–52.

Westwood, S. (1984) *All Day Every Day: Factory and Family in the Making of Women's Lives*. London: Pluto.

Whitehead, A.N. (1938) *The Industrial Worker*. London: Oxford University Press.

Wilkinson, B. (1983) *The Shop Floor Politics of New Technology*. London: Heinemann.

Wilkinson, B., Godfrey, G. and Marchington, M. (1997) 'Bouquets, Brickbats and Blinkers: Total Quality Management and Employee Involvement in Practice', *Organization Studies*, 18, 5: 799–820.

Williamson, A.D. (1993) 'Is This the Right Time to Come Out?', *Harvard Business Review*, July/August: 18–27.

Willis, P. (1977) *Learning to Labour*. Aldershot: Saxon House.

Willmott, H. (1987) 'Studying Managerial Work: A Critique and a Proposal', *Journal of Management Studies*, 24, 3: 249–70.

Willmott, H. (1989) 'Subjectivity and the Dialectics of Praxis', in D. Knights and H. Willmott (eds) *Labour Process Theory*. London: Macmillan.

Willmott, H. (1993) 'Strength is Ignorance, Slavery is Freedom: Managing Culture in Modern Organisations', *Journal of Management Studies*, 30, 4: 515–52.

Willmott, H. (1994) 'Theorizing Agency: Power and Subjectivity in Organisation Studies', in J. Hassard and M. Parker (eds) *Towards a New Theory of Organisations*. London: Routledge.

Wilson, C.P. (1979) *Jokes: Form, Content, Use and Function*. London: Academic Press.

Wilson, D. and Rosenfeld, R.H. (1990) *Managing Organisations: Text Readings and Cases*. London: McGraw-Hill.

Wise, S. and Stanley, L. (1990) 'Sexual Harassment, Sexual Conduct and Gender in Social

Work Settings', in P. Carter, T. Jeffs and M. Smith (eds) *Social Work and Social Welfare Yearbook*. Buckingham: Open University Press.

Witz, A. and Savage, M. (1992) 'The Gender of Organisations', in M. Savage and A. Witz (eds) *Gender and Bureaucracy*. Oxford: Blackwell.

Wolf, N. (1993) *Fire with Fire: The New Female Power and How it Will Change the 21st Century*. London: Chatto and Windus.

Worthington, F., Willmott, H. and Ezzamel, M. (1997) 'Scapegoats, Heroes or Realists?' Paper presented at the 15th Annual Labour Process Conference, Edinburgh.

Wright, P.C. and Bean, S.A. (1993) 'Sexual Harassment: An Issue of Employee Effectiveness', *Managerial Psychology*, 8, 2: 30–6.

Wright, S. (1994) 'Culture in Anthropology and Organisational Studies', in S. Wright (ed.) *Anthropology in Organisations*. London: Routledge.

Zabala, C. (1989) 'Sabotage at General Motors Van Nuys Plant', *Industrial Relations Journal*, 20, 1: 16–32.

Zeitlin, L.R. (1985) 'A Little Larceny Can Do a Lot for Employee Morale', in C. Littler (ed.) *The Experience of Work*. Aldershot: Gower.

Zeitlin, M. (1974) 'Corporate Ownership and Control: The Large Corporation and the Capitalist Class', *American Journal of Sociology*, 79, 5: 1073–119.

Zuboff, S. (1989) *In the Age of the Smart Machine: The Future of Work and Power*. London: Heinemann.

Zurcher, L. (1979) 'Role Selection: The Influence of Internalized Vocabularies of Motives', *Symbolic Interaction*, 2, 2: 45–62.

Name Index

Ackers, P., Smith, P. and Smith, C., 52
Ackroyd, S., 16, 43, 50, 97
Ackroyd, S. and Crowdy, P., 51, 62, 108, 134
Ackroyd, S. and Procter, S., 146
Ackroyd, S. and Whitaker, A., 145
Adams, Scott, 116, 117
Adams, Stan, 2
Adkins, L., 124, 125, 126, 127, 135
Alvesson, M., 118
Alvesson, M. and Willmott, H., 52
Analoui, F., 13, 19, 24
Analoui, F. and Kakabadse, A., 19, 20, 97
Anderton, B. and Keily, J., 81, 82, 84
Anthony, P.D., 161
Aronowitz, S. and Brecher, J., 45
Arvedson, L. and Hedberg, M., 76
Association of University Teachers, 141
Aston Studies, 20
AUT, 141

Bacon, N. and Storey, J., 145
Baldamus, G., 43, 44, 90
Barker, J.R., 155
Barsoux, J-L., 103, 104
Bassett, P. and Cave, A., 145
Bate, P., 89
Bean, R., 72
Beaumont, P.B., 150
Bedaux System, 48
Behagg, C., 31
Behrend, H., 43, 44
Bennis, W., 9
Benson, S.P., 135
Bentham, J., 150
Beynon, H., 46, 133
Big Brother, 83
BIM, 41
Boland, R.J. and Hoffman, R., 63, 108
Boye, M.W. and Jones, J.W., 11, 97
Bradney, P., 99, 107
Braverman, H., 23, 47
Breakwell, G.M., 124
Brecher, J., 44
Brewis, J. and Gray, C., 123, 128
Brewis, J. and Kerfoot, D., 154
British Institute of Management, 41
British Retail Consortium, 81

British Telecom, 83
Brockway, M., 40
Brooks-Gordon, B., 124
Brown, G., 32, 38, 50, 92, 93
Brown, R.K., 20
Brown, W. and Wright, M., 147
Burawoy, M., 26, 42, 48, 71, 88, 92
Burrell, G., 122, 123, 127, 129, 131, 137, 143, 158
Business Week, 131, 138, 142, 143

Cadbury Committee, 2
Carter, P. and Jeffs, P., 141
Casey, C., 152, 153, 155, 159
Cavendish, R., 51, 135
CBI, 41
Chemco, 46
Chadwick-Jones, J., Brown, C. and Nicholson, N., 41
Charkham, J., 2
Clark, J., 156
Clarke, T., 46
Clarke, T. and Clements, L., 22, 100
Clegg, H., 22
Clegg, S.R., 20, 52, 158
Clegg, S. and Dunkerley, D., 20
Cliff, T., 44, 93
Cockburn, C., 50, 59, 122, 124, 125, 130, 131, 132, 133, 135
Cohen, S., 24, 36
Cohen, S. and Taylor, L., 55
Coleman, J.S., 55
Collins, E.G.C., 122, 124, 129, 131, 138, 142, 143
Collins, O., Dalton, M. and Roy, D., 34
Collinson, D.L., 51, 54, 55, 56–57, 62–63, 64, 65, 67, 71, 73, 99, 100, 105, 108–9, 111, 112, 129, 133, 134, 136, 160
Collinson, D.L. and Collinson, M., 124, 137
Confederation of British Industry, 41
Connell, R.W., 131
Coopey, J., 156
Coventry Machine Tool Workers' Committee, 60
Coventry Tool Room Agreement, 60
Cronin, J., 46
Crouch, C., 22, 72

Crouch, C. and Pizzorno, A., 45
Crystal, G., 2
Cunnison, S., 26, 33, 35, 71, 92

Dalton, M., 33
Dandeker, C., 153
Davies, C., 105
Davidson, M.J. and Earnshaw, J., 140
Day, R.A. and Day, J., 20
Deetz, S., 151, 153, 160
Delbridge, R., 161
Delbridge, R., Turnbull, P. and Wilkinson, B., 155
Dennis, N., Henriques, F. and Slaughter, C., 55, 63, 65
Dews, P., 158
Di Tomaso, N., 125, 126, 127, 132
Dilbert, 116–117, 119
Ditton, J., 3, 12, 24, 26, 36, 37, 38, 53–54, 78, 79, 84
Donaldson, L., 20
Donovan Report, 45, 72, 73, 147, 163
Douglas, M., 115
Drew, P., 104, 111
Dubois, P., 39, 45
DuGay, P., 100
Duncan, W. and Feisal, J.P., 104
Dunlop, J.T., 22

Edwards, P., 23, 24, 26, 49–50, 53, 164
Edwards, P., Collinson, D. and Della-Rocca, G., 156, 165
Edwards, P. and Scullion, H., 23, 49, 53, 55, 56, 93, 164
Edwards, R., 21, 47, 48, 159
Eldridge, J., 22, 60
Emerson, J., 107, 111

Filby, M., 51, 124, 126, 135, 139
Financial Times, 132
Finchman, M., 76
Fineman, S., 52, 124
Fitzpatrick, J., 63
Fogarty, M. and Brooks, D., 145
Ford, R.C. and McClaughlin, F.S., 140, 142
Foucault, M., 30, 137, 150, 151, 152, 157–158, 159
Fournie, D., 10
Fox, A., 87, 89
Fox, S., 107
Franklin, P., 2
Friedman, A., 23, 47, 48, 57, 58, 60, 86

Gallacher, W. and Campbell, J., 59
General Motors, 40, 45

Giacalone, R.A. and Greenberg, J., 4, 10, 18, 96, 97
Giddens, A., 132, 133, 153
Glaberman, M., 46
Glacier Metal Company, 33
Goffman, E., 100
Goodman, P., and Atkin, R.S., 41, 76
Goodrich, C., 32, 47, 75, 88, 89
Gospel, H., 60
Gottfried, H. and Graham, L., 51, 129, 134, 135
Greenbury Committee, 2
Grenier, G.J., 156
Grey, C., 151, 153
Guardian Newspaper, 121
Gutek, B., 125, 126, 131, 138, 139, 140, 143

Haavio-Mannila, E., 131
Handy, C., 147
Harlow, E., Hearn, J. and Parkin, W., 141
Hawthorne Research, 18, 33
Hawthorne Works, 97
Hayes, D., 152
Hearn, J., 124, 125, 127, 129, 130, 133, 134, 136
Hearn, J. and Parkin, W., 121, 123, 124, 125, 127
Hebdige, D., 55
Henry, S., 148–150
Herzberg, F., 18
Hickson, D. and McCullough, A.F., 10
Hill, S., 20
Hinton, J., 44, 59
Hirschman, A.D., 102
Hobbs, D., 55
Hobsbawm, E.J., 145
Hochschild, A.R., 101, 124, 160
Holloway, W. and Jefferson, T., 141
Homans, G., 18
Hope, V. and Hendry, J., 156
House of Representatives, 15
Humphries, S., 130
Hyman, R., 22, 45, 49, 72
Hyman, R. and Brough, I., 44

IBM, 48
Independent Newspaper, 121
Independent on Sunday Newspaper, 83
Industrial Relations Act, 1971, 45
Ingersoll Engineers, 156
INK, 40
International Business Machines Inc., 48
IRS, 125, 139
IWW (Industrial Workers of the World), 38

Jackson, M., 44
Jacques, R., 163
Jaques, E., 33
Jermier, J., 30, 40
Jermier, J., Knights, D. and Nord, W., 159
Jones, O., 156

Kanter, E.R., 122
Keith, B. and Collinson, D., 134
Kelly, G., 10
Kelly, J.E., 146
Kerfoot, D. and Knights, D., 153
Knights, D., 52, 153, 160
Knights, D. and Vurdubakis, T., 154, 157
Knights, D. and Willmott, H., 52, 118, 153
Kornbluh, J.L., 38
Kunda, G., 118, 119, 124, 152

La Nuez, D. and Jermier, J., 40
Lane, T., 45, 145
Lawrence, P., 103
Leavitt, H., 9, 10
Lee, R. and Lawrence, P., 10
Levine, A.L., 92
Likert, R. and Likert, J.G., 9
Linstead, S., 41, 65, 109, 112, 115
Lisle, R. de., 123
Littler, C., 47, 91–92
Livingstone, D.W. and Luxton, M., 131
Lovering, J., 145
Luddites, The, 40
Lupton, T., 26, 33, 32, 34, 35, 71, 92, 99, 133
Luthans, F., 8, 9
Lyon, D., 157

MacInnes, J., 146
MacKinnon, C.A., 126
Malone, P.B., 105, 113
Mann, M., 22, 46
Marglin, S., 82
Marks, A., Findlay, P., Hine, J., McKinlay, A. and Thompson, P., 156, 162
Mars, G., 3, 24, 37, 38, 53–54, 83
Marsden, R., 151, 153
Marsh, P., Rosser, E. and Harre, R., 55
Martinez-Lucio, M. and Stewart, P., 162
Martinez-Lucio, M. and Weston, S., 150
Marx, K., 23, 47, 152
Marxist Analysis, 23, 49
Marxists, 23, 47
Maslow, A., 18
Mayo, E., 16, 85–86, 97
McGregor, D., 18, 85–86
McKinley, A. and Taylor, P., 153, 156, 157, 159, 162

Midvale Steel Works, 15
Milkman, R., 44, 97, 156
Mills, A.J and Tancred, P., 121
Millward, N., Smart, D., Stevens, M. and Hawes, 146
Mitsubishi Corporation, 131
Montgomery, D., 32, 44
Morgan, D., 128
Morgan, Glenn., 20
Mulkay, M., 103–4, 111, 114
Murphy, J.T., 58, 59

Nazis, The, 114
Neo-Marxist Approach, 23
Neo-Weberian Approach, 20, 122–3, 152, 164
Neuman, J.H. and Barron, R.A., 11
Newton, T., 158
New York Times Newspaper, 45
Nichols, T. and Armstrong, P., 46, 71, 72, 133
Nichols, T. and Beynon, H., 46, 72, 79
Noon, M. and Delbridge, R., 65

O'Doherty, D., 153, 159
O'Connell, R.W., 133
Ogbonna, E. and Wilkinson, B., 5, 118

Penn, R., 59
Peters, T. and Waterman, R., 18, 102
Pfeffer, R.M., 10
Pirelli Ltd., 156
Plessey Telecommunications Ltd., 67–68, 71
Polaroid Inc., 48
Pollert, A., 51, 135, 136, 137, 146, 150
Pope, A., 121
Pringle, R., 51, 123, 128, 129, 135, 137, 140
Purcell, J., 145
Punch, M., 2, 80

Quinn, R., 122, 131, 142

Radcliffe-Brown, A.R., 107–108
Ramazanoglu, C., 126, 127
Ramsay, K. and Parker, M., 122
Ratner, G., 114
Ray, C., 5, 89, 118, 151
Reed, M., 20, 21
Renold, C.G., 92
Robertson, C., Dyer, C. and Campbell, D., 125, 140
Robinson, S.L. and Bennett, R., 10
Roethlisberger, F.J. and Dickson, W.L., 16–17, 18
Rogers, J.K. and Henson, K.D., 126
Roper, M., 132

Rose, M., 18
Rosenthal, P., Hill, S. and Peccei, R., 156, 161, 162
Roy, D., 26, 33, 34, 65–66, 88, 92, 121, 122, 128, 133, 142
Rubery, J., 60
Russia, 115

Sakolsky, R., 153, 158
Salaman, G., 20
Sargent, A.G., 122, 124
Scott, A., 156, 161
Segal, L., 127
Sewell, G. and Wilkinson, B., 153, 154, 155, 159, 161
Sharpe, D., 156
Sheppard, D., 124, 135
Silverman, D., 20
Sisson, K., 147, 162
Skinner, B., 18
Smircich, L., 106, 151
Smith, C. and Thompson, P., 159
Smith, P. and Morton, G., 146
Smith, S. and Wilkinson, B., 152, 156
Snizek, W.E., 132
Sporting Life Newspaper, 113
Sprouse, M., 2, 39, 41
Stanko, E., 127
Steers, R.M. and Rhodes, S., 77
Stockdale, M.S., 126, 139
Storey, J., 86
Sykes, A.J., 99

Taylor, F.W., 15–16, 17, 26, 85, 91, 94
Taylor, L. and Walton, P., 24, 39
Taylor, S., 157
Tavistock Institute, 33
Terry, M., 61, 72, 73
Thomas, A.M. and Kitzinger, C., 126
Thomason, G., 148–150
Thompson, E.P., 90
Thompson, P., 20, 47, 49, 60, 91, 164
Thompson, P. and Ackroyd, S., 144, 162
Thompson, P. and Bannon, E., 49, 67, 69–70, 71, 72
Thompson, P. and Findlay, P., 161
Thompson, P. and McHugh, D., 18, 20, 86, 160

Townley, B., 151, 153
TUCRIC, 125
Turner, B., 99, 100

Unisys Plc., 142
United Auto Workers, 45
Upper Clyde Shipbuilders, 45

Vaught, C and Smith, D., 61–62, 64
Veblen, T., 13
Von Haller, G.B., 9
Vroom, V., 18

Walby, S., 129
Warhurst, C. and Thompson, P., 97
Watson, S., 39, 40
Webb, Sydney and Beatrice, 32
Weber, M., 122, 152
Weberian Approach, 20, 122–3, 152, 164
Webster, F. and Robbins, K., 118, 154, 155
Westwood, S., 51, 135, 136, 137, 138
Whitehead, A.N., 16
Wilkinson, B., 155
Wilkinson, B. Godfrey, G. and Marchington, M., 156, 161
Williamson, A.D., 143
Willis, P., 55, 118, 133
Willmott, H., 86, 151, 153, 159
Wilson, C.P., 107
Wilson, D. and Rosenfeld, R.H., 9, 10
Wise, S. and Stanley, L., 140, 141
WIRS, 146, 147
Witz, A. and Savage, M., 123, 143
Wobblies, the, 38, 40
Wolf, N., 127
Woolworths, 82
Worthington, F., Willmott, H. and Ezzamel, M., 112
Wright, P.C. and Bean, S.A., 139, 140
Wright, S., 106

Xerox Inc., 48

Zabala, C., 39, 40
Zeitlin, L.R. , 81
Zuboff, S., 154
Zurcher, L., 55

Subject Index

absenteeism, 4, 13, 22, 25, 36, 41–44, 76–8, 84–90
autonomy, 56, 64–8, 73, 88, 89, 154, 162–3
  controlled, 88, 89
  irresponsible, 57, 61–5, 67–70, 73, 164
  responsible, 56–61, 86–9

banana time, 65, 66
'baptism', 65, 66
'blueing', 65, 67

'ca'canny', 32, 38
capitalism, 23, 31, 47–8, 51, 86, 125, 128, 148, 152, 158
ceremonial behaviour, 61, 67, 68
class, 28, 43–50, 71, 130–2
class struggle, 22
clowning, 106–7
compliance, 4–5, 21, 50, 71, 118, 142
control, 5, 31–2, 45, 47, 60, 75, 89
control strategies, 12, 20–1, 29, 47–8, 86–8, 93, 96, 137–43
  cultural, 150–2,
  direct, 58, 86, 90–6, 148
  technical, 68, 150, 153–5, 157
  total, 150
craft workers, 15, 31–2, 56–61, 68, 92
culture, 99, 103, 106, 140–2
  corporate, 18, 98, 118–19, 151–6
  counter-culture, 103, 120
  sub-cultures, 36, 105–6, 120, 128–33

'dead horse', 34
deviancy studies, 10–11, 22, 25–8, 39, 148–9
dialectic of innovation, 7, 74, 89–90, 95–6, 158
Dilbert cartoons, 116–18
dualism, 158, 159
'duck', 84

effort bargaining, 23, 26, 33–5, 40, 43–4, 48–9, 54, 67–70, 73, 87, 92, 158
'embezzlement', 82
emotions, 51, 101, 109, 111, 122, 124–5, 127, 141, 143, 160

femininity, 27, 56, 122, 124, 128, 135–6

fiddles, 24, 33, 34–8, 79
free coal, 84

games, 25, 28, 48, 54, 69
  sexual, 128, 129, 130 136
gender, 28, 34–5, 50–1, 122–3, 125, 128, 133, 137, 143
globalization, 159, 163
gossip, 65
'greasing', 63, 65, 66, 67

'hanging', 65, 67
Hawthorne Studies, 16–17, 33, 85, 97
HRM, 97–8, 147–8, 150–3, 155–8, 161
Human Relations perspectives, 16–18, 31–2, 85–6, 96–7, 122, 153, 161
humour, in workplace, 7, 12, 27, 54, 62–7, 79–120, 126, 135–6, 138–9

identity
  appropriation of, 7, 25, 26–7, 31, 54–6, 65, 97, 100–1, 110, 125, 131–2, 137, 143, 153–4, 159–160
identity work, 160
industrial relations, 14, 21, 22, 33, 38–9, 44–5, 48, 52, 61, 69, 72, 145–7
industrial sociology, 14, 31–52, 54, 121, 150, 158
informal/self-organization of employees, 17–18, 24, 27–8, 33–4, 48, 50–1, 53–7, 59–73, 74, 91, 94, 108, 122, 150, 161–4
innovation
  behavioural, 4, 29
  dialectic of, 29
institutional bargaining, 22

JIT, 154, 155, 161
jokes
  ethnic, 105

labour process, 22, 159
legislative/political context, 45, 96, 140, 145–7

making out, 46
managerial complicity, 78

managerial misbehaviour, 2–3, 36–7, 80,
    112–113
managerial regimes, 75, 85–97, 148, 162
Marxist perspectives, 20–1, 23, 45–9, 128,
    151, 158, 164
masculinity, 27, 51, 54, 62, 122–3, 127–8,
    133–5, 138
militancy, 57, 88

new management practices, 97, 116–17,
    150–5, 165
new organization, 150

OB, 8, 9, 19, 21, 164
organization behaviour
    corrigibility of, 3, 41
    theories of, 1–4, 6, 8, 25, 37, 85, 121–2, 152,
        164
    tractability of, 3
organized crime, 2

payment systems, 33–4, 36, 48, 60, 92–5
perks, 28, 84
personnel function, 121, 140, 142, 148
pilferage, 12, 27, 36–7, 53–4, 79, 81–5, 99
postructuralist/postmodern perspectives, 30,
    51, 126, 128, 137, 150–62
power and politics in organizations, 3, 10, 12,
    20, 97, 122–3, 125–6, 129, 135, 137–8,
    151, 157–8, 162–4
practical jokes, 61–62, 63, 66
product, appropriation of, 25, 27, 31, 75, 81,
    84
psychological explanations, 9, 11, 14, 17,
    41–2, 97, 152
public and private spheres: boundaries
    between, 101, 123, 125, 129–133, 143

recalcitrant workers, 31–52, 67, 88, 89, 164
resistance
    explanations for, 9, 18, 20–3, 47–50, 54, 90,
        112, 126, 136–7, 143–4, 153–60, 162–4
resistance through distance, 112
rites, 63–65
rituals, joking, 27
rule bending, 78

sabotage, 2, 11–13, 25–6, 28, 32, 38–41, 50,
    113
satire, 110–113
sexuality, 7, 24, 51, 64, 70, 99, 105, 121–43,
    160
    harassment, 14, 29, 64, 121, 125–7, 131–2,
        134, 139–41
    romantic relations, 121, 129, 132, 135, 138,
        141–3
sex role spillover, 125
shop stewards, 46, 60, 68–70, 72–3, 79, 163–4
'snapping', 108, 109
socialism, 39, 48, 59
solidarity, 71
stock shrinkage, 27
strike
    on the job, 38
    stay in, 32
'sweating', 34

Taylorism, Scientific Management, 15–16,
    26, 32, 38, 48, 75, 85, 91–2, 94, 102, 148,
    155, 161
teamworking, 150, 153, 156, 163
teasing, 107–10
    reciprocal, 107
    malicious, 108
theft, 36, 79
time
    appropriation of, 25, 26, 31, 41–4, 65–7, 83,
        90, 97, 128
    wasting of, 36
TQC, 154, 157
TQM, 147–51, 154–55, 159, 160, 161
trade unions, 22, 38–9, 45–6, 50, 55, 59, 70–2,
    91–2, 140–1, 145–6, 160, 162–4
trained incapacity, 13
trust relations, 87–90, 97, 155–6

unplanned overheads, 27

Weberian perspectives, 20, 122–3, 152, 164
whistleblowing, 2, 11
work limitation/soldiering, 15–18, 22, 26,
    32–5, 38, 71, 90–1, 94–5, 133, 161